CHAP

POINTS OF DEPARTURE

'Something has to happen'

One evening, midway though writing this book, I called into my local pub by the River Thames and was soon in conversation with a stranger. He was a chemical engineer, who inspected the safety procedures of oil refineries. He described his 'world' and I plied him with questions. He then asked me what I did. I told him I was a psychologist by profession and that I was writing a book about how, living in a world in crisis, we could stay sane, and also perhaps change the world for the better.

I was expecting the usual reactions that followed describing my intention – a bland look and a smile. Instead, he leapt on the topic with passionate intensity: *'Something has to happen, we cannot go on like this: what stops us from acting intelligently? We need a whole cosmic change, we are paralysed. There's a job to do, why are we not doing it? What's wrong with us?'* He had nailed the very subject of my book. 'Exactly!', I replied with a measure of relief at finding someone with an equivalent sense of urgency – and frustration.

A week or so earlier, I had understood how difficult it was for people to speak about what was on their minds with regard to the state of the world. I was at a dinner party where the other guests knew each other well, and I felt an outsider. The conversation ranged over their holidays in Italy, the policies of a disliked government minister, and the art work of one of the guests. At some point, one of the guests, without change of voice or emphasis, reported that he was 'feeling very pessimistic indeed' about climate change, and that it 'was probably too late to do anything about it now'; another guest spoke briefly about the fragility of the food supply chain. There were one or two murmurs of agreement, but then the conversation moved on again, to how best to ride a bicycle while carrying a cello. I was struck by the enormity of the topic raised, the speed at which it was dispatched, the silence of the others present, and the apparent need to get back to 'safe conversation' as soon as possible – not to mention my complicity in all this by not inviting the speaker to say more: the moment was soon gone.

The engineer involved with oil refineries posed a simple but basic question that cut to the core: 'What stops us from acting intelligently?' This is the question at the heart of this book. The answer is not a simple matter of human choice. We also have to attend to the contexts and conditions that we human beings have constructed for ourselves. I'm remembering Winston Churchill's famous reminder that 'We shape our buildings, and thereafter they shape us'.[3] The principle applies to more than our buildings, of course. Our institutions, media, and systems of beliefs – all human creations – also shape us. So, while we may be looking at the qualities and performance of human beings, we shall also need to attend to the

---

[3]   Winston Churchill, Speech on 28 October 1943 (Source: The Churchill Centre).

FUTURE SENSE

FIVE EXPLORATIONS OF WHOLE INTELLIGENCE FOR A WORLD THAT'S WAKING UP

MALCOLM PARLETT Ph.D.

Matador
9 Priory Business Park,
Wistow Road, Kibworth Beauchamp,
Leicestershire. LE8 0RX
Tel: 0116 279 2299
Email: books@troubador.co.uk
Web: www.troubador.co.uk/matador
Twitter: @matadorbooks

ISBN 978 1784624 552

British Library Cataloguing in Publication Data.
A catalogue record for this book is available from the British Library.

Printed and bound by CPI Group (UK) Ltd, Croydon, CR0 4YY
Typeset in 12pt Minion Pro by Troubador Publishing Ltd, Leicester, UK

Matador is an imprint of Troubador Publishing Ltd

This book is dedicated to the memory of Bjørg Tofte (1943–2011), whose spirit, style, love, and courage have inspired me throughout its journey to completion.

I offer the book in fulfilment of my promise, shortly before she died, that I would write what was inside me to write.

TABLE OF CONTENTS

'... the idea of the future being different from the present is so repugnant to our conventional modes of thought and behavior that we, most of us, offer a great resistance to acting on it in practice.'

John Maynard Keynes, 1937

CONTEXT

Being alive today, we realise that revolutions are underway – if not everywhere on the streets, at least across the field of human thought. In this book, we shall recognise what we deeply know already – as we say, 'in our bones' or 'through our own experience' or 'from time immemorial'. We shall also throw light on what passes as 'normal' – the usual thinking of society and the assumptions people live by, often unaware that they are doing so. These matters are also subject to change, in a revolutionary direction.

In Britain, as in a number of other countries, with economic advantages and no war on our actual doorstep, a settled narrative for decades was one of material development, economic growth, and expansion of possibilities. But this narrative has faltered – some will say shattered. A sustainable but expanding economy while meeting carbon-reduction targets is unlikely. We know that climate change is serious, is already happening, and is set to worsen. Prospects of violent conflict re-stimulate past collective traumas in ways too horrific to contemplate. Political upheavals add to a sense of confusion and uncertainty. Not surprisingly, statistics show increases in depression, suicide, and severe mental illness. And the question for many becomes 'Will the centre hold?'.

Staying sane, holding our own centre, and expanding the possibilities of our own lives become high priorities. They are central themes for the book: our own 'future sense', woven into the fabric of a bigger tapestry.

We need to remember that, despite the gloom, upward and hopeful trends also multiply: public campaigns are forcing change and greater transparency, extreme poverty has declined globally, and climate imperatives are finally becoming urgent. Huge, once-unaccountable companies and institutions are under pressure. Corruption is identified more assiduously. Multiple issues of social and international injustice are receiving more attention. Social enterprises are expanding. There is also creative energy right across the arts. Most hopeful of all, perhaps, is the ever-growing understanding of the intimate connections between things, a grand joining of the dots – between agriculture and food, food and health, physical health and emotional well-being, adult emotions and child development, childcare and the social pressures on young parents, work stress and the dominant economic model, economics and politics ... the list could go on indefinitely.

So while the unsettlement is deep, there are also indications of a growing, highly creative, expanding global consciousness – a collective reaching for deeper understanding. The world is waking up.

Future Sense starts from an awareness of these new currents in human thought, and seeks to contribute to them, indeed to move them in a particular direction. Human beings live in the middle of what is happening around them. We always have, of course, but now the village is global; being neighbours can mean living in the same continent; 'neighbours on line' are scattered worldwide. Inescapably, the distances between global issues, local events, and personal lives are shrinking. Moreover, it is dawning on nearly all of us that *the most central and relevant factor in determining the future is the human dimension*. In every global problem, every policy dilemma, every disputed boundary, or every climate conference *the capacity of human beings to act tellingly and cooperatively* is acutely relevant.

Thus, rather than spotlighting the world's issues as if they stand apart from people's lives, *Future Sense* focuses on human beings themselves – or *our*selves (I shall use both forms). As members of *Homo sapiens* alive today, we – along with our predecessors – have created and perpetuated our various global problems. Now, with our predecessors gone, it is left to the generations of us alive today to find solutions. It is an awesome realisation – and some would-be readers will put the book down at the thought of it.

In *Future Sense,* however, the emphasis is not on what we cannot do, but on what we can – beginning not from a desperate or panicked state, but from a place of clarity and self-confidence. We explore in this book five directions we can take – not just for the future of our species, or the state of the planet, though these are important enough – but also for our own benefit and development. Maintaining our sanity in a crazy-seeming world is often a challenge; living a 'good life' is a difficult balancing act; and the complexity of the world reflects the complexities of our own lives – on- and off-line. Our own state of existence is the necessary starting point: if we are to be a resource for humanity, we need to discover our own resources, many of which may be hidden away in cupboards long unopened.

The argument here is that the greater fulfilment of our talents, potentialities, and unique gifts is a direct way of changing the world at the ultimate grassroots. The quality of our own being-in-the-world is relevant as never before in human history.

✳

Like any book, *Future Sense* has roots in its author's own history – and in this case, these are entangled with its contents.

I began post-graduate life as an experimental psychologist in the Psychological Laboratory at Cambridge. I was studying hearing and short-term memory, devising experiments, and conducting them with student volunteers in a soundproof room. I gave it my all, but I was increasingly unhappy – at odds with the whole model of working, and also encountering my own insecurities. Focusing on specific hypotheses, working in isolated conditions, and wearing the symbolic attire of a white lab coat, I had to exclude from view a whole range of 'outside' influences on people's behaviour, despite my conviction that these were significant. Straying *off-piste* was impossible: research occurred on the ski run of experimental orthodoxy. I knew I had to change the direction of my life.

At this point, I was lucky in my choice of colleagues and in the way doors opened for me. I realised that human development and learning lay at the heart of my interests, and over an eight-year period, alternating between the Massachusetts Institute of Technology and Edinburgh University, I was able to pursue studies along 'natural history' lines, following inquiries wherever they needed to go, and building connections between research in applied social psychology and policy-making. I taught myself a form of mainly qualitative research, wrestling with the complexities of human systems. The focus of my attention was the 'teaching and learning milieu' in higher education – the point at which the academic system meets the lives of students, transmits knowledge, develops intellectual skills, and immerses bright young people in departmental and college life. The rigour of the work was different from research life in the laboratory, but no less demanding. Like an anthropologist or historian, I needed to make sense of a mass of information, extract meaning, harness evidence, and present what I discovered to those most critically involved – including university teachers, senior administrators, and students themselves.

My second career move – sideways but still within the broad field of psychology – began nearly a decade later. I encountered, by chance more than choice, the 'gestalt' discipline,[1] and, participating with curiosity and having discovered its thoroughbred nature, I realised it was what I had long been seeking. I saw the way it revealed human experience and went to the deep centre of things, sometimes in a matter of minutes. It opened me to an entirely new way of thinking and of relating to other people.

The German word *Gestalt* doesn't translate well, but roughly speaking it means a 'whole configuration'. Thus,

---

[1]   There are many introductions to gestalt ideas and philosophy, especially as it has been incorporated into psychotherapy. These include David Mann's *Gestalt Therapy: 100 Key Points and Techniques* (Routledge, 2010) and a new introduction by Gordon Wheeler and Lena Axelsson, *Gestalt Therapy*, Major Theories of Psychotherapy Series (American Psychological Association, 2014). In many people's eyes, gestalt therapy is simply another specialist form of psychotherapy and coaching. However, its founders' ambitions were that it would be more widely applied – in education, in organisations, in the public sphere. I believe that much of its thinking can be communicated widely, without diminishing the qualities and carefully nuanced theories of the approach for those invested in them.

we see a house directly *as a house*, not as a collection of windows, roof, garden gate, and drainpipes, which we somehow put together *in order to* see the house as a whole: we see it at once as a totality, as a gestalt. We are 'wired' to take in the world in its organised complexities, as a series of wholes. The gestalt approach stays as near as possible to how human beings experience their reality, and the ways they construct their 'lifeworld'. We are pattern-makers as well as pattern-finders, so *to gestalt* is an active verb as well – forming parts into wholes, sorting items into more complex and meaningful organisations of experience.

The gestalt holistic approach has infiltrated my thinking – as becomes evident here, with the focus of this book being on 'whole intelligence'. Gestalt philosophy leans in the opposite direction to splitting things up into their parts, which is the way in which reductionist science proceeds – with its attention to atoms, elements, cells and genes, and to methods that focus on breaking down complex matters into simpler forms. Gestalt rejects this approach, believing that it depicts a world shorn of much of the complexity, relevance, and troubling unanswerable questions that human beings actually have to face: broken down into its constituent parts, the everyday world as it presents itself to us becomes unrecognisable. Reductionist science has obviously been extraordinarily successful – but for many practical purposes it is too far removed from the 'natural' ways in which people experience reality to be of practical use. Gestalt offers a re-balancing philosophy that opens doors to lived experience that most scientists are trained to keep locked – sometimes throwing away the key as well.

Stimulated by my first encounters with gestalt thinking – so different from my experimental psychology education

– I found my wider research interests beginning to shift. Over a ten-year transitional period, I moved from intensive studies of education, and international work as a consultant and an evaluator of programmes, to going through a gestalt training in America and eventually to practising in my native Britain as a gestalt therapist, coach, and consultant, and subsequently as a gestalt trainer, journal editor, and writer myself.

In moving into this new phase of my career I was working with people across a broader spectrum, more 'whole-life' than in higher education. Yet I realised that gestalt practitioners were in the business of educating too: assisting people to become more effective, authentic, alive, and mindful. As I became a more experienced gestalt practitioner, one area began to stand out prominently: the range and depth of people's intrinsic strengths and skills. Although people might have disturbed lives and could experience distress, almost all had developed strategies for managing their lives. They had learned ways to handle conflicts with partners or to cope with stress, and they were capable of bypassing 'neurotic disturbances' or incorporating them into some inspiring life-direction. I grew more respectful of what people had learned about how to live, and how they experienced feeling more competent and connected when in solidarity with others. I also realised that everyone can 'lose it', and feel incompetent and isolated at times, especially given adverse conditions or contexts that undermine their *joie de vivre*.

*

From experiences along my journey, I have assembled the ideas, anecdotes, stories, and case histories of *Future Sense*, drawing on both professional and personal life. Inevitably, I draw a lot from other people's thinking, but the selection is my own. I have eavesdropped on specialist conversations ranging from ecology to peace studies; neurobiology to the history of ideas; existential philosophy to management studies. My main debt is to gestalt thinking within the frames of psychology and therapy, but this is not a 'gestalt book' as such, nor is it meant to be read as an introduction to the approach. Though deeply consonant with gestalt experience, the language and concepts vary from the tradition.

I am writing for a general readership, for fellow explorers and inquirers – any who are awake to the future, its dangers, and its potential. Those who expect a solid core of detached academic-style argument will be disappointed. Gregory Bateson – the author of *Steps to an Ecology of Mind* – made a pointed remark in his 'Last Lecture': he commented that the 'undoubtedly elegant exchange of intellectual embroidery which occurred at the high table was somehow emotionally dishonest'.[2] He still used his intellect, but he realised – as I have too – that a mode that splits feeling from thought and emotion from intellect is a mode to question, not copy. Similarly, I may not meet what academics will consider an acceptable standard for justifying my conclusions with 'hard evidence'; references and footnotes are kept to the minimum. I have written *Future Sense* as a stimulant to thinking differently; it is a book of practical ideas, an

---

[2]   Gregory Bateson's 'Last Lecture' is in *Sacred Unity: Further Steps to an Ecology of Mind*, a collection of Bateson's writings edited by Rodney E. Donaldson (Harper Collins, 1991), p. 307.

opportunity for readers to think about their own lives, and a proposal for a different kind of activism and new direction for education.

I think of *Future Sense* in relation to its readers – who are all global citizens. Through exploring how people live, acquire tastes, hold beliefs, and take actions, I have realised how much we are inevitably players, never just observers, and how personal 'worlds' are microcosms of the wider world. I intend *Future Sense* as a 'bridge book' between global concerns and the recognisable realities and choices of everyday life.

The book is also an extended appreciation of a priceless human resource – our *whole intelligence*. In the world at large, the ability of whole intelligence to grow rapidly offers a basis for optimism and hope. I think of *Future Sense* as beginning a dialogue, opening up some of humanity's basic qualities for joint enquiry. I hope readers will draw on their own experiences that parallel, contradict, or complement my own.

The *Five Explorations* of the title will be unveiled in Chapter 2. The book is a result of 20 years of investigating these five 'dimensions of whole intelligence'. They form the bulk of the book. I have long been asked to write about them in more depth, and finally have done so. The five perspectives I am articulating in *Future Sense* have largely 'taken over' parts of my thinking and my practice as a coach and consultant, with an ever-deepening impact on my personal life as well. I offer them as key themes, which I believe are worth exploring as gateways to a fuller and more empowered existence. They may also provide new language for fields of human practice in education, social affairs, mental health, and human development.

The writing of the book was never going to be easy, yet the experience has been deeply instructive and rewarding. I now offer it to my readers. I say more about my journey of writing in *Postscript and Appreciations*, at the very end of the book.

conditions in which 'intelligent actions' are most likely to develop and flourish, and not be sabotaged, ridiculed, or ignored.

*

The engineer's questions gave me a nudge. I woke up to the need to share what I have discovered along my career journey and how it is relevant to the global questions.

Professionally, I've looked at how people find their purpose, grow their creativity, and change their direction, and how specialists learn to achieve greater heights in their field of endeavour. I've observed how teachers draw out the best in others, and witnessed artists and performers shining more brightly when their confidence rises. I've been excited when usually sedentary office workers rediscover their sensory and erotic life. And I've listened to people's private longings for a 'spiritual oasis' in a desert of triviality and consumerism, even if they find it hard to talk about this in an era that's stridently secular, and especially when they may have deep misgivings about formalised religions themselves. Out of all that I have noticed, become involved with, or investigated, I have developed a distinct sense of what is possible for humanity: *a deepening of understanding*, collectively and individually, about ourselves and others, and about *what conditions are needed to 'bring out the best' in human beings* – those with whom we are co-creating the world we experience.

We are in a far stronger position than have been previous generations. The extent of human learning about ourselves has multiplied. There is far greater understanding, for instance, about the effects of trauma, or the impact of stereotyping, or the treatment of mental illness than existed 100 years ago. Many ideas of this book would have been rejected at once even a few decades ago, as irrelevant and bordering on the absurd.

I am not an out-and-out optimist about what is possible for humanity, nor do I believe blindly that 'all will be well'. Consultants acquire a sense of humility – accepting the complexities and hazards of the change process, even when it is desired or fought for, or when supposed 'solutions' seem impeccably rational. Developments occur in so many ways that are impossible to predict and, for an outsider, often hard to comprehend. Yet my sense is that humanity IS advancing overall, and collectively we ARE 'waking up' – albeit slowly, and with drifting off to sleep again a not infrequent occurrence.

One thing is certain, though, and is another departure point for the book: human resources and capabilities are under-utilised, and many people under-perform – not through native deficiency or lack of strength, but through lowered self-esteem, or social isolation, or restricted outlooks in which they have become trapped, or because opportunity is simply denied them. Additionally, many of us are distracted by traumatic residues from earlier in our lives. Others amongst us have shattered hopes or entrenched doubts about whether the good will overcome the bad.

While recognising the potential for gloom and despondency, I also know that constructive change is always possible, for I have seen it happen many times. I know that people and groups can learn, alter their priorities, and turn situations around. Life moves on despite stalls and setbacks; the urge to find a way forward is deeply rooted in our being.

*

Several guiding principles are central to the book and to my thinking:

1. *Human beings never exist as psychological entities in isolation – they come entwined with their systems, beliefs, traditions, and cultures.* To grasp human complexities, we need to think like social ecologists and look at people in their contexts or settings. If people are to change, then so also must the conditions and contexts of their lives. We are not only in contexts, we are part of them. Moreover, we act as contexts for others – we help make up their worlds.

2. *We are all of the same embodied animal species and members of the grand tribe called Humanity, and we share more than we realise.* While each of us is distinct and unique, beneath the surface are parallel desires and trends that recur over and over, worldwide. Think of the commonalities among celebrations of births and weddings, the marking of the stages of life, and the experiences of funerals. Moreover, as humans we share with all other organisms the habitat of Earth. Together, we and they make up the miraculous-seeming phenomenon of Life – with all of us dependent on the same threatened biosphere of our extraordinary planet.

3. *People want to discover, re-engage with, or develop further their 'Whole Intelligence' as human beings.* This is evident in their aspirations and in the steps they are willing to take in their lives. Developmentally speaking, this energy for expansions of life and competence is a powerful motive that's expressed and enacted in a myriad of ways. It is arguably the most significant and effective human resource

there is. The promotion of whole intelligence (which I am about to describe) is a necessary step for humanity today. This is the headline conclusion I have reached, and it defines the particular purpose and focus of the book.

Whole intelligence

In the 16th century, an intelligent person meant someone who was 'knowing, sensible, sagacious'. In the 21st century, most references to intelligence have something narrower in mind: we seem to have lost earlier associations of general competence, sound judgement, mature understanding, and wisdom in favour of something like 'pure intellect' or 'acuity of mind'.

The argument of this book is that the 16th-century associations need reinstating. We need a broader conception altogether of intelligence – something nearer to *integrated human competence, overall maturity, and demonstrable good sense*. The conditions of our time require that we extend our definition of intelligence way beyond what intelligence test scores purport to measure, and stop confining our attention exclusively to so-called 'mental abilities', which never operate in isolation from the rest of who we are and how we act.

This agenda is less quixotic than it will appear to some readers. Intelligence researchers themselves – according to a special Task Force set up by the American Psychological Association[4] – have concluded there is 'little

---

4   American Psychological Association's Task Force, *Intelligence: Knowns and unknowns*. www.Irainc.com/swtaboo/taboos/apa_01.html. The quotations are from Ian J. Deary, *Intelligence: A Very Short Introduction* (Oxford University Press, 2001), p. 121.

known about the important human abilities that are not tested by intelligence tests', including 'creativity, wisdom, practical sense, social sensitivity'. An introduction to the psychological study of intelligence[5] let the cat out of the bag at the start: 'In psychology we tend to measure that which can be measured', and that 'if there are some qualities that we value but we feel cannot easily be measured, then our account of intelligence will be limited ...' even though what cannot be measured includes *some of the most valued human attributes ...*' (italics added).

Mental ability tests 'do not measure personality, social adroitness, leadership, charisma, cool-headedness, altruism, or many other things that we value'. The writer, Ian Deary, adds that 'this is not the same as saying that they are useless' – a statement with which I agree. Likewise, I trust that Ian Deary will not dismiss as 'useless' the pursuit of an altogether different kind of inquiry which seeks to reinstate these ignored features of intelligence within its compass, albeit in a more general, discursive fashion than that favoured by academic psychology. The more radical exercise, of course, would be to question whether measurement is useful or even necessary in all circumstances and in all conditions and whether the pursuit of numbers may sometimes cloud our wider vision of what makes sense. There might be other means of promoting understanding of human beings that also have value in practical ways.

When people refer to a team as being *good to work with*, because they seem *far-seeing and clear-headed* or *smart*

---

[5]   Deary, *Intelligence*, pp. 1, 2, and 16.

and competent, or they *show a lot of common sense* – when they're saying that certain managers can be relied upon to *figure out what's happening*, or are *savvy and know what to do* – they are drawing on evocative metaphors and terms to help them pin down overall qualities which are difficult to specify but are nevertheless appreciated and respected by others, and understood as important. These qualities link to our direct experience of what it means to 'be intelligent'.

As a senior manager tried to explain, 'I'm much more interested in whether applicants have got this "something" than in their academic qualifications'. Of course, we can understand that attempts – in recruitment, for instance – to 'measure objectively' have been partly to avoid the potentially discriminatory nature of assessing this 'something'. But that good reason does not trump every other consideration.

When someone is identified as *'not being on an ego trip'*, or as *'straightforward in explaining their ideas to others'* or as *'having their act together'*, or having *'all-round good judgement'* in making decisions, these general attributions are also demonstrating qualities of maturity and capability to function effectively in the world. These qualities contribute to high performing engagement in practical affairs. They are the kinds of qualities that fit within the more inclusive conception of intelligence that suits the needs of today's world and is advocated here. Being fast thinking conceptually, and capable of grasping new terminology and applications of technology more rapidly than others, are important capabilities, but they are not sufficient in themselves. To place them in supreme position, and to applaud them in isolation from the wider human qualities depicted here, is to skew attention away from other important aspects of overall competence. Remember that financial wizards of extraordinary cognitive facility also helped land the world economy in deep trouble.

As conceived here, then, 'whole intelligence' is *deliberately* an holistic and inclusive general concept, which attempts to gather together a number of valued human qualities and varieties of capability, high level skills, and attitudes to commitment and competence that people demonstrate. (Throughout this book, I shall abbreviate 'whole intelligence' as *whi* – pronounced as 'whee'.)

If we went for a formal listing, whole intelligence – or *whi* – might include such qualities as *practical understanding; sensitivity to present conditions; a capacity to discern the dynamics of complex situations; ability to make informed choices; a clear sense of what a group can and cannot do; and a recognition of other people's humanity and potential* – but the list would be far from exhaustive. One could add to it more or less indefinitely.

Making extensive lists is another way in which human beings try to wrestle some order out of overwhelming complexity. Like measurement, list making has its uses. But lists, categories, and measurements are not the only ways of understanding or experiencing. I can enjoy a good meal without studying the lists of ingredients; I can happily watch a sporting contest without knowing all the statistics of past performance. In other words, I am suggesting that whole intelligence or *whi* has a useful general meaning and usefulness in practical fields of application, in part *because* it does not attempt to divide up and specify all the numerous different high-level human skills, capacities, and manifestations of competence in some long and unwieldy list, but preserves a useful, 'broad brush', everyday holistic meaning that has recognisable relevance to life and work.

Whole intelligence makes sense because when we meet examples of it in practice, we are affected by it – we are impressed, or respectful, or perhaps even relieved to encounter it being demonstrated. Many a boss's face has been preserved through the more available whole intelligence of an assistant, making a timely remark that 'saved the day'. Many a meeting has been successful through someone recognising what needed to happen in order to prevent the occasion from 'going off the rails'. Specialists realise that solving a problem may take them beyond the precise boundary of their expertise. Some will draw back and say 'we cannot go there', even if this violates common sense considerations; others, true to the spirit of *whi*, will respond as the situation requires. Likewise, many projects could have failed, and many resources been wasted, if no one present at the planning stage had had the courage to express their inner doubts. When someone *does* speak up, and puts into words what everyone in the room 'knows really', and a whole dubious plan collapses like a house of cards, here is surely an important contribution that should be thought of as intelligent. Why would one *not* consider that such a timely intervention was intelligent?

Drawing on *whi* can slow a headlong rush to accept a cobbled-together compromise; can switch discussions from the trivial to the significant; can lead to capturing in some vivid image what half an hour's meeting has failed to deliver. Whole intelligence can cut through blockages in negotiations like sun breaking through on a dull day.

✳

Even if I'm deliberately not attempting a neat, single, watertight definition of whole intelligence, I am wanting in this book to show there is nothing arcane, mysterious, or unachievable about it. As with so many human qualities (like tolerance), attributes (like a 'musical ear'), and specialised experiences (like downhill skiing), one needs to 'get inside it and live it' rather than merely grab hold of a simplified description and pretend that defining something constitutes understanding: it doesn't. We best know that *whi* is important by encountering it directly in others or perhaps from learning from our own shortfalls in accessing it reliably.

In other words, to be fully known, *whi* has to be lived, observed, and explored – not read about. This presents a contradiction for me, in writing here about *whi*: I am willing to proceed despite it. I regard whole intelligence as a concept that gains credence and power through its 'fitting the bill' – or having 'face validity' in the jargon of psychology. Arguably, it's a concept that we have needed for a long time, during which 'intelligence' has lost a lot of its earlier robust and down-to-earth resonance, and instead become equated with IQ scores or intellectual achievement alone.

It is possible that psychologists, in the intensity of their longing to be regarded as scientists, have discarded other traditions prematurely – notably, in my view, the intellectual legacy of William James. Though often defined as 'the father of American psychology', James seems to have been comprehensively ignored. In my investigating what I am calling 'whole' intelligence, because of its relevance, I like to think he would have approved.

Understanding *whi*

Another point of departure for this book came from reading Iain McGilchrist's *The Master and his Emissary*.[6] This widely praised and controversial work has influenced my thinking about whole intelligence, and it provides another means for approaching an understanding of it. McGilchrist's book takes off from discoveries in neurobiology, his 20-year long immersion in the research findings about differences between the two hemispheres of the brain, and the speculative connections he draws between brain functioning and some trends in cultural development.

Building on pioneering work by Roger Sperry on 'split-brain' patients (for which Sperry was awarded a Nobel prize in 1981), a mass of studies have confirmed that the right and left hemispheres of the brain function in different ways, albeit in perpetual collaboration and with considerable overlap in what they do. The two 'half brains' are connected by a wide bundle of nerve fibres – the *corpus callosum* – which is sometimes surgically severed to give relief to those suffering from serious epileptic seizures. It was this group of patients that Sperry studied, exploring experimentally the differences between the hemispheres.

McGilchrist's thesis, meticulously supported by evidence, is that while the hemispheres 'cooperate', they also 'compete'. He uses the analogy of a pianist's two hands playing independently but in a 'working relationship', each with their own 'modes of operation', both necessary though different from each other. He explains: '…each hemisphere attends to

---

[6]   Iain McGilchrist, *The Master and his Emissary: The Divided Brain and the Making of the Western World* (Yale University Press, 2009). Quotations from the book come from pp. 27–8, 30–31, 210, and 228.

the world in a different way – and the ways are consistent… the right hemisphere sees things *whole, and in their context'* and 'underwrites *breadth and flexibility of attention*', whereas the left hemisphere 'sees things *abstracted from context, and broken into parts*, from which it then reconstructs a "whole": something very different' (italics added).

While McGilchrist's way of describing brain functioning can seem highly idiosyncratic – in seeming to impute 'motives' to brain tissues – his clinical observations are acute, and relevant to grasping features of whole intelligence. Conventional notions of intelligence place emphasis on the left hemisphere's attention to 'the three Ls language, logic, and linearity'. Whole intelligence includes these but also includes what McGilchrist describes as the right hemisphere's attention to 'the live, complex, embodied, world … with which we are deeply connected'.

Stimulated by McGilchrist's ideas, I realised that in the present cultural climate there is an assumed dominance of abstraction, precision in language, and model-building, while the kinds of conscious experience associated more with the right hemisphere tend to attract less recognition and less status or cultural approval – with direct participation, bodily experience, and unique and particular attention all tending to be considered – especially in education – as secondary in importance, as inferior, and even as possibly on the way to becoming obsolete.

Any idea that our wholistic, participatory, and bodily sensibilities are somehow less important than our capacities based on intellect and our measured IQ, is a notion that I shall be questioning throughout the book. *We need both kinds of knowing and competence, and we are collectively endangered if we forget this reality of our human condition.*

*

To draw this chapter together, here are some final introductory points, some already expressed.

1. *There have been limitations in the study of intelligence.* Psychologists have measured what they can, even attempting to include 'multiple intelligences', but these have not helped much, as they still constitute attempts to separate and list a number of different constituents – with inevitable questions then arising as to whether some of the items count as an intelligence or not. Psychologists have admitted to failing in the greater project of understanding the roots of practical, multidimensional competence, maturity of thought, and clarity of mind. A different approach seems justified given the manifest importance of human competence, especially at a time of supreme urgency for humanity.

    Just as with terms like 'beauty' or 'respect', or 'insight' – all weight-carrying words – whole intelligence reveals itself as necessary and valid mostly through reference to practical examples, and personal, direct experience of human situations. In answer to the wish for definition I refer readers to the rest of the book. This offers an extended account of *whi* in action – and what its development entails.

2. *Whole intelligence includes the intellect but is a broader concept.* Investigating the human experience of whole intelligence is a different way to approach the quality of our mental and physical life. What gets categorised as 'mental health' is closely related to what I'm describing as living with whole intelligence. However, mental health draws

on notions and outlooks taken from medicine, while the starting point and emphasis here is on enhancing human performance, strengthening all-round competence, and the need to draw upon and develop further people's high-level skilfulness in managing their lives, work, and participation in the world.

Whole intelligence is for everyone. Lots of children display a junior, developing version of *whi* and take us aback with their clarity of insight – cutting through lack of candour and stating things without pretence. Whole intelligence is not confined to one age group or gender, or to those who have trodden the educational path a stated distance. It is not confined to the intellectually gifted and, anyway, intellect needs to be integrated with other features and a wider range of strengths to be of practical value. Many people who have fallen foul of the educational system or exist on the fringes of society seem nevertheless to have access to qualities of whole intelligence.

3. *One obvious way to grasp what whole intelligence entails is by noting its absence.* We have all witnessed actions taken that are short-term fixes or that strike us as inauthentic – initiatives that lack insight or worth, or are sloppily conceived or anaemically delivered. The suggestion here is that people are a lot more canny, and capable of noticing 'what does not feel right' than is generally acknowledged. I believe the majority of us are naturally attuned to register examples of missing *whi* – thereby revealing a considerable sensibility of what *whi* entails, enhances, and makes possible.

4. *A long-term goal for humanity needs to be learning more about* whi *and how we can support it.* We need to

learn more about what happens in successful win–win negotiations and creative breakthroughs, and what helps promote unlikely reconciliations and extraordinary achievements. Humanity urgently needs to discover and refine new ways to stimulate, encourage, and expand the range of whole intelligence and the conditions that support its development. In effect, we need the equivalent of a software upgrade for the species as a whole.

Whole intelligence can grow and be augmented. We just need to remember that the primary access to it is through building our own understanding of it over time – by engaging with teachers and relevant ideas, and through personal and collective learning and examples set by others. Short-term structured courses and other quick-fix money-making promises of immediate change are likely to be insufficient and give a false picture.

Finally, greater whole intelligence is less something to discover than something to recover. *Whi* exists as a potentiality and is something we can nurture in ourselves and encourage in others. As a well-known Buddhist writer and teacher, Pema Chödrön, has written '…you begin to connect with the intelligence that you already have, it's not like some intelligence that's going to be transplanted into you … If you're going to be a grown-up – which I would define as being completely at home in your world no matter how difficult the situation – it's because you will allow something that's already in you to be nurtured'.[7]

---

7   Pema Chödrön, *Start Where You Are: A Guide to Compassionate Living* (Shambhala, 2004), p. 240.

CHAPTER 2

THE FIVE
EXPLORATIONS MAP

The beginning of exploring

Some readers will have an instant rapport with whole intelligence, or *whi*, and it will make immediate sense. Others will be wary: they will want to know more about *what* it entails; *to what extent* is it necessary, useful, and practical; and exactly *how* this form of intelligence is to be widely communicated. Some will also question whether *whi* can be understood and experienced by reading a book.

On all these counts, it is time to explain what I mean by the *five Explorations* named in the title, and which I have not yet introduced: *they are five different Explorations of whole intelligence.*

I remember Robert Hupka's stunning photographs of Michelangelo's Pietà, in St Peter's Basilica in Rome.[8] Allowed access to the sculpture during building works, Hupka took photographs from many different angles. Viewing them, the effect is cumulative: each image reveals

---

[8]   Robert Hupka, *Michelangelo: Pietà* (Crown, 1987).

something particular, with one's appreciation of the whole being cumulative, and conspicuously 'greater than the sum of the individual photographs'. This is what is intended in this book: each of the Explorations offers a different angle of view on whole intelligence.

In this chapter I introduce the five Explorations as a group: I explain how they arrived rather unexpectedly in my working life, and the subsequent path I took in developing my understanding of them. In later chapters I discuss them one at a time.

For a long time, I saw the five Explorations as freestanding and independent of one another, but they criss-crossed and interwove so much that I realised that this was no 'five-category model' in the making. I was a little disappointed – this would have been more straightforward and easy to assimilate. But it was obvious that the boundaries between them were fluid, almost arbitrary. Realising that whole intelligence could not sensibly be divided, I could have given up talking about them as a set of five. But I found that as different *perspectives* on the whole, as five part-wholes, they offered something informative, and that describing them one by one still had significant advantages, especially in first encounters with them.

So that is how they appear here – as five mutually supporting Explorations, each of which, once embarked upon, is found to lead naturally to the others, until they come together to constitute a single unity. By taking separate routes, the territory of *whi* comes to be known in an overall manner, rather like learning one's way around a new city. The separate journeys appear distinct from one another at first, but later they do not.

To each of the Explorations I have given a name. They are

called *Responding to the Situation, Interrelating, Embodying, Self-Recognising,* and *Experimenting,* and these are the titles for Chapters 3, 4, 5, 6, and 7. Identifying them grew out of a 'making sense' process in the course of working with several different clients. For the sake of simplicity I present the story as an encounter with someone I shall call 'Jane'. Later I applied the ideas and thinking to other professional fields beyond therapy – notably, in coaching and consultation. In my thinking I have since regarded them as properties or processes which apply to all human systems and relations. But in a way it all began with Jane's story and my experience of working with her.

Jane, an artist, came to see me 'out of curiosity', and a sense that 'several things were bugging [her]'. She told me her life was 'basically fine'. Fifty years old, she had a 'successful marriage overall'; her two sons were now both at university and 'independent', and she was relishing the opportunity to work more with her painting than she had been able to do for nearly 20 years.

What therapists call her 'presenting issue' was about her work. 'I live to paint', she said. 'This is my life and I cannot imagine doing anything else'. She described herself as a landscape painter, exhibiting regularly and selling her pictures for good prices. While her life as an artist was successful, especially compared to others she knew from art school days, Jane had long wanted to paint portraits, and here she experienced considerable fear and frustration. She regarded it as the most rigorous kind of painting and a challenge she was drawn to, yet she had 'enormous resistance' and had never pursued her dream to the point of actually completing one.

Another concern was her migraines. These she described as 'visitations' – they could knock her out for over 24 hours. Medical treatment had not helped much, and she wondered whether it was the kind of thing therapy might help. I made no promises.

As a gestalt therapist and coach,[9] I was attending to my whole experience of listening to Jane – noticing where my attention was drawn, where she seemed most alive, and the emotional timbre of her speech. As usual, I was also checking on what she evoked in me; by close attending to my own bodily experience and feeling state, I would more likely pick up something that was missing, odd, or not congruent, and this could be useful information.

By the end of the first session, I was already wondering how the therapy might go long term, and doubting whether I had heard all the story. However, given it was the beginning, my focus was on building a connection, noting first impressions, and communicating the boundaries around the work – what I would and would not be doing or allowing, and my expectations regarding missed appointments and the like.

I find it difficult now to recreate exactly the order of what happened next. But I recall that about two months into the

9   I retired from working as a psychotherapist in 2008, but continued my coaching practice. The experience with 'Jane' took place around 1993–1995. I describe my approach to coaching in 'Coaching for Whole Intelligence', in *Contact and Context: New Directions in Gestalt Coaching,* ed. Ty Francis and Malcolm Parlett (GestaltPress, in press).

therapy (which lasted for just over 18 months), I was still trying to find some patterns, or deeper meanings, in the work we were doing together. I was puzzled. The sessions seemed richly diverse, different from each other, both in tone and in how we worked together; and Jane reported that she was well satisfied. But the sessions seemed unrelated somehow – overriding themes had not announced themselves; I still felt as if I was missing something.

I discussed Jane with my (then) peer supervisor, a very experienced therapist, and expressed my uneasiness; she was reassuring – I needed not to strain after deeper meanings, but just to stay open and be ready for them to appear; undoubtedly they would. And she was right, some ordering soon did appear, I want to say 'of its own accord' (in fact, the phenomenon of incubating ideas in sleep is well known). At any rate, one morning I woke up and seized a note-pad at once; and I wrote down five words 'that came to me' from the mystery place of first waking.

I did not realise it then, but this moment was to prove significant in my subsequent professional history and personal life. The words I wrote down that morning have stayed with me ever since, and seem to have demanded me to investigate them, to teach and write about them – and now to write, years later, a whole book with them at the centre.

The words that appeared – almost identical to the list I gave at the beginning of this chapter – helped me to stand back from the therapy with Jane, but at first I was not sure to what they related. Were these words about Jane and what she was doing and experiencing? about what I was doing? about what we were creating together? Or were they simply a random set of terms I had somehow latched onto in my half-awake state, which had no significance?

Whatever they were, I kept thinking about them. They helped me capture something about the varied work I was doing with Jane and they began to order my experience, and then to open doors in both my thinking and my practice. Many years later, they are still opening doors.

✳

The first on the list of five was *responding*. What was Jane responding to, I asked myself? Lots of things, seemed the first, rather uninteresting answer: Jane and I had been concentrating on the issues that were uppermost for her at the time of each session – like conversations with her husband about moving house, issues with renting her studio, scandals in the village, and new paintings ready for sale. Each session seemed to start with what was in front of her.

As a Belgian colleague, Georges Wollants,[10] describes the therapy process, Jane was bringing to our sessions her 'situation'. I was not looking at Jane's 'personal psychological life' in some abstracted fashion – focusing on symptoms and syndromes as they appear neatly parcelled in a diagnostic manual. Rather, of foremost interest were her experiences of her 'world' or 'life-space'. What she was offering me were glimpses of her life unfolding in real time: her specific, unique circumstances, surroundings, and changing horizons. Any idea that her 'psychological traits and characteristic behaviours' could be extracted and kept distinct from her life and world, seemed bizarre – both unnatural and unrealistic.

I was being 'let in' to scenes of her ever-changing personal world. Its content seemed as much 'outer' (relating

---

[10]   Georges Wollants, *Gestalt Therapy: Therapy of the Situation* (Sage, 2012).

to her peopled world, her family, her studio, and her paintings) as 'inner' (her private thoughts and feelings). I could see that any division of 'outer' from 'inner' world was arbitrary and unhelpful: life happened in the joining and interplay between the two. They had to be held together if we were to do justice to her experienced life. For instance, Jane described one of the 'stable structures' in her life – her village – but it was hardly an objective, constant, and factual structure in her life: one day the village was a 'middle class enclave', another time it was 'just a boring collection of houses stuck in a valley', and on one occasion it had temporarily become a 'combination of haven and heaven'.

In other words, Jane's overall situation as she was experiencing it was changing all the time; and so was her responding, as various events and family developments fluctuated in their overall importance. I realised that, in her responding to these changes and to what was happening around her, there were rich seams for inquiry: her response to a row with her husband was in a sense more telling than the facts of the row itself. How had she handled it, and the wider impact: did it trigger a migraine, or did she just 'laugh it off and get on with things', as if it had never happened? This was sometimes her response to setbacks, and one that 'worked for her'. I questioned whether it always would.

Teasing apart what she did – in other words how she responded – how she 'self-organised' and managed her life, how she frightened or reassured herself, coped with problems, or pushed them aside – were all important in that they mattered to her and revealed more to me about her ways of organising herself. As her therapist, I saw part of my function as being to bring a fresh eye and a different curiosity in ways that acknowledged the changing conditions of her life and how she variously coped, commanded, and compromised.

So I discovered, with some excitement, that thinking about Jane's responding to situations in her life offered multiple entry points: to discovering, *first*, how she 'danced with' various events of her life; *second*, how she could fall back into habitual patterns that were self-damaging or obsolete; and, *third*, what resources she had that she could draw upon – but which she did not usually access; and how these latent 'responses in her repertoire' could offer new possibilities for her when encountering challenges.

Realising that her repertoire was not fixed and locked in to particular situations seemed to empower her; it gave her strength and confidence; she realised she was more of an agent who could take responsibility for how situations developed, rather than 'being a passenger carried along by events'.

Turning to the second word on the list, *interrelating*, opened different doors. It was an obvious part of my thoughts about Jane. The quality of relationship between us was all-important. Relating together is an obvious part of the therapy journey, even if different schools of therapy think of it in sharply different ways. Also, how she described relating to others was one of the chief ways in which Jane revealed her world to me.

As is the case with many clients, Jane's life was richly peopled, but at times she could feel isolated. However, she explained that, even when she was alone, her family were 'always with her' – as, in lower key, was her first art teacher, who had inspired her to go to art college: he was a mentor, and had bought several of her landscapes. Her relations with her husband and sons, with art dealers, purchasers of her work, and friends, were all significant – and most of the time these relationships seemed uncomplicated; the therapy was in part about exploring difficulties when they did arise. Jane had a few close women friends with whom she shared times of hilarity and 'letting off steam', but also occasional conflicts.

A whole set of questions arose for me when I focused on her relational life. To whom did she relate most satisfyingly, or with most difficulty – and what were the conditions that made for her 'feeling most herself'? With whom had she identified as a child – including 'lost' presences in her family's history – and how, unawares, might she be re-living family ties and styles? How did she let the opinions of some people influence her so much, while she ignored others' advice?

Her relating with others offered a rich vein to explore – including in her life as an artist. She had told me how she approached people who might commission a painting and 'flirted a little' with them – which made her feel uneasy afterwards; how she drew on her friends' support (or didn't sometimes, thereby denying herself nourishing contact) when she was feeling low; how she remembered her dead brother, also an artist; and how she felt cherished by her husband, who supported her painting and was her most reliable critic as well as her business advisor.

In her sessions, of course, there was also her evolving connection with me as her therapist – a live example of relating to which we had immediate access and could investigate directly: were we really meeting? How was she 'editing' what she said to me, and did she need to? What was she looking for from me? And how was I behaving like (or unlike) her father or some other male figure?

Our relating together had changed rapidly soon after we began: she relaxed and softened as she registered I was not a doctor in a white coat, nor someone with a 'technique' that required her to conduct herself in a designated manner. She was moved when I occasionally reported some of my own experience while listening to her – how I was impacted at a feeling level; and she was astonished that I was so attentive to small changes arising in the 'space between us'.

With regard to interrelating, I have left the most important point to the last. Jane blossomed in her therapy for many different reasons, or so it appeared, but at the end of her therapy, what she chose to emphasise, looking back, was the quality of listening both ways: each of us listened and took in what the other was saying. She did most of the speaking, and I sought to give her uncluttered attention, my empathic presence, and freedom from judgement. She felt respected and followed carefully, and when I spoke my own truth of experiencing being with her, I also felt listened to and understood.

In focusing on interrelating, I realised the dimension brought together a variety of observations which I had not assembled into any pattern hitherto. I was intrigued.

I next turned attention to the third word which had 'spontaneously arrived', *embodying*. I realised that here was another point of privileged access to Jane's experiencing. As a gestalt therapist, I knew not to focus on words and spoken narratives alone: there were always other dimensions –

sensations, movements, gestures, postures, and feeling states that needed to be attended to. Some announced themselves in some dramatic fashion – like an energy slump or burst of laughter, or some sudden filling of the eyes with tears; others were more subtle, deeply felt, and Jane had to 'tune into' them – like finding a station on an old radio.

Focusing on Jane's physical experiences, and attending to her 'felt sense'[11]– the overall feeling in her body, often centred in the diaphragm, was a departure from our being 'talking heads' that took Jane by surprise. Generally, Jane paid little conscious attention to subtle changes in her feelings and the sense of her changing emotional life; and she had not realised how much they might be affecting her painting, and *vice versa*. Concentrating on feelings and body sensations awoke a deeper sense of herself as a physical being – sometimes tired and listless, sometimes focusing too hard and straining her neck and head, which led quickly to a headache – that could become a full migraine.

I realised that among all those I worked with, their embodied life was central. I was always seeking 'more actual' methods than relying on 'talking about'. Also, it was more grounded and real to recognise that, in the dialogue between us, there were two people present, two bodies, two sets of feelings; and differences also in terms of energy and present state. For instance, Jane might be very excited and I could feel unmoved – was this significant? Perhaps she was more ambivalent than she announced, or I was limited in my empathic reaction. Sometimes she would say something she regarded as unimportant but I was excited because it was something I had never heard from her before – an emerging insight or fresh outlook perhaps, or a sign we

---

11 Eugene Gendlin, *Focusing* (Bantam Books, 1982).

needed to change direction. These moments were often rich in meaning and connection between us.

As with all of us, Jane's situations and relationships were suffused with feeling tones of one kind or another. Thus, she could be excited and lively, or deadpan serious, or smilingly content as she entered into reporting some feature of her current situation – which included me, of course, but also perhaps a still reverberating episode with someone else – like her son, having driven him back to university the day before. Yesterday's experience could remain with her, still somehow being registered in her body, and now 'woken up' in the telling of what happened.

As the therapy continued, we paid more attention to her non-verbal experience – talking was less urgent. In the course of the therapy, she became more skilled in heading off migraines – by resting, and through increased body awareness. She paid more attention to registering her felt sense in difficult situations; she was able to deal with distressing matters sooner, for having 'tuned in'.

I realised that Jane was a lot more embodied than many of my clients and students. More often people seemed to regard their bodies as 'things' they had to maintain, exercise, feed, wash, and empty, and, when they were causing trouble, take to a doctor. The idea that the body also provided an endless stream of information about themselves in relation to the world seemed never to have registered in their minds; nor – for some – was there any conscious connection between how and what they ate and their health or body mass.

I was also struck by the way that *embodying* and *interrelating* were both present and relevant at the same time.

✳

We also built in times when I would suggest that we took a longer view of the therapy – 'what she had learned', or 'what the next step was for her'. Here we were engaged in *self-recognising*, the fourth on the list, which seemed to sum up another way we researched her lived experience. These reflective times – often with space and silence between us – provided an unhurried, un-pressured time to quietly observe what she needed, what felt 'right' or 'not right', and what she had assimilated and integrated; or alternatively was 'still nagging' at her.

Sometimes she felt a need to update her image of herself, and revise her life story. 'I'm not that kind of person any more', she said several times. At other times I invited her to look with concentration at exactly what she was doing: 'I'm telling myself I can't do it, and the reality is that I can – I did it last week!' Sometimes I invited her to look at what she was currently noticing, attending to, or ignoring. And sometimes we compared notes on 'what was missing' in a session – which entailed both of us doing some self-recognising.

Of course, throughout therapy there is inquiry into 'self' – broadly conceived to include self-image, sense of identity, and those less varying patterns or 'selves' – as in 'my shopaholic self' or 'my "work" self in contrast to my "home" self – and which merge into social roles. Ideas of self often imply a 'central core', and definitions of that can sometimes become obscure. I think of 'self' rather as simply a useful pointer to the live and changing scenery of our unfolding existence. Thus, I would encourage Jane to 'listen deeply to her truth', or invite her to notice how she 'spoke to herself', or ask her about the ways she 'took in discordant ideas' or 'gave herself time to know her direction'.

How people 'relate to themselves' is not a standardised process: some people gain access and perspective by walking the dog at dawn, others go on retreat, and one man I coached used intercontinental flights as occasions when he 'stood back from his life' – the only time he felt relief from others' demands upon him.

I realised practices of refined self-observation entwined with the other varieties of experiencing. For Jane, gaining sense of 'where she was at' came up more richly in conversation with certain people, while with others she got nowhere. As the interpersonal neurobiologist Dan Siegel describes, 'The mind we experience in our own subjective world can become filled with frustration if the other person does not see and acknowledge with positive regard our own inner world'.[12]

So far, the new terms had offered up fresh insights. I now turned my attention to *experimenting* – the remaining word I had written down. My first thought was that experimenting was endemic to all therapy and coaching.

For Jane, a newcomer to therapy, the whole journey was an adventure – she was wanting to 'take new steps' and test herself, and as an artist she knew all about the extremes of either 'going too far' or 'playing too safe', both of which meant her paintings did not really 'work'. In therapy, witnessing the flow of her emerging consciousness, I would ask myself

---

[12]   Daniel Siegel, *Pocket Guide to Interpersonal Neurobiology: An Integrative Handbook of the Mind* (W.W. Norton, 2012), 2-3.

at what point she was drawing back into a familiar, safe, and known thought, habit or decision. And I would wonder how and whether to support her venturing into the riskier waters of the unfamiliar, sometimes with no guaranteed ground to stand upon? When was it advantageous for her to take a risk, and when was it foolhardy, at the stage that she had reached?

Experimenting was at the heart of our inquiry together. Sometimes, too, in a session, we would 'try something out'. Thus, in preparation for a difficult negotiation with a particular gallery, I role-played the gallery owner, so that she could practise how she would talk to him. On another occasion, I vacated my chair so she could 'view herself through an imaginary therapist's eyes'. At such times, the therapy room became a rehearsal space, with playful atmosphere yet serious intent – an act of live investigation, a form of action research. Most of the experimenting was small-scale: for instance, when exploring her anxiety, I invited her to see what it was like to pause, breathe deeply, and attend to her feet on the ground: what difference did she notice?

In part we were building up to her embarking on her first portrait commission. We had been exploring what held her back from painting portraits. Jane realised her hesitancy may have been connected to noticing that long ago her art teacher – the same one who had enthused about her landscapes – had seemed non-committal about her first attempts to draw portraits. However, seeing more clearly how the difficulty may have arisen made no difference to Jane's fear. She was still scared to start. I realised that 'talking about' the issue was insufficient, so we planned an experiment.

She brought in some photos of her son, whom she wanted to portray. I encouraged her to begin the drawing in the session. I was able to observe, and quietly 'held the space' – that is, I stayed in the room, provided an attentive presence, and focused on her. I invited her to think aloud; she reported the moment-by-moment shifts in how confident or nervous she felt. We allowed time to 'feel the edge of the fear' and to breathe and stay connected. We also gave space for the feelings of embarrassment and awkwardness that arose when she 'remembered' I was watching her. I shared some examples of how others could feel exposed in this way, and commented that Laurence Olivier had continued to feel stage fright throughout his acting career; she was reassured. The drawing began to emerge. At one point, Jane wanted to scrap it, rip up the sheet of paper she was drawing on. I persuaded her to take a break, and she walked outside in the sun for a few minutes. She came back and was soon taking the drawing to the next stage.

In the form of therapy in which I was trained, gestalt therapy, such experimenting has a central place: it's about 'going live and trying things out' and stepping forward into a 'manageable unknown' with the support of others – 'support' I later defined as 'that which enables'.

I realised that experimenting interweaved with the other dimensions. It was another way in which we interrelated; a lot of the experiments were bodily (like breathing and grounding) and all called for situational thinking: here I was arranging the context to support a possible new and previously untried happening – a new mode of responding.

✳

As Jane's therapy came towards its end, both she and I registered how she had become more *embodied* and could more accurately now impede migraines; how our *interrelating* had become more fluid, and how she was more effective in noticing (*self-recognising*) when it was time to stop painting for the day, or when she needed to 'complete a step' and could lay down her brush with a feeling of finality. She became, in present parlance, more 'mindful'; she was less likely to lurch from one activity to another without checking to see if she was ready to, and she spotted more quickly when she needed to pause and stretch – like her cat did. This was a step into more *self-recognising* too.

Other connections were to her *responding to her situation*: she talked things over with her husband, and they decided that village life, as attractive as it was, no longer 'fitted' their lives, now that their children had left home. In effect Jane was updating herself, taking note of her changes, and also what was developing in her painting interests. She was enjoying the sense of feeling more in touch with herself, and some earlier spiritual leanings were resurfacing, though she felt uncomfortable with the language of many church services. She noticed a rising curiosity in Buddhism. And she was painting some portraits at last, and enjoying the challenge of continuously *experimenting*.

At my insistence, she also looked at where I had 'missed her' or had inadvertently set her off on a false track – part my own *self-recognising*, of monitoring my effectiveness. I was aware of sometimes being too tentative; and she realised she had not given herself enough time for integrating as she went along. While choosing to stop therapy had to do with her moving house, it would also give her time to 'catch up with herself', allowing the realisations of therapy to 'sink in'.

Jane's journey, and my travel with her along it for a short period of her life, proved deeply instructive for us both, albeit in different ways. For me, many years later, I remember the first thrills of fitting both of our experiences into the framework of the five dimensions. They related to her life and being, and they afforded a simple template or schema for me to consider further my own practice.

Later developments: the question of 'abilities'

I began thinking how these five domains of experience formed part of everyone's life, and were central to what I was doing as a therapist and coach. Thus, all my therapy and coaching clients had '*situations*' – complex problems about access to children, or their business about to go bankrupt, or something else that grabbed and held their attention. Many were caught in *relational* dilemmas – whether with spouses, bosses or teenage children – or, of course, with me. Our travel together in the therapy or coaching vehicle meant our relationship kept moving; remaining stationary was not an option.

In addition, most of my clients could gain access to their *bodily 'feeling state'*, even if not all at the same speed or with similar enthusiasm. Sometimes I might be cautious in opening up greater body awareness in my clients – especially in coaching situations, but I knew that attending to my own *embodied* reactions and senses was essential to my being fully present. All those I worked with, as well as I myself, could benefit from more profound integration, making greater sense of their lives, and awakening to 'who they were now' – in other words, *recognising themselves* anew. And it was helpful, too, to think of my clients and me being present at the threshold of newly emerging life, with the therapy or coaching itself being an ever-present and changing *experiment*.

I began to use the five different perspectives as a simple checklist, looking at the same issue or set of events from five different viewing points. Thus, for example, a critical business meeting could be appraised as follows:

1. Did we *respond to* the actual situation – get to the nub of what needed to happen? Were people taking responsibility, having a sense of ownership, exercising leadership?
2. Did we *relate together* well, sharing information and handling differences effectively? Were we authentic rather than playing games? Was the meeting satisfying?
3. How *embodied* were we? Did we give credence to our 'gut sense' and were we in touch with ourselves at a feeling level? Or, alternatively, were we merely 'talking heads', as if that were sufficient?
4. What did we learn – or *recognise* about ourselves, individually and as a group – about the ways we took part in meetings of this kind? As a group, did we make intelligent choices? Were we 'on the ball'?
5. Did we take any new steps, or *experiment* with something fresh or different, or simply recycle the familiar themes or habits without question, playing safe?

At this point, I began to be enthusiastic about the idea that this five-fold way of thinking had utility right across my coaching, therapy, and organisational work, and that the dimensions could be applied to very different kinds and sizes of human system – and could serve as something like a simple language, transferable and multi-functional. Thus, to get a full picture – whether of a joint project, coaching session, international conference on climate change, or a peace process – the checklist of different inquiries could bring attention to matters that might otherwise be overlooked or side-stepped. They could also raise my consciousness as to which dimensions were problematic – or 'missing' – in a client's life, or in the therapy or coaching.

The usefulness of the concepts seemed to lie in being 'rough and ready', yet relevant and straightforward. I had discovered – it felt like a discovery at the time – a kind of simple summary picture that made sense to me, and subsequently to a number of others, some of whom picked it up immediately as a map for their practice.

As I continued to explore the five dimensions, I realised how interconnected they were, and also how they were mutually dependent upon one another. They were separate enough to serve as good raisers of consciousness but any move to fence them off from one another as hard and fast divisions was highly suspect. In fact, over time, I realised, further, that *each needed to be 'in play' for the others to become fully available.* For instance, going back to Jane, she had needed to feel safe enough to talk freely to me, or to *interrelate*; otherwise, how could she have explored her *embodied* fear, and then – through *experimenting* – have learned how to overcome her fear? This in turn enabled her *response to her situation* to change, and for her sense of herself to evolve to a new stage – which she *recognised in herself.*

In other words, they were all closely linked, mutually enabling, and interdependent.

At first I called the above dimensions the 'five abilities',[13] and the name stuck. However, I thought that using the term 'ability' might suggest that a person possessed some private store of some 'thing-like' psychological substance, implant, or fixed characteristic that was located somewhere inside them and which, fed by sufficient motivation, produced high performance.

I wrote a piece for myself about a world-class men's tennis champion and realised that 'ability' was a summary concept that was actually misleading when considered in isolation. Ability was not simply an internal 'force' or 'cause', nor was it an 'underlying property'. The tennis champion's early coaching, financial sponsorship, and 'lucky breaks' in terms of opportunities were all intimately linked to the emergence of his 'overall ability'. He had coaches, managers, his family, his partner, agents, PR staff, a masseur, his accountant – just to mention a few – all working in the background on his behalf. Also, he needed others to play and train with: if there were no others remotely at his level available or willing to play with him, with whom could he practise? He needed tennis courts; the organisations that set up tournaments; sponsors; a tennis-watching public. These are all 'enabling' and contribute to his high performance becoming visible and actual.

I realised there was no way one could separate out the 'playing ability' itself from the 'impact of the intimate family milieu' with tennis playing at its heart, and that the tennis player was deeply embedded within his *enabling infrastructure*. I had

---

[13]   Malcolm Parlett, 'Creative Adjustment and the Global Field', *British Gestalt Journal*, 9/1 (2000), pp. 15–27.

grasped something even more important for my long-term thinking: namely, that none of our personal life 'components' – skills, qualities, morals, longings, fears, hopes, or dreams – exist in isolation. In time, I realised this applied equally to *whole intelligence*, or *whi*. Each of us is embedded in a culture, in contexts of language, in local identifications and national institutions, and in the whole context of our lives. Our so called 'internal' qualities and psychological features exist always within such frameworks and infrastructures, and *there is no exact cut-off between 'oneself' and 'one's intimate contexts'* – certainly no exact border between 'inside' and 'outside', unless we impose one arbitrarily, without concern for the essential subtleties.

A second realisation was this: just as the tennis player's performance and capacity to play championship-level tennis would not survive intact if the enabling infrastructure were dismantled, so human beings are also more than 'influenced' by their surroundings: to a significant extent, we *embody* our surroundings, and depend on them absolutely. Of course, we also help to fashion them by our cumulative actions and choices.

To sum up, we live in continuous intimate connection with our 'infrastructure', whether it is *enabling* or, sometimes, *disabling*, or, in most cases, not completely one or the other. So whole intelligence is not confined to the psychological realm: we are talking about something far more fundamental – the way human beings collectively make their world; and what best enables them to live in it.

∗

By way of introducing the following five chapters and *Explorations* (having moved on from using the term 'abilities') I want to share my experience of what I have noticed people reporting – about the times in their lives when they have felt most effective, competent, satisfied, and fulfilled. They report such occurrences happening ...

1. When they are given or take responsibility for something in a context that feels worthwhile, and that may involve exercising leadership; and also when they feel encouraged or enabled to handle situations within their competence, in ways they consider as most fitting for the specific circumstances. (*responding to the situation*)

2. When they collaborate or participate with others in conditions that feel mutual, respectful, and friendly, where people are not harbouring stereotypes and prejudices, and where there is open, shared, and honest communication between themselves and others – recognising that differences, misunderstandings, or conflicts are bound sometimes to arise, but do not have to be destructive of the connection. (*interrelating*)

3. When they feel able to tune sensitively into their embodied condition – their needs, emotions, desires, and fears, as well as sources of pain and discomfort – and can take steps to support their health and maintain their physical wellbeing and life-balance; and also when they feel able safely to express their feelings through movements and gestures as well as in speech; can enjoy a rich sensory and erotic life; and can exist in conditions where they feel in harmony with the rest of the natural world. (*embodying*)

4. When they are able to access their thoughts, emotions, and short and medium states of mind; are unafraid to discover 'blind spots' and recognise what they need to

learn; can take in what is useful to take in from others about themselves; are able to remember and gain access to all that they have learned about how to stay sane, and maintain their poise, health, and equilibrium in an often crazy-seeming and stressful world. (*self-recognising*)

5. When they feel supported to express their full creativity, innovative powers, originality, artistic talent, and wild ideas, while savouring core stabilities that anchor them, and are able to stay with the unfolding present, to relax, to allow themselves to be spontaneous, improvisational, playful, and to 'refresh' their lives and routines. (*experimenting*)

Together, these five encapsulations – which summarise the dimensions, varieties, or reflections of *whi* – constitute a map, to help the traveller or reader. The next five chapters (and Explorations) are like a certain kind of travel, designed to stimulate curiosity. They incorporate ideas, suggest skills, give examples; they attempt to throw light on whole intelligence in ways that are of use to individual human beings and more widely, to humanity.

*

I remember how one day, towards the end of writing the manuscript in draft form, I stopped to look at the project as a whole. I asked myself a fundamental question: 'What are the *defining values* that characterise the five Explorations? Or, what end, or destination, do I have in mind for each of the different Explorations?' I realised I had never asked myself these questions – nor acknowledged that the answers were bound to be personal in nature. Inevitably, my values were part of what I was bringing to the enterprise, and must have lain in unarticulated form at the core of my approach from the start, maybe from the very waking moment when I scribbled down the list all those years ago. I just had never thought about my *values* so explicitly, to the point of putting them into words.

I allowed the question of defining values to sit with me, as I brewed a pot of coffee. Then I realised that, actually, I knew clearly what values underlay this work: I just had not known that I knew them. As they came rapidly into focus, I wrote them down. They represent the five core values that are associated, for me, with the five Explorations as described in the remainder of the book: they do not represent *all* my personal values, or all those I discern and respect in others' lives and work. But if I ponder each of the five *whi*-dimensions, and what fuels my commitment to each one, these are what are significant.

1. In the case of *Responding to the Situation*: I want to celebrate ACCOMPLISHMENT and humanity's genius. We have the capacity to adapt to a vast range of circumstances, address and solve problems, take on great challenges, and handle emergencies. Human beings can rise to heights of practical, intellectual, and artistic achievement – like building cathedrals, writing symphonies, finding the Higgs boson – and stay committed over time to worthwhile long-term projects, like eliminating malaria. As human beings we are able to create things of beauty and to master skills, endure difficult conditions, organise ourselves and others to transform potential into high performance, and turn situations around and start again. We have the capability to act responsibly with courage, conviction, authority, and resilience. (*Some*

relevant opposites are incompetence, mismanagement, maladministration, corruption, waste of talent, duplicity, ignorance that could be easily avoided.)

2. In the case of *Interrelating*: I am recognising the central importance of FRIENDSHIP in all its forms, allied to four c's – compassion, companionship, comradeship, and effective collaboration. Friendship is basic to all expressions of love, affection, empathy, and warm relating to others: whether in the dance of courtship, or in successful long-term partnerships, or – scaled up – in establishing and reinforcing peace between nations. There are synergies of connection that arise from our joining with others, becoming mutually dependent and trusting one another deeply, and from people reaching out to suffering others, acting with generosity and selflessness. The spirit of friendship is manifest in mutual respect, in acceptance of differences between people, and in the restoration of goodwill when relations are damaged – making peace and reconnecting. (*Some relevant opposites* are dehumanising and abusing others, violent conflict, psychopathy, cynical manipulation, bullying, stereotyping, narcissism, isolation, anti-social actions, and callous indifference to the fates of others.)

3. In the case of *Embodying*: I am expressing extraordinary gratitude for the gift of LIFE, which is evident in the miracles of our bodies' functioning, self-regulation, and capacity for self-repair; evident too in the birth and growth of children, in the power of the erotic, and in the strength of the life force. It is evident in our own species as well as in other life forms within Earth's biosphere, with its countless ecosystems, life-cycles, diversity, and spectacular beauty. There are the rhythms of activity, of relaxation, of sleep,

and of lifelong breathing and beating of our hearts. (*Some relevant opposites* are desensitisation to the body's needs, repressive sexual attitudes; deliberate harming, mutilation, and chemical abuse of human bodies, whether self or other inflicted; ecocide, habitat destruction, disregard for the natural world, and denial of its significance.)

4. In the case of *Self-Recognising*: I am respecting the development of WISDOM, reflected in the multiple ways we come to 'know ourselves', or can become more conscious, reduce stress, and integrate life's experiences – all with the intention of finding coherence, meaning, and sense of direction. Many engage with some philosophy, teaching, or communal method of personal inquiry, drawing on ancient traditions of mind and body awareness, or invoking the poetic, numinous, and 'sacred'. Others opt for therapy, silent reflection, 'getting away from it all', or 'taking stock' outside the mainstream conditions of materialistic, consumerist, society. For me, wisdom is about living integrally, in accord with one's values, acknowledging existential questions, and maintaining humility in recognising how little we know. (*Some relevant opposites* are 'burn-out', stress, mindlessness, 'denial of any need to look at oneself', anxiety, narcissism, hubris, fear of self-learning, and 'not remembering to remember'.)

5. In the case of *Experimenting*: I am recognising the power of PLAY and its gifts of spontaneity, enjoyment, inventiveness, and the experience of freedom in creative life. Playfulness promotes vitality, curiosity, and humour – all central to our living with artistry, pleasure, delight. A playful willingness allows for taking risks with what is stale, questioning the automatic supremacy of the habitual. Play entails a readiness to stay within agreed limits – like

the rules of sport – thus supporting us to act ethically, anticipate consequences, and to realise the value of the tension between two poles: maintaining structures and turning them upside down. (*Some relevant opposites* are rigidity of belief, excessive fear of the unknown, following precedents blindly, making changes without preparation, inability to shift frames, shaming those who question the *status quo*, lack of capacity to laugh.)

Though a personal choice, the five values that underpin the five Explorations are far from idiosyncratic. They enjoy very wide acceptance and remind us of shared humanitarian priorities and preferences. It is the contention of this book that we forget them at our peril. They are not peripheral and unimportant, but represent key human principles and attributes which we need to harness, and find new ways to incorporate them within human life.

The scope of the global challenge to human beings is vast. Yet, as the values articulated here, and which inform the Explorations of the book, become increasingly the common currency of human beings, our chances of creating a sustainable global future will increase dramatically. If, on the other hand, we take for granted the presence, 'normality', and inevitability of the '*relevant opposites*', the chances of a high-performing human world dramatically reduce: our fate as a species will be sealed.

It is my view that more and more of us are finding the question of fundamental values is the key to unlocking future possibilities. The ones explored here are necessary if not sufficient, and they deserve more detailed inquiry.

CHAPTER 3

RESPONDING TO THE SITUATION

The First Exploration

This chapter and the four that follow, have aims in common: each is a search for deeper understanding of a critical dimension of whole intelligence. *My aim is 'recognisable relevance' and to aid reflection, not to present a condensed argument for the benefit of speed-readers. The asterisks denote possible pause points. Each Exploration gives an overview of the* whi-*dimension that is the focus of the chapter, and points out qualities that are hidden, under-used, or philosophically devalued.*

Each chapter seeks to promote ways to strengthen and support the emergence of more whole intelligence (or whi) *into the world – concentrating on the unique qualities of each dimension.*

Arguably, responding to the situation, *the First Exploration, embraces all the others. It certainly captures most explicitly the ultimate subject of the book:* our personal responses to the global situation. *The core motive for the First Exploration is the move to greater ACCOMPLISHMENT. Accomplishment has relevance for all of us as we move in and out of our many life situations.*

There are already specialised discussions taking place in similar subject areas: for instance, about leadership, scenario planning, and management strategies; but these receive little non-specialist attention – they isolate themselves by jargon that holds a wider readership at bay. Yet 'situations' are basic to all life – as are our 'responses'.

The Big Question remains visible throughout: What needs to happen for humankind to respond more intelligently to the global situation – with a particular focus, in the First Exploration, on the climate crisis? The Exploration investigates key elements of whi-*responding: how people and groups organise to make things happen, deal with emergencies, experience their power, take responsibility, exercise leadership, and set new trends in motion – or, alternatively, fail to grasp what needs to happen, accept their disempowerment, or deny their responsibility.*

Varieties of situation, varieties of response

A president of an organisation steps into an ongoing dispute at exactly the right moment, and prevents waste of time and effort. A group that's defining policy options wakes up: an opportunity to achieve a goal could slip away unless acted upon swiftly, so they act promptly, sweep away obstacles, and win an unexpected contract. A teacher realises her class is restive and distracted; she chooses a different topic than the one she planned, and captures their attention for a memorable lesson. These are all examples of skilful responding – of this dimension of *whi* in action.

Responding to situations with sensibility and insight is of key significance: a human practice to treasure and emulate. In acts of real accomplishment and refined leadership, reading situations accurately and the exercise of sound judgement are crucial. There are three basic points to understand about this dimension of whole intelligence.

FIRST, its everyday nature. Responding to situations is an ordinary part of life. In a single day we are in many situations, maybe at one point handling an office dispute and 50 minutes later making fools of ourselves at a children's party. We know this about ourselves: that sometimes deliberately, sometimes automatically, we shape our responses according to the situation we are in, the role we have at the time, and what is 'appropriate' for the occasion. How we are in one place may not do for another – though it is also true that sometimes an office dispute might benefit from carrying over some 'playful energy' from the children's party: it might be the key to unlocking some missing sanity. Most of the time, though, the majority of us stay within the assigned compartments of our social repertoire, organising ourselves according to hidden rules of etiquette and expectation, as well as meeting our personal need.

SECOND, the varieties of skilfulness involved. Responding to situations relies on one's insight or capacity to judge when a meeting needs to end, for instance, or the point at which a designer should go public with her design, or when to call out to an adventurous child who might be in physical danger on a railway platform. Such common occurrences require threefold skilfulness on our part: we must be able

1. *To stand back and regard the situation as a complex and organised whole.* There may be other comparable situations, but each one is unique. We have never experienced any situation before in *exactly* the same form.

2. *To use our 'situation-reading' to discern what kind of action to take* – or refrain from taking. We realise our responses will change the situation, and become part of a 'new' one. Situations change, constantly.

3. *To carry through the required steps.* According to the situation, what we need to do may emerge in seconds, hours, days, or a longer time frame altogether.

The three stages outlined are necessary steps in a *whi*-response. Thus, when Srdja Popovic, the Serbian activist, began the 'Otpor!' ('Resistance') movement against Slobodan Milosevic, he saw the big picture of apparently unassailable state oppression. Then he spotted how unusual, attention-grabbing, funny and enlivening kinds of mockery of the authorities, and other non-violent resistance that appealed to people and put them in no great danger, could have a cumulative empowering effect. In due course, after their influential actions in helping to remove Milosevic, Popovic and his friends set up 'The Centre for Applied Non-Violent Action and Strategies', with a (now) global outreach, fuelling ideas in over 50 countries.[14]

THIRD, its inevitably personal nature. Intelligent responding to situations is never a simple mechanical process or adaptation. It includes some 'creative adjustment'[15] – active participation in bringing about a result. Even in cases

---

[14]   Jon Henley in *The Guardian*, 8 March 2015.

[15]   Creative adjustment is a key concept in gestalt thinking. 'Managing our lives involves more than mere adjustment: calling it creative signifies that the adjustment is an active process of "approaching, laying hold of, and altering old structures … Reality is not something inflexible and unchanging but is ready to be remade"'. Parlett, 'Creative Adjustment and the Global Field', quoting from Frederick Perls *et al.*, *Gestalt Therapy: Excitement and Growth in the Human Personality* (Julian Press, 1951).

of enforced compliance, we have our privately held attitudes – of rebellion, eagerness to please, or 'inner hardening' – that are part of our total response. In other words, we always have input, however much we are 'compelled' to do something. There is also a subterranean or unconscious pre-determination of what we do as well. These responses in embryo often precede our conscious choice: self-organising emanates from deep within us, and we are inherent organisers of our reality.

Human beings are able to switch direction when stuck rather than plough on regardless: to do so can be life saving. I always remember what a survivor from the Nazi concentration camp at Dachau told me, when I had the privilege of interviewing him. He described how he had worked out, by canny observation, that the best chance of surviving was to change the course of each day – altering his physical situation by volunteering for exhausting and dangerous jobs outside the camp, which took him physically out of the locations and time frames in which most people were rounded up to be taken to the gas chambers. Almost certainly, his situation-reading, his creative adjustment, and his intelligent and courageous choices saved his life.

If we pay close attention, we can discern the many-layered nature of our responding: the ways we are first impacted, and how we tend to engage, avoid, approach, hesitate, or grasp what to do. I remember asking a client what he wanted to do next in his life. He thought about the question and gave me a thoughtful answer. However, something did not quite settle within me as I listened to him, so I asked him a supplementary question: 'Okay, that's what you want to do. But what do you *really* want to do?' His reply was immediate: 'Well, what I *really* want to do is ...' and he went on to give a different account altogether, with more energy and interest. We tapped a different layer of his response to his situation in life.

Describing how we respond to situations can be slippery and complex. Basic adaptability is part of what defines our humanity, and it has played a massive part in our evolution as a species. We can be inspired by people who adjust to the most extreme situations – like protecting loved ones in a war zone, saving a fellow sailor in a small boat in a storm, or surviving being trafficked and forced into prostitution. We are looking at human engagement with reality that can sometimes ennoble people, and sometimes, of course, the opposite. The capacity to continue to respond intelligently in dire situations is worth celebrating. We may remember with pride our own *whi*-responding in difficult conditions, and we can also wonder how we would cope, if confronted by extreme adversity.

In emergencies, human beings can often surprise us: they become especially resilient and adaptable; they even surprise themselves, discovering how resourceful they can be. It's often 'when the chips are down' that people discover how they can *really* organise themselves to cope. Business and political leaders sometimes admit to preferring crisis times to everyday management: paradoxically, life seems simpler, since one 'has to do what the situation requires'. They don't drift off or get distracted – routines are suspended for the duration.

Many international initiatives that seem directionless or moribund might unfold much more rapidly if they were regarded as emergencies. If the scale of our ecological crisis was re-cast *as a serious global emergency* – which it is, of course – there might be more chance of galvanising swift intergovernmental agreements. The possibly apocryphal story of the slowly boiled frog is relevant here. Suppose the extremity of the damage to the biosphere was being registered anew – with the effects of the last 300 years appearing, as it were, overnight – a powerful sense of global emergency would surely arise. The situation would be seen as *demanding* an immediate response on the scale, say, of a huge undetected asteroid about to hit Earth.

Many out-of-the-ordinary situations change by the day, sometimes by the hour or minute. With a rescue mission – say for miners trapped underground – the responses required need constant updating. The big picture includes the emergency services' reactions, the public's outpouring of support, and the narratives and shared understandings which come to define the situation. These all add to the totality of what is happening, an ever more complex and layered situation, perhaps with news media becoming as centrally involved as the miners and rescuers themselves.

The changeable nature of situations – including emergencies – is demonstrated when, a few months later, there's a whole new picture. For example, the miners' fate – if they are not rescued – may be shocking and seen as an appalling loss. Yet a year or so later, the tragedy may be recast as having stimulated a necessary safety change that had long been held up. Alternatively, of course, it might seem an even greater disaster in retrospect – for instance in its longer-term devastation of a whole community's morale.

Standing back, and regarding a complex situation from a distance may inspire in us thoughts of a different response we might have made: 'Had we known then what we know

now!', we might say. What characterises responding with a high degree of *whi*, however, is the capacity to be able to stand back *in the present moment*, to understand a greater spread of interacting influences at the critical time, not merely with the benefit of hindsight.

As we know, complexity frightens many people or may lead them to naïve conclusions or impulsive actions. Responding with *whi* invites us to stay with the complex, often mixed or paradoxical nature of what is occurring, and not to be scared of 'not knowing' for a period of time. Often the best responses need longer to take shape, for the dust to settle.

To appreciate the unique nature of situations – a central feature of this Exploration – I have found Kurt Lewin's 'whole field' view of how we experience reality to be the most helpful perspective; Lewin did more for developing a situational approach than has perhaps anyone since.[16] He points out that in perception there is no clear and crisp boundary between the person and his or her surroundings: notions of a division between 'inner' and 'outer' are simplistic, and they split reality in ways that are not borne out in people's actual lived experience.

Thus, two strangers whom I meet while out walking – I'll call them Ali and Sam – are standing next to me by the River Thames. I may *assume* that they will be seeing exactly the 'same scene' as I am. But even on the simplest investigation

---

[16]   Kurt Lewin (1890–1947) was the founder of social psychology and a brilliant pioneer of action research. See Alfred J. Marrow, *The Practical Theorist: The Life and Work of Kurt Lewin* (Basic Books, 1969).

this proves not to be the case. This is not surprising: for a start, we cannot be standing in exactly the same physical location as any other person at the same moment, so our angle of viewing will inevitably differ. In other words, not even the sensory input is identical, as we also know is the case from eye-movement studies of how we scan a visual field. Further, in terms of what we look at and notice, where our interest takes us and the associations and memories that are evoked in us in looking, we all differ. Ali and Sam will have experiences – or perceptual organisations – that are different from each other's, as well as from mine.

Other divergences are inevitable. After all, the three of us have three different life histories; each of us has a unique genetic inheritance, upbringing, school experience, and a separate physical body. We are likely, too, at the time of looking at the river, to be in different states of mind and feeling, and in our degree of attentiveness. Given our separate observing states, three non-identical experiences of looking are not surprising, even if all three of us – Ali, Sam, and I – take 'what we observe in front of us' as 'the reality'.

Of course, there can be overlaps. Let's suppose Ali and Sam live together, and I ask them what 'stands out the most' for each of them. They might speak of noticing dogs that people are walking at the time. Perhaps they are jointly thinking of getting a dog, but specifically what they'll notice will still differ: Ali may be thinking of the *types* of dogs that are running by the river; Sam may notice their *level of obedience.* And in my own looking I am a lot more interested in the speed of flow of the river and the water level: given that I live in an area which floods, and it's been raining non-stop, the dogs – at least today – are virtually unseen by me.

Kurt Lewin describes a person's perceived and constructed 'version' of reality as the 'field' – which can also be regarded as a person's experienced situation or milieu. The terms in use are not so important, but Lewin's fundamental truth is significant for this Exploration: *the way we regard and make sense of the world around us is something we actively construct:* it is personal, and is related to our needs and interests at the time.

This truth is ignored in much everyday thinking, with ideas of an 'objective and agreed upon reality' still existing as a basic assumption in common currency, complete with the presumption of near-identical perceptions between people. This distorts at the outset our understanding of how people and groups engage with the world. Far from living in an identical reality, we are always constructing a personal 'version' that relates to what is currently important to ourselves.

In placing emphasis on the unique qualities and immediate and long-term priorities of people's experiences, we can see how the two terms 'responding' and 'situation' are impossible to separate neatly, or to allocate to two definite categories. This is because for each participating person or group, lived reality is of one 'whole experience', and *in our responding to any situation, we become part of it ourselves.*

This was demonstrated when a manager, Beatrix, was faced with a tricky situation at work, which she recognised was both fluid and complex. She pondered various scenarios, and realised that taking any step immediately would compromise the situation, because her actions would become an extra part of the situation before she had understood in detail what had already happened. Moreover, the more she might try to alter the course of events – that is, the more extensively she responded – the more she and her actions would add layers of additional complexity.

She decided to wait – which was itself a response, of course, but a minimalist one at this point. At the weekend she had the chance to make some calls, which helped her take in the big picture – including a row between two staff members, someone's broken trust, another person's distress, a project deadline, and a key colleague missing on vacation. Standing back from it all, Beatrix weighed her options. By Monday morning, she had a clear set of steps; she knew what she would do, and how she would consult with some other managers who ought to have been involved before but had shrunk away. What unfolded became manageable, and she was now willing to be at the centre of what happened next. Demonstrating *whi*, she calibrated her responding to the total situation, notably through her sense of timing, and a clear sense of how she could have 'made matters worse'.

We've seen that people can be resourceful and effective in the face of difficulties. Yet, this is dependent on context: in unfavourable conditions, human beings can also feel powerless, victimised, or ready to snap. There's always a continuum, in this case ranging from the most resourceful end – with people rising to challenges in a spirit of great enterprise – right through to the other extreme, when people verge on a breakdown or collapse. People need to be thought of as capable of moving up and down the continuum – our responding is never a fixed matter.

We are not machines, and situations can be 'turned around' as much by changes in what is happening in the wider context, as by any personal bootstrap operation. One needs to think of all the factors in play at any one time, and how changes *either* in a person's own meaning making *or* in the environmental conditions can sometimes make a notable difference – with both happening at the same time being the most common pattern.

There's another source of complexity regarding someone's position on the continuum. 'Consistent positions' often prove illusory. I remember several clients who presented themselves as distressed and unable to cope, but whom I discovered, in other places and roles, were operating successfully as confident-seeming executives or as holders-together of large families in crisis. The human capacity to respond to situations is far from predictable – there's no dial-reading set at 'confident' or 'unconfident', implying that the label applies across the board.

If we do not think of people as 'fixed', but think of them as affected by (1) the prevailing conditions, and pressures emanating from the wider context; (2) their overall state of health and emotional wellbeing at the time; and (3) the dominant needs or preoccupations that are current concerns, then, one might ask, what is the sense in all the labelling, measuring, and putting people into categories that goes on in our societies? In a sense, these all hinge on the assumption that a person is 'basically the same' across time and space, with their 'characteristics' possible to consider independently of the context or environment they are in, and of which they are part – in other words, *without regard to their situation.*

I would suggest that the contrary statement is equally if not more true: that people are basically *different* all the time, and *vary according to the total situation which they are currently experiencing – as well as, in part, constructing.*

The above re-thinking underlines a key feature of this *whi*-dimension and the First Exploration. Humanity needs a more complex view of performance, ability, and accomplishment, as such terms are commonly understood. Too often, these are attributed to 'personal characteristics' or the 'strengths of a team', and we can see that this is often only half the story, if that. As explored briefly in the previous chapter, with regard to the championship tennis player, the presence or not of an *enabling infrastructure* is as critically important as any 'characteristics' or 'strengths' considered in isolation.

Sophisticated leaders demonstrating *whi* already appreciate these points and take them for granted: they know the dangers in making too swift judgements about others, and they realise that situations and human beings' responses can vary over time, and that changes are always possible. They recognise that the potential for change is there in everyone. *Holding the context AND the individual – or team – in mind together* means we need to recognise not only how an individual (or team, or organisation) performs, but also how they might be functioning if the social pressures, or incentives in the context, were arranged in a different configuration.

Two paradigms in opposition

We have taken note of how situations change, often rapidly, and how they call for versatile responding. Such unpredictability and variation in responding is, of course, an uncomfortable fact of life for those whose working lives hinge on creating bureaucratic order, listing specific protocols, and devising detailed frameworks for standardised responding in different categories. These are the priorities of 'technical rationality', as named and described by the late Donald Schön, a much-appreciated colleague at the Massachusetts Institute of Technology. Professor Schön is remembered now particularly for two influential books, *Beyond the Stable State* (the 1970 BBC Reith Lectures), and *The Reflective Practitioner*.[17]

When I first met Donald Schön, I was questioning the merits of evaluating social and educational programmes based on test results alone. My view was that, while the tests may be called 'objective', the ways in which people chose to *select* and *use* the tests and then *interpret* and *selectively report* their results, were laden with human judgement. I questioned whether, if these largely hidden 'subjective' judgements were taken for granted and left unexamined, there was any logical basis for the fierce denunciation – on the grounds of their 'subjectivity' – of other kinds of qualitative human judgements, for instance, those of teachers regarding their students' potential. Schön was approaching similar questions on an even broader scale. He was interested in the professions, and in professionals' specialist skills. He pointed out that complex skills and competence involved more than could be systematised or written down precisely.

We agreed – coming from our respective interests – that skilfulness was involved in responding to the unique qualities of situations, people, and problems. Schön believed that setting up systems and standard operating

---

[17] Donald A. Schön, *Beyond the Stable State* (W.W. Norton, 1973) and *The Reflective Practitioner: How Professionals Think in Action* (Basic Books, 1983).

procedures might allow for more efficiency in some areas, but if they were extended indiscriminately deep into the realm of human expertise, eventually more would be lost than gained.

Schön reminds us that 'problems are interconnected, environments are turbulent, and the future is indeterminate'.[18] For him, as for me, the place of 'human judgement' was crucially important. Yet the climate and pressure at the time he was writing was urging everyone in management, and in educating professionals, to think in 'more scientific' ways, to systematise and quantify wherever possible, and to *reduce* the element of human judgement as much as possible. The aim of achieving 'objective', quantitative measurement was becoming the dominant – and sometimes it appeared the sole – priority.

The roots of technical rationality lie in the scientific revolution of the 17th and 18th centuries. In the 21st century, the scientific outlook arguably has become the most prestigious and powerful mode of thought in existence on the planet, easily eclipsing the great religions in size and influence, and being taken over in modified form in 'business thinking', management, and public service institutions as well. At the time when this new-style kind of professional education first came in – the shift of outlook reaching its peak in the 1970s and 80s – there was often strong resistance from professional groups: for instance, from doctors, architects, lawyers, librarians, psychotherapists, managers, and engineers, all of whom regarded their skilfulness as coming from accumulated practical experience, acquired over years of perfecting their craft, artistry, or engagement with real-life situations.

---

[18] Schön, *The Reflective Practitioner*, p. 16.

This practical kind of knowing, which was not considered 'scientific', became suspect. It was no longer considered adequate to rely on professionals' claims to *implicit* knowledge, that is, 'what practitioners had learned from experience' and applied to specific situations; let alone was it acceptable to rely on the reputation and length of time that a professional had practised. Instead, in any field calling itself 'professional' there needed to be a 'theory base', something *explicit* which could be taught and learned in universities, advancing knowledge which was less concrete and more abstract, less to do with particular 'cases' and more to do with what could be generalised. It had to be capable of being written down, formalised, and examined 'objectively' – that is, by pencil and paper means within an academic framework, rather than by observing skills in actual practice.

The new-style professional approach downplayed what was applied and particular, and elevated the theoretical and generalised.[19]

✳

For most people, including me, numerous benefits have arrived in our lives through adopting technology – improvements in countless practical ways. Many will see this whole movement of business thought and the wholesale

---

[19] Having lived myself through this revolution in the early 1980s, in relation to psychotherapy training, I can see the many advantages that have accrued: greater accountability, a greatly extended theory base, and a far more consistent and comprehensive 'coverage' of what professional practice entails. I have also experienced a decline in the perceived importance of 'learning by doing'; a tendency to think that one can learn psychotherapy through reading books, and a mistaken idea that passing a written exam is indicative of competence to practice.

shifts in operating procedures as evidence of progress, an overall success story to celebrate.

Those of us who question technical rationality are not rubbishing technology or the scientific method *per se* – well, I am not, nor was Donald Schön. Nor am I ignoring the expanded opportunities and life choices that have come about through the applications of technical rationality to manufacturing, financial operations, merchandising, ticketing, and many other fields of application. My doubts about technical rationality are more long-term and philosophical. I'll mention two:

First, is it possible that the pendulum swung too far in devaluing cumulative experience? Have we developed ways whereby understanding of the subtle complexities of the organisation's relationship to its environment are lost, through people retiring at the height of their powers and having accumulated a maximum degree of know-how? And – again regarding professional expertise – are there ways that it is harassed out of existence by the requirement to follow prescribed procedures to the letter, or the requirement to document every step taken? I think it is possible, as Schön speculated might happen, that at least in some areas of professional work, more has been lost than gained.

Second – more troubling still – is the possibility that the overwhelming endorsement of technical rationality has helped establish a prevailing and normative mindset: one which may spread more widely – undermining our human capacity for intelligent responding, and for taking responsibility in complex and dangerous conditions. I am suggesting that our collective competence to deal with the most complicated and non-standard situations may be weakened by assuming that problems and complicated issues can be handled best – or even *only* – by recourse to reductionist methods, and by assigning situations to categories and systems of classification that have been pre-specified. Perhaps advancing technical rationality as the most prestigious – and only legitimate – endeavour is leading to wholesale forgetting that we possess extraordinary human gifts for adapting to awkward and unprecedented situations, and also for seeing them in their complex entirety, rather than in some simplified or 'bullet-pointed' form, perhaps massaged by statistics.

Exponents of technical rationality do not deny that the world is complex, changeable, and difficult to systematise. But that does not stop them from insisting that orderly systems can be built. They simply construct the equivalent of an artificial 'platform' that sits on top of all the chaotic and unpredictable complexities beneath: the platform – based on sets of assumptions and operational definitions – allows system-builders to build further predictive models, simulations, virtual realities, scenario-planning and a host of other artefacts. The platform itself remains constant and certain-seeming – as only abstractions can. It enables systematisers to categorise, pre-figure, and quantify in ways that suggest order and predictability – or to enforce an orderliness that accords with their purposes. Disregarding variability and unpredictability becomes a habit of mind. Effectively, the platform becomes 'the reality'.

Needless to say, I have profound misgivings about the wholesale adoption of an outlook that contradicts the situational emphasis that is one of the hallmarks of whole intelligence. While many operations and procedures can be systematised in ways that are prescribed, there are others that cannot be – including some of the most troubling global policy questions. These tend to be unique, changeable, complex, and difficult to classify or compartmentalise; the lived world is often messy, corrupted, politically complicated, non-standard, and conflicted.

Specifically, with adoption of the technical rationality mindset and its assumptions, a more sinister spread of side effects may be inevitable. Notable, for instance, is the tendency to standardise and lump together unique situations and force them into categories, thereby assuming that all respondents that end up in a particular category are essentially the same – the 'one size fits all' solution.

Likewise, unpredictability and uniqueness get to be seen as challenges to overcome – as irritating departures which 'don't fit the system', and therefore receive less weight or attention. If they are undeniable, and very obtrusive – like floods arriving – there is then the possibility of over-reacting in some kind of panicked response. In these cases, the situational perspective is brought out of its mothballed status and applied out of necessity. But it's not that simple. Having adapted to reliance on checklists and protocols, and operating with computer models on screens rather than engaging with the situation on the ground, those in charge discover they lack the requisite experience or support needed for flexible handling of the situation – 'professional judgement' has been comprehensively devalued and the 'canny old-timers' laid off.

There is also a creeping effect of increased detachment – justified by supposedly achieving 'extra fairness' – in the management of certain kinds of human practice. Thus, an administrator – such as a local representative in a far-distant country deciding on visa applications – no longer exercises professional judgement, for the whole process has become centralised in London: he or she is meant simply to administer a remote, non-influenceable system, which means that it is also inflexible – intended to be 'fairer', but questionably so, given that it ignores individual circumstances. This is similar to what has happened in the courts, where imposition of fixed sentences for some crimes reduces judges' flexibility to use their 'discretion' and 'experienced eye' to make case-by-case differences.

In autocratic regimes there are often regimented systems which punish behavioural variance. In Britain and in many other countries, such steps may be politically unacceptable, at least in terms that appear crass, yet conformity becomes the *de facto* requirement anyway. If the whole weight of priority is towards system compliance, and technical conformity, even small departures from the expected procedures are likely to get 'punished' – the systems do not allow for variation, and the normative 'system-compliant responder' is rewarded.

The power of technical rationality – say in a manufacturing setting – to remove ambiguities, increase rigour, incorporate diagnostic procedures, and provide problem-solving techniques is not in question. It is when the same thinking becomes institutionalised and built into the very fabric of policy formulation, engagement with social problems, and the ways in which people work together on a joint project, that it shows its weakness: it runs up against the facts of situational variability and the complex and subtle nature of our response making.

Instead of remaining fixated on promoting technical rationality, Donald Schön proposed that professionals engage in a reflective process about their actual practice and the phenomena they were dealing with – including their 'complexity, uncertainty, instability, uniqueness, and value-conflict'.[20] These all prove 'troublesome' in the unwavering pursuit of further technical rationality and, at the same time, feature strongly in every major global problem area.

Within a technical rationality frame, language changes too. Abstract terms like 'validation', 'diffusion', 'accountability', 'facilitation', derive from verbs but become detached and float around as new abstract entities once the change from verb to noun takes place. Such language acquires a formal status, and needs to be learned if one is to advance in the world that speaks it. Someone completing a grant proposal told me they had to study the terminology like learning a foreign language in order to write 'appropriately'.

However – as political memoirs, for instance, reveal – official-speak is also disposed of immediately once officials are by themselves, unobserved, off-air, or in the company of close colleagues. Two forms of language come therefore to co-exist, rather like Latin and the vernacular of the Middle Ages: the one people speak formally, and while on show; and the other how they speak privately. Behind the scenes, 'an implementation process' becomes 'getting the damn thing fixed'.

As has often been recognised, language is never 'value neutral'. I was reminded of this by some writing by David Zigmond, a medical general practitioner in London, who also works psychotherapeutically in conjunction with the mental health system. He is a fierce critic of recent changes in the

---

[20] Schön, *The Reflective Practitioner*, p. 49.

delivery of mental health care in the British National Health Service, including the choice of language used. He writes:[21] 'If the language of our culture becomes restricted to the technical, the commercial, the procedural and the defined, then our patients – people, like us! – are seen as merely biomechanical problems to be controlled, managed, traded or disposed of'.

Zigmond points out that health-carers are also more and more affected by the language in use: they 'communicate now – almost entirely – in dull narrow administrative, technical words: of conventions, clusters and codes; of quantifiable procedural activity and description … designating the objectively generic but excluding the humanly variable'.

Finally, in considering technical rationality – including its tendencies to specify categories and sub-categories, to create 'orderly procedures', and to work towards totally quantifiable data – I am remembering Iain McGilchrist's views on left- and right-hemispheres of the brain. He suggests that the left-hemisphere-related *desire for a generalised order* has established itself more and more as a cultural priority, with 'abstracted' summations of human phenomena preferred to the particularities of single instances. Abstraction is, of course, simply a different variety of reduction – substitution of what is particular, concrete, qualitative, and complex by something simpler, more general, and more condensed.

I am suggesting that any drawing away from the complex actuality of a situation into the realm of abstraction has its

21   David Zigmond, *If You Want Good Personal Health Care See a Vet. Industrialised Humanity: Why and How Should We Care for One Another* (New Gnosis, 2015).

losses as well as its gains; the difficulty is that the gains are trumpeted, and the losses hidden. For instance, an abstracted version of something can be misread as providing a basis for practical purposes. A notorious example is the glorious abstraction that is the London Underground map – which can seriously misinform visitors to London, if they attempt to use it to locate their geographical position above ground. I suggest that many mathematical models, simulations, standardised protocols, and other systematisations and abstractions provide the equivalent of the London Underground map – that is they are useful for powerful if limited purposes.

Some express enthusiasm for a trade-off between two ways of thinking – 'the best of both worlds'. On the one hand, there are abstractions, systematised procedures, generalised categories: in short, the simplified and more easily administered orders of technical rationality. On the other hand, there are complex, highly differentiated, and singular instances more suited to the subjective richness of situational thinking. Could the world not use both approaches to good effect? Might there not be some way of allowing them both to operate, if not together, to be used in parallel, or for different stated purposes?

I'll return to this possibility following the next section.

Planetary questions – and human 'response-ability'

The ways we *respond to the total global situation* have obvious contemporary relevance. Here the 'situation' is of a different order of magnitude to those we've addressed so far, prompting different areas to visit in this Exploration.

Mark Lynas, George Monbiot, Bill McKibben, Joanna Macy, and George Marshall are just some of those sounding loud alarm calls. Mark Lynas,[22] for example, confronts us with the extent of humanity's global impact: he explains how 'for the biosphere as a whole the Age of Humans has been a catastrophe … .The Earth is now in the throes of its sixth mass extinction, the worst since the ecological calamity that wiped out the dinosaurs 65 million years ago'. Lynas argues convincingly that human beings need to *take responsibility for our actions at a planetary scale*' (emphasis added). This requires our taking 'conscious and collective decisions about how far we interfere with the planet's natural cycles and how we manage our global-scale impacts'.

His message was eminently sensible in 2011, and it remains so several years later. However, there's no guarantee that the world's governing elites will collaborate and make the necessary definitive, far-reaching and courageous political and economic decisions, *or that their populations will back them if they do*. Several years after the publication of his book, far less has been done than most climate scientists consider essential – that is, if we are to stave off devastating changes to the climate, let alone be in a position to begin reversing the damage to the biosphere.

Of course, admonitions to 'act responsibly' or to 'take responsibility' often fall on deaf ears; they sound censorious and finger wagging, and do not have a good record. They are also ineffective. Think of all the people who continued smoking despite repeated warning messages on cigarette packets and a mass of evidence regarding its lethal effects; even physicians in full possession of the medical facts would carry on smoking, *knowingly* 'not taking responsibility' for their own health. They

---

[22] Mark Lynas, *The God Species: How Humans Really Can Save the Planet* (Harper Collins, 2011).

would likely claim that they 'were dependent on it' and while they knew it would kill them, they 'could not help themselves'. In a sense, this is an apt parallel to the human dependence on the existing ways of organising society and the global economy: we know we are damaging the health of the Earth's biosphere by our continuing with our unsustainable ways, and yet act as if we are 'unable to help ourselves'.

The reality is, though, that given a powerful enough multi-pronged campaign, much is possible. Numerous people _have_ given up smoking – at least in Britain. An enabling infrastructure was created through a sustained multidimensional response to a major public health hazard – the dangers of 'passive smoking' being recognised as real. A similar multi-pronged climate change campaign could also be initiated. It would need the setting of national and international objectives, with a whole range of initiatives launched as a rolling programme. As Kevin Anderson (a distinguished professor of energy and climate change) has written:

> The one thing we know about the future is that it will be different. If we do nothing, we will be hit by devastating impacts and unmanageable adaptation needs. If we choose to act to avoid the worst, the mitigation will have to be very significant, which itself will lead to major social change. _Therefore, our role now is to think differently, to achieve greater clarity, to foster a greater imagination and stop saying that it is impossible._ There remains real hope to instigate meaningful and timely change, but each day we choose apathy over action that hope diminishes'.[23] (emphasis added)

---

[23]   Kevin Anderson, 'To meet international commitments on "avoiding dangerous climate change," wealthy nations must reduce emissions by over 10% each year', _Svenska Dagbladet_, Sweden, 7 November 2012.

✳

One can understand the frustration of clear-thinking environmental activists, who cannot understand why people do not 'take responsibility when it's obvious they have to'. As the chemical engineer did at the very beginning of the book – such active campaigners and thinkers can get heated: 'How can people be so intransigent, oblivious, recalcitrant – to the point of our collectively behaving like damn fools?' These are the questions asked provocatively in George Marshall's *Don't Even Think About It*[24] and Margaret Heffernan's *Wilful Blindness*.[25]

The question 'Why is knowledge of climate reality being resisted?' is also the dominating question for Sally Weintrobe and her mainly psychoanalytic colleagues writing in *Engaging with Climate Change*.[26] In explaining the apparent lack of a sense of urgency, they cast the net wide. Thus, one contributor, Stephan Harrison, notes that the opposition of 'climate deniers' comes from vested interests, with 'a vigorous misinformation campaign by sceptics', just as happened in the campaign against smoking. While the scientific smoke screen produced by the tobacco industry provided an early example of determined and deliberate undermining of strong scientific evidence, so equally there has been a campaign to cast doubt on the scientific evidence on climate change.[27]

---

[24] George Marshall, *Don't Even Think About It: Why Our Brains Are Wired To Ignore Climate Change* (Bloomsbury, 2014).

[25] Margaret Heffernan, *Wilful Blindness: Why We Ignore the Obvious at our Peril* (Walker and Co., 2011).

[26] Sally Weintrobe, ed., *Engaging with Climate Change: Psychoanalytic and Interdisciplinary Perspectives* (Routledge, 2013).

[27] Stephan Harrison, 'Climate Change, Uncertainty and Risk', in *Engaging with Climate Change*, p. 236.

In passing, putting commercial considerations ahead of all other obligations is a striking instance of a totally non-*whi* response to the climate crisis: short-term, tunnel-visioned, and already proving self-destructive, as public outrage mounts against those who have funded so much spurious research. Attempted repudiation of the overwhelming evidence for human-implicated global temperature rise is not an intelligent response. Admittedly it is difficult for those whose commercial mission has been to find more and more sequestered carbon and make it available for human beings' use, but this egregious example of lamentable responding to a world situation is a reminder of the need for all the dimensions of whole intelligence to be in play: as well as this being an unintelligent *response*, there is also a lack of *self-recognising*.

Other contributors to *Engaging with Climate Change* locate the problem of inaction and passivity firmly within the unconscious processes of individuals. They look for psychoanalytic explanations. Thus, one of the authors suggests that 'Mother Earth' has been long treated like an 'environment mother' who creates a 'sense of the world as sustaining and there for us to use without undue concern'; or encourages 'the belief that the planet is an unlimited "toilet-mother", capable of absorbing our toxic products to infinity'.[28] Such explanations may be intriguing, and may stimulate our thinking, but on their own they are not likely to lead to public policy changes.

However, another writer, Paul Hoggett (a professor of politics who is also a psychotherapist), takes a more situational approach. He suggests that the apparent anomaly between 'expressing concern' and doing 'little about it' makes sense, given that often (a) there are 'no public recycling schemes,

---

[28]   John Keene, 'Unconscious Obstacles to Caring for the Planet: Facing up to Human Nature', in *Engaging with Climate Change*, p. 146

no sympathetic party to vote for'; (b) people may have little belief in their own ability to effect changes 'and there are no wider networks of like-minded people'; (c) the 'framework of government policies, taxes and subsidies either fails to incentivise pro-environmental behaviour ... or provides a disincentive to such behaviour (for example, public transport is too expensive to use)'; (d) 'people perceive there is little they can do to make a difference because they believe either that it is too late or that the key changes need to be made by others' (e.g. one's own or other governments).[29]

On the subject of responsibility, I remember my own reaction when I came across early gestalt writers who re-cast it as *response-ability*. The different spelling made a difference: it lifted a heavy feeling in my chest that appeared when I heard I was 'not taking responsibility' for something. I felt less deficient in moral terms. I knew the different spelling did not rule out requiring people to account for their actions – and this included me; but the change of expression invited me to take a deeper interest in people's *ability to respond* in a particular situation, and what might be being triggered within my own history if I realised I was 'avoiding responsibility'.

I realised that, in part, the ability to respond is dependent on the situation seeming manageable. If the odds are heavily stacked against a person's capability to act or to make a difference, pointing the finger of blame or condemning others' actions may not be justified. For instance, few people

---

[29] Paul Hoggett, 'Climate Change in a Perverse Culture', in *Engaging with Climate Change*, p. 56.

condemn hostages who read out statements they are forced to read, given their lives are – literally, in this case – on a knife-edge; martyrdom is not for everyone.

As Paul Hoggett found, if the wider context creates disabling conditions, even a strong personal or group wish to do something practical can be set backwards. In such cases, responding to the situation appears 'too difficult'. Ordinary citizens can be labelled 'irresponsible', but a more insightful conclusion might be that they are less 'response-able' than they could be if the surrounding context – or social infrastructure – were more enabling and less disabling.

Part of responding with whole intelligence, then, involves *redefining the situation and taking a wider, longer-term view of all the 'forces' at work.* Regarding the climate crisis, arguably this is happening, albeit slowly – but the chief vehicles for educating the population, the news media, have consistently underplayed the seriousness of the situation, in connection with climate change and the damage to the biosphere.[30]

Frustration at the lack of an intelligent-seeming response was palpable following the collapse of the Copenhagen climate summit in 2009. World leaders *en masse* assembled – at a peak of concern, expectation, hope, and world attention – to

---

[30] Shortly before *Future Sense* went to press, the *Guardian* newspaper in Britain embarked upon a concerted campaign to raise consciousness of the climate issue. The retiring editor, Alan Rusbridger, wrote that he had 'very few regrets ... except this one: that we had not done justice to this huge, overshadowing, overwhelming issue of how climate change will probably, within the lifetime of our children, cause untold havoc and stress to our species. So, in the time left to me as editor, I thought I would try to harness the Guardian's best resources to describe what is happening and what – if we do nothing – is almost certain to occur' http://www.theguardian.com.

come to global agreements, and they went away with very little accomplished. The global leaders, who could not have been oblivious of the massive significance of their failure, 'were pulled back by the gravitational force of their contexts'[31] – that is, by how their publics and industrialists would react back home.

The failure of the news media to keep this topic 'on the boil' after Copenhagen – which they can mostly do when they want to – is in part their own failure to 'read their whole situation' intelligently; notably, they appear not to grasp the extent of their own power and persuasive influence, as being among the chief global providers of information and shared public narratives. However, they themselves appear not to feel 'response-able', given their need to sell newspapers or win audience share, and not to offend their proprietors and advertisers. This highlights the need for courageous and timely interventions, and for understanding the dynamics of a more intelligent, wider-angled vision. Realising that the contextual constraints are hardly ever straightforward is an obligatory first step.

A markedly different approach is demonstrated in one of the more successful grassroots movements that have sprung up in response to the global environmental crisis. The Transition Network[32] defines its role and purpose as

---

[31]   I am grateful to Hugh Pidgeon for bringing this evocative sentence to my attention.

[32]   Transition Network. Quotations from https://www.transitionnetwork. org.

follows: 'to inspire, encourage, connect, support and train communities as they self-organise around the Transition model' – the model being one of preparing for a different kind of world in the future.

Transition writers emphasise how human beings 'are already entering a period of huge change – turning around the story of ever increasing material well-being for each succeeding generation. *Our only choice is in how we meet the situation*' (emphasis added). In other words, the Transition Network is tapping into underlying concerns about the future, and it is fuelled by the longing of a great many people to 'do something' and 'make a difference'. The network activates people's endowed potential – their ability to respond to situations, and specifically to an emergency regarded as worldwide. Taking in the global picture – which is daunting and devastating in its implications – is handled here by emphasising the scope of local action. People can make at least a small difference, witness their impact, and experience a sense of accomplishment. The whole enterprise is human scale. Participants are invited to exercise initiative, help define objectives, and bring their enthusiasm and individual inputs – in effect to access their whole intelligence. The set up encourages those with expertise to exercise leadership, and for those with many different skills to become engaged, involved, informed, and included. And I am noticing as I write this, the repetition of 'in-' is striking.

The originators of the Transition Network stress the continuity between initiatives and changes at a global level, and the need to 'design a "transition" or process of change ... where all sectors of society can still live well with much less fossil energy'. They reject outright the model of choice of the large corporate and governmental variety: that of rolling out a standardised programme, centrally orchestrated, and hierarchically led. Instead, their thinking embraces local leadership, development of local communities, and wide participation.

The language of taking direct responsibility sits easily with their goals: in the words of Rob Hopkins, the principal originator, 'it's about what you can create with the help of the people who live in your street, your neighbourhood, your town. If enough people do it, it can lead to real impact, to real jobs and real transformation of the places we live [in]'.

Strengthening *whi* in the practice of responding

In this First Exploration, we have seen that whole intelligence also has the meaning of 'intelligence applied to the whole'. Responding to complex situations requires engaging with a bigger picture, the totality, or a long-term strategy. Some parts of the total response may involve specific quantitative analyses, or specialised procedures that are definitively attending to parts, rather than a whole. Ultimately, however, all these need to fit into a bigger picture, a comprehensive understanding, which is qualitative and subjective – however much this is under-played, or '*always* justified by the hard data' – as one emphatic CEO insisted.

The capacity to engage with the whole of something – say, a major international incident, or a crisis in the family – calls for adroit and skilful attention to a complex situation. Formulating coherent and imaginative choices in responding to it are intrinsically challenging, yet also satisfying – like solving a complicated puzzle. Such opportunities stimulate and educate those who are engaged in it. The task is also one of helping to write the narrative – or to rewrite it – thus taking ownership of the meaning.

However, the scope of manifesting – and growing – whole intelligence in this way is often confined to a privileged few: those in leading positions of influence who – whether alone or operating as a tiny kitchen cabinet of people thinking in unison – are the only ones who are actually able to look at the 'whole picture', including its external context and its internal workings at the same time, and as an entirety. Though many leaders already displaying *whi* make vigorous attempts to ensure widespread consultation and participation among their staff, I suspect that a majority of senior executives and others holding power still take for granted that the bulk of the workforce will be excluded.

Yet when only an elite cadre has privileged access to information, can read situations, and decide the strategy, there are serious long-term consequences. The remainder of those involved – those regarded as 'the lower echelons', worker bees, foot soldiers, or lower level managers in a hierarchical system – in having little access to the overall picture, disengage from the complexity. Reality is what the higher-level leaders define, while off by themselves. The rest feel as if they are getting an edited version, about which they may well be cynical.

Top-down proposals rarely galvanise strong endorsement from those excluded from the actual decision making. Those excluded lose their 'response-ability'. Not sharing responsibility also isolates leaders and fails to capitalise on the capacities and whole intelligence of others. Wars have been ill embarked upon through deliberate bypassing of the wisdom of regional experts – as well as, sometimes, the good sense of a massive demonstration on the street. Here we see an abrogation of *whi* with disastrous consequences.

*

If the pattern is that skilled 'whole situation thinking' is confined only to a small minority, this increases my concern that – unless highlighted, reinforced and expanded immeasurably – *high level skills and abilities relating to 'perceiving the whole' may go the way of lost traditions.* The consequences of too few people having the opportunity to think in big-picture ways may be leading to an overall decline in competence – and neglect in cultivating *whi* – when those skills may be the most required in conditions of increased uncertainty in the future.

The absence of a strong tradition of whole thinking may be especially serious in institutions such as corporations or government departments – or certain families for that matter – where hierarchical systems of management and decision making are still taken for granted as necessary and 'normal', and especially when there's reliance on single individuals or an elite group. Higher education institutions, too, if they allow knowledge to become ever more specialised and compartmentalised, could be providing – in contradiction to what they pretend to exist for – a system which effectively rewards a *narrowing* of capacity, rather than an *expansion* of ways to 'handle big and complex problems'.

I am speculating that it may prove to be a colossal error in history, and one continuing to be made in the field of responding to the climate crisis – that so much of the problem solving is confined to scientific experts, politicians, civil servants, and others who speak to each other in language that is formal, legal, institutional, academic, and / or bureaucratic. This supports the hierarchical tendency to create an 'in group of the knowledgeable'. The intergovernmental-type language is 'stripped of soul' as a senior manager recognised – and represents another kind of exclusion from total participation. In its recognising the need to engage with a broad, inclusive audience, one senses that the Transition Network – as discussed earlier – is ahead of the game. Fundamentally, the issue is about sharing power.

My conclusion is that, *if actually able to respond*, people are more likely to want to be *responsible*. If more people are given opportunity to grow and deepen through greater power sharing and evolving and decision making, with many more 'town meetings' of the kind found in New England in the USA, and other ways of creating mass engagement – as happened, for instance, in the Scottish campaign for independence – more people may become engaged and resourceful problem solvers. They will unearth their aptitude and potentiality for responding – meaning that they will become more situationally aware, will ask more questions, and creatively adapt to unique circumstances.

Given the seriousness of the climate situation, millions – even billions – of people need to become involved. Opening consultation and study to a far wider global community of potential activists could be made a priority. Changes of language and presentation would be a start.

Luckily, at the grass-roots level, there is plenty happening, but the need for some linking between the two kinds of approach is sorely needed. Otherwise there is continued disjunction between those who decide policy and those who are not informed and not believed to be interested enough to engage with it. The evidence, however – both in the Transition model and in the Scottish independence campaign – suggests that given the chance to make a real difference, and to connect policy making with their own experience – a far greater number are more than willing to respond to the situation with enthusiasm.

CHAPTER 4

INTERRELATING
The Second Exploration

FRIENDSHIP, the value underlying the Second Exploration, has its own impetus and intrinsic rewards; it's a vast source of strength and human hope, and the basis of all that we regard as humanitarian. Arguably, this Exploration is an extension of the first. But here the 'situations' are specifically to do with our relating together – human to human or group to group.

Perhaps the most pertinent question here is about the loss of trust, ease, and quality of engagement that can – and frequently does – occur when differences are not resolved. When communication breaks down, human suffering is often a result. We know from our own experience that sometimes, even with goodwill, finding common ground with another person or with a group is beyond our reach; misunderstandings, distancing, or conflict can result. If friendship is the attracting value of the Exploration, enmity is its antithesis. The pursuit of war, genocide, and terrorism represent humanity's most egregious departures from sanity, in which all considerations of friendship are set aside. Yet we can recognise that much of the vindictiveness and violence which can ensue derives from feeling oppressed, or from fears of invasion, of being robbed, or otherwise devalued – rather than from some free-standing destructive impulse.

The contrasts between peace and war lie in the background

of my thinking throughout this Second Exploration. As the book goes to press, there are numerous conflicts around the world – all of them distractions from engaging adequately with a destabilised biosphere, and global economy – as well as, of course, each having a fallout of damaged relationships between states, communities, religions, and ethnic groups in the wider network of the whole-world community.

Through interrelating we experience the potential impact of greater whole intelligence in perhaps its most vivid form. In grasping the complexities of intimate relationships; in exploring the endless varieties of love; in appreciating our creative impulses in the company of others; and in managing our potential destructiveness, there is much to discover about how human beings engage with each other constructively rather than destructively. The continuing question for the Second Exploration is: 'How can we relate to others with greater whi?'

First realisations

When I think of demonstrating whole intelligence in relating with others, I think of Malik, as I shall call him here. He was a gifted consultant and experienced observer of people, especially in situations of conflict.

I recall a meeting with him, early in our relationship, when I was slightly in awe of him. I arrived with some points of disagreement lined up to talk about. He had argued for a proposal which I thought was going to damage the organisation in which we were both members, and I was aroused with a sense of protest. We sat down and I began to speak. I noticed I was a little accusing in my tone of voice, and somewhat tremulous.

Malik did not look away or appear defensive. At one point, the phone rang: he apologised, explained to me that his assistant had just arrived, having been off sick. He picked up the phone. After a brief word or two, he returned to our conversation, having signalled by his movements and manner that he had 'not really left' and was ready to resume. He 'heard me out' without interruption. At the end, he said, 'Thank you. I need to make sure I've understood your point of view correctly', and he repeated back to me what I had said, asking for any corrections, if he had misheard me or not understood. He summarised what I had said perfectly. Malik then responded with a clear statement of how our views differed – which I agreed summed up the difference – and as I left, he thanked me for coming and said he would like to think about his position in the light of my comments. Altogether, I felt respected, and my contribution valued. Looking back, Malik provided a master class in both how to listen and how to acknowledge differences without closing any doors: he demonstrated whole intelligence in action.

If we are to learn as a species to collaborate to maximum effectiveness, and also to confront our capacity for inhumanity, spitefulness, and hate, interrelating should be at the very centre of learning and research. This is not so. However, the good news is that, for any new-style education that might be forthcoming in the future, there's a curriculum at hand. A huge body of practical 'know-how' already exists. Among psychologists, relationship counsellors, neurobiologists, peace-educators, group therapists, many spiritual teachers, international mediators at flash-points, and practitioners of 'non-violent communication',[33]

---

[33] Marshall B. Rosenberg, *Nonviolent Communication: A Language of Life* (PuddleDancer Press, 2003). The book describes a very useful approach that deserves to be learned by everyone.

one discovers remarkable areas of overlapping knowledge – for instance, around trauma, the need for people to feel respected, and the dangers of stereotyping. This basic know-how needs to be gathered together in a critical mass, recognised, and encouraged to 'go viral', with a necessary contagion of arriving sense.

Without doubt, the complexity in relating between people is immense: there is an elaborate 'grammar' of social engagement and etiquette, with immense cultural variation. There are questions of power differences, and the effects of yearnings and fears that stem from our human past. A *whi* approach to interrelating requires an appreciation of the different 'frames' and layerings of experience that occur in relating to others.

It was not until my late twenties that my fascination with human relationships converged with what I was doing professionally.

I was deeply involved in researching experimental educational programmes in university and college settings, and was noticing huge differences in the ways in which teachers related to their classes, with a whole variety of effects upon students, learning, and performance. Some instructors and professors were courteous towards their students, one might almost say 'tender', which surprised me; others seemed oblivious to there being any human connection at all in their teaching. One engineering professor used to eat his lunchtime sandwich in an unwholesome fashion while teaching his laboratory class.

While differences in personal style were important, the contexts of relating together were also influential in what happened. I recall a particular senior professor of physics – a brilliant and appreciated lecturer. His exposition was polished, humorous, full of enlivening anecdotes, and his lectures were popular. But, faced with small seminars, he needed to change his mode of relating with his audience; when he did, he came across as dull and pedantic, and his students soon lost interest. It was an early confirmation that one could not look at people relating together in isolation: one needed to look more widely, for instance, at how people *think they are supposed to relate* in the context in which they find themselves.

Towards the end of this period I began my gestalt training. This prompted seismic shifts in me. There were skills and practices communicated – and modelled – by my gestalt teachers that were new and different. I learned rudiments that had passed me by in my own social learning. I realised how easy it was to fall into certain traps. For example, I often thought I could tell what others were thinking – when actually I was wide of the mark. In the training, checking with others was encouraged and the lessons were obvious. There were other demonstrations of how we largely invent our reality. Our views of others' actions and attitudes can only be provisional or tentative speculations at best. Our observations pass through our own selective filters – acquired in the miscellaneous subcultures we have known, starting with our family of origin and other formative milieus. Once we realise this, we can hear pronouncements – for instance about the attitudes of another person – as saying more about the one observing than the one observed.

In my training, I also realised for the first time that the *quality of the contact* – the health, mutual satisfaction, usefulness, and significance of what happened in a two-person situation – was not something that 'just happened'. I discovered it was not like some chemical reaction in a test-tube, as in the popular metaphor, 'the chemistry was, or was not, right between us', but was something in which I myself was centrally implicated and could help fashion. Better relating together could happen as a result of simply reporting the truth of one's own experience rather than hiding it behind a mask, provoking mystery.

I was also discovering for the first time, and well into adult life, that speaking someone's name and maintaining eye contact brought directness and more life to the interchange. I also learned the merits of reporting to someone, rather than just saying it to myself, that 'I do not think I have been listening carefully enough, so please could you repeat the last point you made?' and that, in a coaching session, reporting my feelings was sometimes better than holding them privately. I realised I could say: 'When you were describing your sense of elation, I was struck by how my own feelings were different ... I felt sad' – which might help the person being coached to acknowledge her own sadness and recognise that it was not an emotion she needed to suppress all the time.

I gathered that short statements often carried more 'weight' than long ones; and that lots of questions people ask are not genuine questions. For example, 'Why did you not simply call the police?' often means that the speaker has in mind that the person recounting what happened *should* have called the police. The person's feeling is of being criticised, but the fact of there being criticism is often denied – as in, 'Oh, no, it was just a question', said with innocence. Inner confusion results, and muddies the waters of communication.

I discovered, too, that if I said, 'You must be so relieved that the project is completed', I was planting a meaning into the conversation that was my own in origin, rather than the other person's – and that the meaning was yet another guess, fantasy, speculation on my part, and needed to be portrayed as such. Thus I could have said, 'I'm guessing you might feel relieved ... is that the case?'

There were many of these small extra clarities, and changes of speech habits, that I discovered made a difference to engaging with others. The bigger learning for me was threefold:

First, I was realising that this activity I thought I knew about – relating to other people – was a lot more complicated and multidimensional than I had imagined.

Second, I was being invited to raise my sights, to take in a bigger picture – a kind of crash course in advanced civility. I realised that attending to the shape, colour, and texture of relating to another person is part of the totality of the message conveyed: the content can be blurred or muddied if said without feeling, or confused by slipshod verbal shortcuts. The subtleties of how people affected one another were obviously a rich field of enquiry – and everyone could benefit from knowing more about it.

Third, I discovered how important it was to pay attention to the circumstances of each meeting, and to pay close attention to questions of timing, perceived relevance, and whether the necessary conditions were in place to enable a successful meeting of minds – or perhaps hearts. Blundering in, as often happens with someone who either has, or imagines they have, more power – authority, seniority, higher rank, or right to be listened to – signifies an absence of *whi*. Speaking with complete disregard of the availability of the other party to be able to hear what one has to say is more or less to guarantee a mismatch, a failed communication. I learned that often I needed to slow down, to inquire, to build more baseline understanding of where my conversational partner was in their attention, and to discover by direct inquiry their readiness to hear what I had to say.

*

The learning never stops. I had a reminder of one the most common pitfalls on a recent flight to Norway. The interrelating 'lesson' began when I boarded the plane. I was in an aisle seat, and a couple were already installed in the two other seats. They scowled as I struggled with putting items in the overhead locker, and when I made a small comment about the locker being surprisingly small, they ignored me. No hint of any conversational interest was forthcoming, and soon I was reading and snoozing. I 'forgot' them, though when they were asleep and I was awake, I took a look at them and remember deciding – on all the evidence to date – that they seemed unhappy, impolite, and unfriendly. Of course, I should have caught myself in the act of *fantasising* on the basis of a tiny bit of data, and in the further act of *believing my fantasy was true*, an error so common that statistically it might be considered normal – but which is a small step down a very long and slippery road to relational confusion and ineptitude.

As we approached Oslo, all three of us were straining to see out of the window; it came as a surprise when the woman of the couple turned to me with a smile and asked me whether it was my first visit to Norway. Soon we were chatting amiably. I was struck by her animated expression, the sparkle of her eyes, and the fact that they had just flown via London from Tobago, where they had been on vacation, celebrating their silver wedding. Her husband took her hand, and eyed me with interest. Of course, any conclusion that they were 'genuinely happy' would be another leap in the interpretive dark. But what happened showed I could still fall into relational habits that were unintelligent – in this case, allowing my initial irritation at their lack of conversation at the beginning to contaminate my later thinking.

Changing my thinking

Inevitably, exploring this second *whi*-dimension best occurs through live studying of our meetings with others. I am remembering Matthew, a long-term friend and fellow coach, who arrived to see me at short notice. His father had just been diagnosed with inoperable cancer, and Matthew had flown at once from California (where he lived) to visit his father – he thought possibly for the last time. He arrived in Europe with hopes and expectations.

I make Matthew tea, and we sit and talk. I am listening deeply, with great attentiveness – the same kind of professional attention I bring to a coaching session with a client. Being 'professional' does not mean distancing myself: I like to remember what the notable philosopher Martin Buber said – that one can only 'know the wholeness of the person' if one does not leave out one's 'subjectivity' and 'does not remain an untouched observer'.[34] So I am touched and affected, and also may want to say something about *how* I am affected, bearing in mind that while not wanting to interrupt his flow, I also do not want to 'leave myself out of the equation'. After all, Matthew is opening his heart and speaking to *me*; I need a readiness and willingness to meet him in all his human fullness with all of my own.

Buber's message is very different from the advice Sigmund Freud gave to beginning psychoanalysts – that they model

---

[34] Martin Buber, 'What is Man?', 1938, translated by Ronald Gregor Smith in *Between Man and Man* (Macmillan, 1947; 1965), p. 148.

themselves during treatment 'on the surgeon, who puts aside all his feelings' and maintains an 'emotional coldness'.[35] This particular advice from the pioneer of therapy may still persist among a minority of professionals, who think that 'to be scientific' requires treating the client more like an object than a fellow subject who is the author of her or his life; but it has been quietly shelved by most psychotherapists.

With Matthew, I listen as he describes his 'longing for real communication' with his father, a type of connecting which he feels he never has experienced. He describes his three-day visit, largely alone with his father. Though he is likely to 'die in months', his father wants to talk about impersonal matters – cricket being foremost. Along with not mentioning his illness, he also fails to acknowledge that Matthew has flown to see him at short notice, an out-of-the-ordinary event.

I am listening and imagining the scene between father and son, each with their separate preoccupations and wishes for their meeting. The needs that were organising how they responded to each other remained unspoken. I felt a wave of regret about the lost opportunity for intimacy. Sadly, the experience of many men, including fathers and sons, is that intimacy and showing love for one another has a very narrow bandwidth for expression. Much does get transmitted, but indirectly – which can be a profound limitation.

The meeting with Matthew reminded me of the journey I had travelled in my own thinking. I mused to myself as follows: 'You

[35]   Quoted in Morris N. Eagle, *From Classical to Contemporary Psychoanalysis: A Critique and Integration* (Taylor and Francis, 2011), p. 85.

can understand how people – including Freud and still a large majority in psychology, medicine, and other professions – can picture what's happening as an encounter between two people, each with a separated mind and individual needs, operating as if there's empty space between them, across which messages are transmitted and received, bouncing back and forth as in verbal ping-pong'. This was once my own understanding, and on this model, Matthew's disappointment would be accounted for by 'lack of contact', 'not getting through', or an inability 'to connect' – in other words, missing one another, the ping-pong ball constantly landing on the floor.

Later in my career, as a result of both discovering the emerging field of interpersonal neurobiology,[36] and listening to well-informed colleagues, I underwent a complete shift of perspective. I realised that the 'space between' the two parties is full of taken-for-granted connectivity. Regarded this way, Matthew and his father are no longer seen as 'disconnected' at all: they have years of shared history, privileged knowledge regarding each other. How could these two possibly be considered as 'not connected'? The old model suddenly seemed out of date – like an old-fashioned telephone exchange.

I had already written about encounters between people being like 'dances', and the ideas began to fit together. Each meeting is 'co-created': it's not a product of one person alone. In long-established relationships, both parties know the style, the safe conversational topics, the no-go areas, and each party's expectations arise from a small selection of possibilities. A two-person conversation – like Matthew and

---

[36] See Daniel Siegel, *Mindsight: Transform your Brain with the New Science of Kindness* (Oneworld Publication, 2011). I have also been influenced by the writings of Lynne Jacobs, Frank-M. Staemmler, Mark Fairfield, Gordon Wheeler, Rupert Sheldrake, and Bert Hellinger.

his father – unfolds according to the 'steps' of the dance in question and has a familiar (family-like) ring to it.

The difficulty for Matthew was that he wanted to change the dance. He hoped that proximity to death might shake loose the old routines, and they might dance to a new tune or at least rhythm. But Matthew found – as most of us do – that he lapsed into dancing his familiar steps. He felt helpless to do anything about it. Theoretically, he could have flouted the dance routines – but the old man was frail, it would merely have upset him, and could have meant they ended on a worse footing, not better.

Matthew and I decided to take a more considered, more complete, view of interrelating – as revealed by what had happened for him.

First, we recognised that encounters of all kinds are influenced by their contexts (as discussed in the First Exploration). Thus, a conversation between two people live on TV is likely to be very different from one held in private. If it had been his father's actual deathbed, all might have been different.[37]

Second, in co-creating the joint situation, or dance, each dancer is adapting to the other's steps and both are seeking a way to move together in a mutually satisfying way. This can only happen successfully if the parties 'read' one another's intentions – and this reading is not a conscious speculation regarding their thoughts, but something far more automatic

---

[37]   Matthew later reported that as he accompanied his father dying, he was massaging him, cradling him, expressing his love, and felt his father responding in 'an incredibly loving and tender way'.

and basic. With the discovery of 'mirror neurones', we now have a neurobiological explanation for our extraordinary capacity to adjust to each other: so we very rarely bump into each other in crowds, for example. As the neurobiologist, Dan Siegel, explains: We 'make maps in our brains of the internal state – the intentional stance – of other people'; we embed 'the mind of another into our own firing patterns, ... resonate with their feelings ... sense not only what action is coming next, but also the emotional energy that underlies the behavior'.[38]

Third, in speaking of two (or more) parties dancing together, the most common perspective puts the emphasis in the wrong place. To remain focused on the separate status of the two 'body-minds' engaged in the dance, and to think of the two individuals' dance steps originating in two different nervous systems, is misleading. Human beings are more connected and more mutually dependent than the 'entirely separate organisms' model assumes. As the philosopher Mary Midgley has suggested, the 'idea that people are solitary, self-contained, indeed selfish individuals ... [once] looked rational because it reflected the atomic theory of the day, a theory that similarly reduced matter to hard, impenetrable, disconnected atoms like billiard balls ...'.[39]

I realised, eventually, and it took some while to grasp, that the idea of our being separate single organisms that can exist independently, misses the point. We cannot exist separately or entirely autonomously and still survive. We are 'en-cultured' beings, right from the earliest age, bound into the common language and cultural assumptions of the community into which we are born; we could never have survived other than by being cared for, fed, and culturally included.

---

[38]   Siegel, *Mindsight*, pp. 60–61.

[39]   Mary Midgely, *The Myths We Live By* (Routledge, 2004), p. 9.

We can begin here, then, to appreciate what is sometimes called 'the relational outlook'. Here, the fundamental realisation is that our interplay – our relating to others, our connectivity to others – is not some secondary process 'added on' as the 'interacting-with-others function' still regarded from the viewpoint of solo psychology. Instead, our 'joined up-ness' occupies the central position: rather than thinking of ourselves as entirely separate individuals *we are, first and foremost, interconnected and interdependent*, and *we cannot exist otherwise.*

While hermits may choose to isolate themselves, and while there are times when all of us wish to be alone, isolation is never the norm. Thus, it is forced on people as punishment (solitary confinement) or to drive captives half-mad (for interrogation purposes or as part of torture), or it comes about through loneliness and loss of a 'secure base' of connection in a community. Just as it takes a village to raise a child, so it takes a village to hold distressed persons, to care for the elderly, to provide places of peace and healing and stimulation where people can engage in relaxed and playful recreation.

What was missing for Matthew and his father were other presences, offering support, acting as catalysts, sharing their own experiences. This meeting with Matthew came as a useful reminder of why I had gravitated years before to working predominantly with groups rather than individuals in therapy.

Central to a more *whi* perspective is recognising the extent to which our usual individualistic assumptions can lead to dangerous simplifications. They are still dominant in general thought.

I see a parallel in the way ecological thinking took decades to be understood and fully taken on board within biology. The idea that animals studied in a laboratory could provide all one needed to know about the animal's physiology, for instance, has taken a long time to be superseded: now the whole emphasis is on regarding the organism and its habitat as intricately interwoven, as a single system.

A comparable insensitivity to context exists in the case of what I'm calling solo psychology – thinking that everything can be contained within an individualised psychological focus. I have come to think in terms of a web of complex neural connectivity – centred in two brains, yes, but not necessarily confined there. Just as there is an unmeasurable but manifest 'intelligence' embedded in a woodland ecosystem – so that the whole woodland works together as a complex organised whole – so we might consider an equivalent intelligence at work between human beings. The idea of a shared 'relational field' that embraces any two or more parties who are conversing, working, or living together is far more useful and revealing than the earlier thinking, as existed before the discovery of mirror neurones.

I realise that this more ecological-type approach stretches many people's thinking. They may be deeply reluctant to abandon ideas of entirely separate organisms existing apart, contained intact within their own distinct boundary. As I have intimated, it has taken me years to begin to redraw the lines in my own thinking, with a continuing desire on my part to uphold the separateness between any two parties. Yet this is belied by understanding – most obviously and least controversially – how a mother and a newborn baby operate together as a single system of continuous intimate interdependence, with proven physiological effects upon each other.[40]

Regarding two parties as a single working unity, indivisible and organised as a complex entity, and *seeing this as the natural order*, means letting go of the powerful individualist assumption that has long dominated Western philosophy. The experienced reality, however, is that, notably in dancing, deeply conversing, or in love-making – in the words of David Bohm – the 'barriers have dissolved, [and] then there arises one mind, where they are all in one unit, but each person retains his or her own individual awareness … It's actually a single intelligence that works with people who are moving in relationship with one another'.[41]

Strongly, then, the kinds of connectivity that exist between mothers and their babies also apply more widely than we have imagined. One thinks of those deeply in love, or of the intense bonding which can occur between soldiers in combat, where the felt connectivity can be so powerful that it can eclipse other kinds of loyalties. Here the suffusion across boundaries is most obvious. But one can also think of what happens when we receive an email from an intimate friend or lover – how we exist during the reading of it, and maybe for some time after, in a state of shared connection, as if the other's presence and one's own receptivity are momentarily joined in one seamless relational event. Likewise, after receiving an email that emphasises difference between us, we can also feel effects upon

---

[40] I recommend any book or YouTube video by Dr Edward Tronick. See, for instance, Ed Tronick, *The Neurobehavioral and Social-Emotional Development of Infants and Children* (W.W. Norton, 2007).

[41] David Bohm, in conversation with Joseph Jaworski, in Joseph Jaworski, *Synchronicity: The Inner Path of Leadership* (Berett-Koehler, 1998), p. 100.

our own state of being: a different flavour but still a reminder of how connected we are to one another: a few words on a screen can transform our mood, and our relational openness or defensiveness, and degree of arousal.

Fields of connection have 'whole properties' and induce an encompassing shared sense of togetherness – or, of course, felt apartness, but often jointly felt. As those who lead or chair any group discover, the group's 'relational field' needs to be looked at in a unitary manner as a phenomenon in its own right. We need to recognise the totality of the group as a whole, which is not merely a medley of assorted separate participants.

This way of thinking – moving into more 'whole' perceiving of human beings in their togetherness – may not fit easily into the normal thinking expounded in reductive science, but perhaps there needs to be deeper questioning of the latter's taken-for-granted dominant status. With ecosystems operating in the way they do as working totalities, and with human beings operating in strongly bonded relationships that have a particular overall joint character or 'feel' to them, which people can access through their bodies, the thinking has to change its focus. The presumption that we should minimise or even deny the existence of such observed phenomena becomes unreasonable.

In terms of whole intelligence, one can question whether following uncritically the 'scientifically approved' model of human reality is wise in all conditions and circumstances – especially given that the scientific community reveals itself at times as 'all too human'.[42] That we have a 'distinct psychological life', unique to ourselves, seems obvious – yet is it more complicated than that? Might the existence of a shared 'relational field' be more than a metaphor?

---

[42] See, for instance, Rupert Sheldrake, *The Science Delusion: Freeing the Spirit of Enquiry* (Hodder and Stoughton, 2012).

Science has a habit of denying what lies beyond that which is currently understood. Even Isaac Newton had this problem. His ideas about apples falling and the gravitational force were so new that he was reluctant to publish his ideas, writing in his *Opticks*, 'This principle of nature being very remote from the conceptions of Philosophers, I forebore to describe it in that book, least I should be accounted an extravagant freak and so prejudice my Readers against all those things which were the main designe of the book'.[43]

The influences of roots

The benefits of interrelating with greater *whi* soon become clear. Using one's empathic skills to 'listen and understand where others are' or to 'recognise at once what is called for in a critical encounter' enhances the quality of meetings. Collaborations and business negotiations become more proficient and pleasurable, leisure times with friends fuller and more flowing. Paying greater attention, and accepting one's own responsibility and place as a co-creating party to what is happening, help reduce relational difficulties when, inevitably, they arise.

We all know times when relations misfire. Someone has not felt respected, or has experienced being 'missed', or has felt insulted – or worse, humiliated – by another party; and, in reaction, they have bridled or become irritated, withdrawn some attention, or gone into some introspective self-condemnation ('I am not good enough'). A misunderstanding

---

[43] Quoted in Murray Gell-Mann, *Selected Papers*, ed. Harald Fritzsch, World Scientific Series in 20th Century Physics, Vol. 40 (World Scientific Publishing, 2009), p. 380.

can be enough to set in process a cycle of mutual reactivity. Some shift any 'awkward' conversation onto safer territory, effectively burying both the issue itself and their commitment to take part further. If two parties do not have sufficient recognition of what has happened, or insight enough to stop, recoup, or gather themselves together to explore what happened, a relational failure is probable.

My friend and colleague, Gordon Wheeler, argues that, given basic facts about human socialisation, it is inevitable that we find difficult the differences between ourselves and others.[44] He reminds us that from the moment of arriving in the world, we are being formed – culturally and linguistically, emotionally and cognitively – by what's around us: that is, by 'the medium itself ... that we were most immediately steeped in'.[45] Our development as infants and children is an extraordinary multidimensional journey of learning, during which our brains and nervous systems continue to develop physically, and our capacity to engage with the world around us changes in parallel. Thus, *biological and social development proceed together, as a single process*: we do not develop biologically and *then* go about absorbing the embracing culture into which we have been born and which we have experienced; our very brain development is dependent on our cultural immersion.

[44] Gordon Wheeler, 'Culture, Self, and Field', in *The Bridge: Dialogues Across Cultures*, ed. Talia Levine Bar-Yoseph (Gestalt Institute Press, 2005), pp. 43–66.

[45] This evocative phrase that I have always remembered is from Henry James, describing the childhood that he and his brother William James experienced. It has always appealed to me, conveying some of the feeling that my own upbringing evoked – and maybe others' too. Henry James, *Autobiography* (Princeton University Press, 1983).

The basic patterns of our cultural, linguistic, familial, and social environment become the networks of assumptions that we take for granted as *the way the world is*. Our basic security, our sense of what is 'normal' and 'right', our very way of making sense of reality, begin to be established in our first months and years. And once these are established, we take them for granted as 'givens', as part of who we are, as our 'normal'. So when we sit down to engage with someone from a very different culture, who may speak a different language, and perhaps has a different appearance, it can be useful to imagine that there are not just two persons sitting there, but two cultures. It is a meeting between two different paths of development, two versions of making sense of the world, and two sets of culturally formed assumptions about how to relate to others – and about what is true, or funny, or insulting, or sacred, or appropriate to talk about.

Two points arise from this way of viewing cultural difference, it seems to me, that mark out the means for enhancing whole intelligence in our interrelating. Again, I am drawing on Wheeler's ideas. The *first* is that we cannot obliterate cultural differences. They are too deeply ingrained – all we can do is to acknowledge that they are there, negotiate around them, recognise the differences, and *enter into a dialogue*.

The *second* point is that, in the presence of 'strangeness', a frequent impulse is to retreat to what is most familiar, and most reassuringly 'normal' – which brings people back to their root assumptions, and a place of known safety. So that when two parties are there as strangers to each other and seeking to connect, and *find themselves NOT doing so*, then each party may be *less* inclined to reach out into the uncertain space of encountering the other's strangeness. Instead, they come back to what they have known the longest, and feel most certain about – the place they feel is most safe; in effect, they retreat into themselves. So the more tense and difficult the encounter between the two persons, the greater the likelihood of cultural mismatches appearing, with perhaps both parties inclined to be *more* inflexible in their beliefs, and perhaps insisting that *their* 'take on reality' has to be 'the right one'.

This example of a possible runaway process can result in an escalating misunderstanding about what is happening and can lead to entrenched conflict. But there are numerous ways to prevent a downward spiral. Mediation by a third party is obviously one of them. But one or other of the parties, recognising what's happening, can also bring about a change in the dance between them. They can make a unilateral move – perhaps sharing that what they are together experiencing may be a mismatch and that they need to honour the two sets of cultural assumptions that may be at the root of the differences. Perhaps too, at a procedural level, there might be an agreed suggestion to 'take time out', or for the two parties to 'cool the temperature of the meeting'. They might also change from attending to what they disagree about to acknowledging things on which they are likely to find agreement. These kinds of intervention are exactly what a *whi* approach to relating can offer: sensible compromise, standing back to see a bigger picture, unlocking from an ego-defensive and often childish reactivity, and realising one's own contribution to the pattern of communication which has become established.

While acknowledging the hazards and problematic aspects of people relating across cultural divides, we should not overlook an equally powerful phenomenon: the joining energy between people, the wish to affiliate, the longing to reach out for contact and communication, and the indefatigable seeking to find common ground. This side of the picture needs also to be appreciated and understood, if a fuller and more intelligent appreciation of interrelating is to take root.

Many travellers have had the experience of being in a foreign setting where there is no common language, but nevertheless they have enjoyed memorable connecting, complete with gestures, laughter, eye-contact, manifest warmth, and mutual recognition of shared humanity. Many cultures put emphasis on being generous to strangers, opening one's home, offering food, and going an extra mile to help us on our way. Whatever its origins, the fact of our pull to meet, collaborate, and engage with one another can induce a sense of awe if we stop to think about its prevalence and global magnitude.

Every day, around the globe, countless millions of conversations, ceremonies, informal gatherings, business meetings, musical events, confrontations, shared meals, and sexual liaisons are taking place. There's a buzz of ceaseless global talk happening on a planetary scale that is literally '24/7', given that the Earth rotates and roughly only a third of the world's population are asleep at one time. Life on the planet could not go on without this wealth of collaboration and mutual encountering. Great cities work as organised complexities only because human beings are highly skilled in interrelating, including surmounting disagreements and finding ways to re-connect after conflicts, mishaps, and misreadings of each other. We largely take for granted these multiple webs of collaboration and mutual understanding.

*

Holding in mind the prevalence and power of the energy to join, connect, and befriend, it is even more astonishing that, as a species, we can organise ourselves – often at vast expense – to set about butchering others in the world community of human beings, because we hate or fear them, or want to exact revenge or punish them, or have power over them.

In the context of *interrelating*, war, violence, and choosing to inflict deliberate human suffering represent the antithesis of demonstrating this dimension of whole intelligence. Whether it is someone driving a vehicle loaded with high explosives into a crowded marketplace and detonating it, or someone sitting at a computer monitoring a drone's approach to its coordinates, there is something extraordinary happening, which demands urgent investigation. Both of the examples are choices, planned and orchestrated, both with a sense of 'right being on their side'; and both involve premeditated killing which the great majority of human beings accept as 'normal' – even whilst knowing there are other ways to manage and contain disputes, resolve conflicts, and seek justice for wrongdoings. Even more puzzling is how mutual working and neighbourliness can exist so successfully and for long periods; they can also break down and turn in a matter of days or weeks into lengthy periods of hatred, violence, and mad, mutual destruction.

As impossible as it may seem to question the dominant outlooks regarding 'the inevitability' of war and terrorism, and acknowledging the dangers of appearing naïve and ludicrously idealistic if one does so, there is also a need fearlessly to stay with the agenda of new understanding and of thinking afresh. Humanity evolves, and values and perceptions alter. And if we are to survive long-term, as a species on the planet, we have to continue to evolve.

If we liken our interrelating to a tree, we can see at once the numerous *branches* of how we can relate: formally (as at a business meeting), intimately (with our partner in bed), dutifully (say, with elderly relatives), playfully (with children), sternly (with those who have not honoured a commitment). If we turn our focus to the *roots* of the tree, we are reminded that our most ingrained patterns of interrelating are long-standing and stretch deep into our histories – the cultural and family conditions in which we grew up, and how these, in turn, were influenced by previous generations and the legacies of ancestors. I am suggesting that attention to 'improving relationships' is directed too much to the individual leaves and twigs, while the roots receive less attention than they deserve.

Thus, what arises between people – or between groups or countries or religious communities – sometimes has surprisingly little to do with what they think they are doing and choosing personally or collectively in the contemporary world. Instead, they are acting under the influences of the deep roots: hidden pressures, family politics, inculcated traditions, longstanding grievances, and handed-down history. Even if many of these influences are not thought about consciously, they are powerful in shaping our present relationships.

Shakespeare's play, *Romeo and Juliet*, reminds us that as individuals we are always members of various groups and that each membership exercises a particular pull upon us. The two central characters in the play are divided by two sets of loyalties: to their respective families, traditions, and lineages, and to each other. Shakespeare reminds us of the costs of disavowing one's family. But – in present day terms – there are numerous other loyalties that count: loyalty to nationality, social class, sexuality, ethnicity, or political beliefs, or to anything else 'that we've stood for' or have allied ourselves with, or that has formed part of our identity. Going against the grain, politically, or in terms of religion, or in any of the above regards, can lead to ruptures of the expected order of things, and are often strongly felt – as uncomfortable at least, and sometimes resulting in bitter conflict. At an intimate level, Montague and Capulet-type entanglements can still have a powerful influence on what seems relationally possible, even in cultures that give emphasis to the idea of complete freedom.

There is often history hidden from view, or long considered as past and irrelevant. Thus, for Georgina – who had been shunned by her family because she partnered with someone who shared her own extreme politics, which were so different from those of her parents and social class – the impact of a great-aunt who had died years before appeared to have contemporary resonance and relevance. The ancestor had been kept at a distance by her family for marrying someone 'wholly unsuitable', just as Georgina was seen by her family to have done. The clinical evidence suggested strongly that she may have made an identification with the fate of her (now deceased) relative, and had made choices – out of awareness – regarding her partner and her politics which brought about the same result two generations later.[46]

---

[46] Such conclusions make some psychologists uneasy, especially when connections across several generations are postulated. They are unhappy because the exact 'mechanism' for this kind of intergenerational transmission has not been identified – at least in accordance with conventional scientific views. However the emerging field of epigenetics may throw light upon something which, in the relevant areas of clinical and coaching practice, is now well documented. By way of introduction to 'constellation' work, I recommend Vivian Broughton, *In the Presence of Many* (Green Balloon Publishing, 2010) and John Whittington, *Systemic Coaching and Constellations* (Kogan Page, 2012).

The links – between people in families, or in small long-term communities – are often stronger than we might think. In similar fashion, whole populations – notably those whose members were once slain or treated unjustly many decades ago – may well carry some collective grievance, which is shared and helps to bind them together, and which is communicated to later generations. It's part of that comprehensive process of unwitting absorption of a culture that happens in the transition of children growing up and wanting to become adult members of their communities.

So just as a family feud can pass from one generation to the next, so can national stories, insecurities of ethnic groups, and deeply felt beliefs of religious minorities. They can be parts of a deeply felt history that carries inter-generationally to those who follow. Old themes can always be fanned into flame again, for instance, by nationalistic leaders intent on increasing their political power. All they need to do is draw attention to scars left behind or rehearse historic statements of grievance, realising that a whole sense of communal identity can thrive on keeping these old themes alive and current. As a neighbour of mine – a wise, elderly Spanish woman – wryly observed, 'they hate people without even having met them'.

The impact of 'root-level' disturbances in the general field of world politics is evident, and has obvious relevance in the emergence of conflict and inter-communal violence. But these phenomena are not just 'out there'. They are also prevalent in most people's day-to-day lives.

The story of two consultants, Inger and Stig, is a good example. They worked together for several years in the same organisation, became close colleagues and confidants. The collaboration was strong and easy. Then Stig decided to leave the organisation to move to a senior position in another firm of consultants. There was some light-hearted joking between them about his 'joining the enemy': after all, the two respected organisations, located close to one another in a major European city, were commercial competitors – at times bidding for the same contracts. There was no strong rivalry between them, as organisations, but neither were they active collaborators. Inger and Stig recognised at the time of Stig's leaving the organisation that their relationship was bound to change; 'rationally' they accepted that career paths can alter. They parted on good terms with appreciation and sadness. They then did not meet or have any conversation for several months.

When they did meet next – in an ongoing group outside the business setting altogether – they recognised their connection was 'different now'. The friendship was intact but felt 'less free'; there was an inbuilt limitation on what they could speak about freely. Even casual questions about work lives had to be carefully considered, and keeping confidentiality became a little obsessive. They did not want to disturb the good feelings each had towards the other: but 'something had changed'. Ending up with a boundary of difference between them, Inger and Stig managed to negotiate it gracefully. However, had they felt even stronger affiliations to their respective organisations, or if there had been more overt competitiveness between the two firms, the result might have been different.

Inger and Stig's experience reminded me that we do not operate as completely 'free' agents *ever*. Ideas that we should be able to 'be completely free' derive from the kind of solo psychology discussed earlier.

This view, which I have suggested leads to thinking along lines contrary to whole intelligence, is not just a psychological theory. Individualism as a doctrine and outlook is pervasive: inevitably, it propels most of us in the direction of believing that we are separate and autonomous human beings – that we operate in the world economy primarily as competitors or independent producers and consumers. It is a basic assumption, a model of human existence, adopted most enthusiastically by the USA, and increasingly followed around the world and regarded not only as the norm, but as one that many consider beyond question.

When the famous French diplomat Alexis de Tocqueville[47] travelled to America in 1831, he reflected on the word 'individualism' as a term that had been 'recently coined to express a new idea'. It seemed to Tocqueville that those he observed 'form the habit of thinking of themselves in isolation and imagine that their whole destiny is in their own hands … (They) do not care about one another and treat one another as strangers … Each man is forever thrown back on himself alone, and there is a danger that he may be shut up in the solitude of his own

---

[47]   Alexis de Tocqueville, 'Of Individualism in Democracies', in *Democracy in America*, ed. J.P. Mayer, Vol. 2 (Doubleday, 1969), section 2, ch II.

heart'. What individualism did was to lead 'each citizen to isolate himself from the mass of his fellows and withdraw into the circle of family and friends; with this little society formed to his taste, he gladly leaves the greater society to look after itself'.

He regarded it as different from common egoism, or selfishness, which he characterised as 'exaggerated love of self' that 'springs from blind instinct' and is 'a vice as old as the world'. Individualism, by contrast, is 'due more to inadequate understanding than to perversity of heart' and is approached in a 'calm and considered' fashion – that is, regarded as normal and not as selfish.

The dominant assumptions of our time may be individualistic, with a view of ourselves that many have taken on without real examination – like the idea of having 'selfish genes' and a 'me first' outlook – but the longing for connection and togetherness exists as a strong counter to this. In waking up, as a species, to the fact that our survival rests on achieving unparalleled levels of collaboration and international cooperation, and a massive reduction in the incidence of war and violent conflict, it is not irrelevant that a taken-for-granted view of human beings as fundamentally separate and variably connected has gone for so long unchallenged, and still for many appears as an absolute given. Yet the ideology does not *have* to undermine our confidence in the strength of our relational, interconnected, and mutually dependent status; the more these latter views are investigated, the more they make sense, and grow more coherent, as they have done in my own understanding. The need to move on from an outdated picture is obvious, given a time such as ours.

From war to peace

In addressing the causes of war, violent antagonism, and the destructive behaviour of human beings, I have found it useful to draw upon the thinking of a political scientist, Benjamin Miller,[48] who describes a war–peace continuum. Though I have slightly modified his typology, I remain faithful to his intentions. He distinguishes five positions along the continuum: *Hot War*, *Cold War*, *Cold Peace*, and two degrees of *Warm Peace*.

Hot War is where there is actual use of armed force. This is the war of blood and fire, of shooting, killing, and destruction let loose. In Miller's restrained language, the idea in hot war is to 'destroy the military capabilities of the adversaries'.

Cold War is where there is absence of hot war, but 'hostilities may break out at any time'. There is no atmosphere of peace – it is a 'stand-off', a state of armed readiness and acute suspicion.

Next on the continuum is *Cold Peace*, where war is 'possible but not in the short run'. Armed conflict is 'unlikely … but it still looms in the background' as a long-term possibility. Diplomacy proceeds, but efforts 'stop short of full-blown reconciliation'.

In *Transitional Warm Peace*, the likelihood of war is considerably lower than in cold peace because 'most, if not all', of the issues have been resolved. States have reached agreement, and relations are good. War is 'not out of the question in the longer run', if there is something like a change in the 'ruling elite' in one of the states, but it is unlikely.

---

[48]   Benjamin Miller, *States, Nations, and the Great Powers: The Sources of Regional War and Peace* (Cambridge University Press, 2007).

Resilient Warm Peace is where there is complete trust, sharing of perspectives, and a full range of collaborations in many different fields of activity. Going to war against each other is inconceivable, even if there are uncomfortable disagreements from time to time.

Miller's continuum has far greater applicability than considering relations between states. We do not have to head for the international stage to investigate warlike and peaceful behaviours – they exist on our doorsteps. Thus, frictions and disputes may arise with a neighbour about the height of a hedge, the felling of a tree, or the siting of a greenhouse. I am suggesting there are some structural similarities between international diplomacy and diplomacy on the street, or at a church committee meeting, or in a household, or in the bedroom.

Thus, icy stand-offs (cold war) can exist for years between neighbours or colleagues in an office. Impatient horn blowing of a driver in a hurry can sometimes lead to road rage (approaching hot war). Two hitherto close colleagues can fall out, both convinced they are the aggrieved party, but continue to work together for the sake of the business, their connection feeling forced rather than heartfelt (cold peace rather than warm peace). States of cold war can exist in families and university departments – and even in organisations devoted to promoting peace.

Perceived by those at a distance, many disputes seem trivial, or not worth fighting over. Outsiders can sometimes be baffled by the unwillingness of those in disagreement to work towards a resolution – or even to contemplate mediation. But speaking to and getting to know those directly implicated, one finds hurt, suspicion, accumulated resentment, and a sense that the issue DOES call for making a stand. The experience of battling with a neighbour over payment for damage to a fence may indeed look to outsiders as being trivial, but it may nevertheless trigger severe health problems or a decision to uproot and move house.

Examples of spite, rancour, ill will, and other offensive behaviour can be found not just in family settings and shared living spaces, but also in most organisations. A friend describes her place of work as 'full of intrigue, people not speaking truths, backbiting, grievances, staff leaving without explanation, secrecy, and insincerity'. These phenomena can occur at any level of human system, right up to those established systems in the international arena that we call sovereign states.

The ubiquity of warlike behaviours is matched, of course, by many indications of peace-making that are part of the general urge to affiliate, cooperate, and collaborate – the good ordering of civilised society the world over. Among the many examples of this behaviour are offering of thanks and of hospitality, the giving and receiving of gifts, building or smoothing neighbourly relations, and more definite steps of building or re-establishing peaceful conditions such as making up after rifts or quarrels, 'shaking hands on it'-type makings of new agreements, acts of contrition, formal apologies, acts of mercy, reaching out to former foes, and, when all else fails, agreeing to mediation or joint therapy or binding arbitration.

The uncomfortable truth is that given certain conditions we are all capable of 'going to war', launching attacks, and making enemies of people, especially when we feel provoked or badly treated or threatened. However, equally, so are we all capable of taking steps towards peace. In situations of conflict most of us can learn to spot our own contributions to destroying good relations and have the ability to set about re-establishing trust and goodwill.

We have identified both the power of affiliating and bonding, and also of distancing from others. I had an experience that was very educative in realising how these two topics were related. I organised a residential workshop on the theme of 'Projection', with 14 participants. On arrival, I assigned them randomly a red or green badge, and suggested that in the interval before the workshop got underway, they should only talk to those wearing the same colour badge.

By the time they all had arrived and had moved into the room we would be using, the two sub-groups (seven participants in each) were already forming. Spontaneously they took up positions at two ends of the room. I gave them no instructions. However, both groups, reds and greens, began in similar ways, with the participants absorbed in getting to know the others in their sub-group. At both ends of the room there was a good atmosphere – I could sit back and imagine I was listening to two bubbling mountain streams.

At a certain point, about 20 minutes later, they began to look around the room, to peer at me and to glance at the other group. Despite not having spoken, they obviously knew the other group comprised participants they would meet shortly. Left alone, how would they join together? I imagined they would find a way of meeting, and I was happy to let this be spontaneous and un-programmed.

Each group then began to fantasise about the other one, at first with natural and warm curiosity, as if interested in 'meeting the neighbours'. But in further talking *about* each other, there was a subtle shift – from a short-lived 'We–you' feel to something more like a 'We–they' position *vis-à-vis* the others. Then comparisons began, first in jokey style:

'We're definitely the better group' or 'I am glad I'm red, I wouldn't want to be green'. The next stage, a few minutes later, included some judgements – statements like 'I really don't like the look of them' or 'They look unfriendly'.

I was surprised and concerned, and began to wonder at what point I should intervene to stop what was designed as a small, open-ended inquiry to launch the course in lively fashion. A few minutes later, as one group started shouting some remarks of a competitive flavour down the room, including one person shouting about 'coming to get you', I called an immediate halt and brought them together. They each paired up with someone from the other sub-group, to discuss what they had learned. This took some while, and the session ended with a general mixing so that everyone finally met each other.

While the participants ended feeling satisfied, I was left with troubling questions. One stayed with me. What would have happened if I had continued the experiment for another 10 minutes? My fantasy was that insults would have escalated; to be sure, these may have fallen well short of what passes as normal in some football stadiums, and often on the internet – both contexts where people 'escape' into anonymity and feel 'freed' from normal social constraints – but might there have been more ugly signs of conflict?

When I voiced my fears about seeding a 'tiny war', the participants did not dismiss the possibility altogether. They did not know, but they acknowledged how caught up they had been in the experience, and how strongly they had identified with their own group and saw the other group in the most distant of terms.

The splitting of human beings into 'us' and 'them' is the first big step towards creating a fantasy picture, an imaginary world of goodies and baddies. 'Identification with' is to be aligned with, or to join together; while 'alienation from' involves distancing from 'the other'. And with this distancing goes a small, subtle, and yet discernible reduction in the personhood of the other, or others. They become less 'people like me' and more 'others, unlike me'. And the more detached and unlike me they seem to be, the easier it becomes to regard them either as *dangerous* – thus, fear-inducing; or as *abnormal* – offending our sense of what is normal judged by our standards; or as *unimportant* – so that we don't need to learn anything from them that might disturb our sense of ourselves.

When we join and identify with those who are similar in one or more respect(s), we also use them as supports in maintaining our own identity. We share an identification, a 'common home'. Even when identifying with an organisation at a distance, I am in a small way relating to others, joining 'them' and perhaps acquiring a sense of being 'we' – upping my connectivity and decreasing a sense of isolation I might otherwise feel.

The greater the loyalty *we* have to *our* membership group – the more likely we are to make the 'others', or non-members, into *de facto* competitors. 'They' get to be regarded as different and – swiftly sometimes – as 'alien'. All of us are part of the phenomenon of identifying and alienating. It takes an enormous shift in consciousness to transcend this dynamic, to step outside it, to recognise it, and to avoid being caught in it.

Great leaders – Nelson Mandela and Martin Luther King come to mind – have made this journey, and it is a large part of the towering respect they command. However, many of us easily go the other way: we exaggerate 'us and them' differences in order to reinforce the sense of 'we-ness' within our own group, party, or organisation. Even Harriet, a peace organiser, is inclined to try to galvanise her groups into collective action, by emphasising 'what we are up against'.

So, strong affiliations – nationalist, political, sporting – help create divisive conditions. Partisanship and separating of 'our side' from the 'other side' become normalised. It is a climate in which small numbers of people feeling actual hatred for others (it might well be towards *any* others) are less likely to be challenged when they seem to deny altogether that the other side, team, or grouping are 'human beings like us'.

In cases of communities bound together by shared hatred, a primary dynamic is still one of strong affiliation, supporting not just 'us and them' but 'us *versus* them'. Throw in words like 'scum' or 'vermin', and the progressive degrading of the other becomes intensified. Signs of the other's goodwill and humanity are eclipsed. The identification and then the splitting become near absolute. Bridging such divisions can seem a Herculean task. Phrases such as 'creating enemies' or 'whipping up hatred' therefore carry more than a little truth in them.

The potentially divisive nature of strong affiliations is a big subject. Dismantling our identifications is not easy. I have one small postscript, though, to the experiment with which I began this section, which throws light on what can happen. Even when the 'reds' and 'greens' joined up and, removing their badges, formed one group of workshop participants, their original identification remained as a powerful organiser of their sense of identity within the group. As I recall, it took two to three days fully to erode these initial allegiances to 'their' badge-colour, even with a lot of mixed contact time and enjoyment of their contacts with 'opposite colour participants'.

Out of curiosity, at the end of the six-day course, I invited them to reconvene in their original badge-colour group to see what it felt like to be back with the others in it. I imagined they would be interested too. They categorically refused to do this – their dismantling of the original division was by then complete and they were not remotely interested in reconstituting the sense of distance and separation they had experienced at the start. Some claimed they could not recall their original colour or who was in which group – a shifting sense of identification that happens much of the time in numerous settings: as many stories of present-day Anglo–German, and US–Japanese friendships confirm.

As Albert Einstein wrote, 'You cannot simultaneously prevent and prepare for war'.[49] Human beings generally, as well as communally, give little attention to war *prevention* – or to the active pursuit of warm peace. I suggest this represents a conspicuous failure of whole intelligence, and that it is within our power often to do something about changing the collective mindset, if not globally, at least locally. There seem several steps to deepening understanding that could happen.

---

[49] The full quotation is 'You cannot simultaneously prevent and prepare for war. The very prevention of war requires more faith, courage and resolution than are needed to prepare for war. We must all do our share, that we may be equal to the task of peace'. Quoted in *Einstein on Peace*, edited by Otto Nathan and Heinz Norden (Simon and Schuster, 1960), p. 397.

1. Acknowledging polarities

Alongside war, genocide, and terrorism – these ultimate acts of dehumanising the other, culminating in butchery, mass gassing, or indiscriminate slaughter – one can witness or read about a whole catalogue of person-to-person violence associated with exploitation, rape, pillage, and abuse: all malevolent practices that take away or trample on the personhood of others. All involve the objectification and demeaning of the other, and in this way they work against the connection between people. Connection is made through respecting each other's individual subjectivity and personhood, and within a dialogue or satisfying conversation exploring our similarities and differences in a spirit of mutuality and curiosity.

As already noted, both extremes – identifying with and standing alongside others regarded as similar, and holding others at a distance as 'alien' – are part of our lived, ordinary human world. They represent two ends of a continuum and we know – most of us at first-hand – that human beings can occupy different places along this continuum at different times. Often the roots of deep respect for others and interest in their lives and worlds exist alongside seeds of dislike, feeling threatened, envy, or resentment – and we emphasise the differences between us. Many people recognise the circularity trap that beckons us if we indulge the latter sentiments.

I attended a lecture by Albrecht Mahr, a human relations consultant to the United Nations, in which he described visiting prisoners in Rwanda who were serving sentences for taking part in the brutal killings of the 1994 genocide. He was expecting to encounter a tough, bloodthirsty, and disturbed-looking group of people who were 'very different from the rest of us' and perhaps guilt-ridden, twisted, or depraved-looking. In fact, he discovered they were quite ordinary, friendly, and open human beings, indistinguishable from the many other Rwandans that he met; they could not explain fully 'what had come over them' that they could kill former good neighbours in the way they had.

We know from the Nazi period in Germany that conditions can arise, and become socially acceptable, where crimes can occur that are 'unspeakable' in other conditions. Because others are fully engaged in them, there is a collective weakening of the pre-existing constraints in operation, and a new and different norm is established: what is forbidden becomes permissible, or even encouraged. Many people who follow the crowd find themselves behaving in ways which at other times and in different social conditions would not be permitted and would be actively discouraged.

So the first realisation is that none of us is entirely free of these disturbing contrasts, or of the potential to act in ways that could be war-like. Polarities – such as between gentle and violent, or peaceful and warlike – can easily be treated as if they are dichotomies, rather than continua with two ends, as if in a long-term relationship there could only be two positions: 'I love you, I hate you' – this, we know, is grossly simplistic. The reality, of course, is that there are numerous states in between, a continuum with gradations along it. Our experiences are layered: remember the man whom I asked what he *really* wanted to do. Similar confusions often arise relationally – as in 'I hate you, but really I love you' – which, expanded, may mean 'I am currently furious with you because of … But I DO love you and that's not affected'. We can similarly register in ourselves the warlike and the peaceful, and everything in between deep respect for others and wanting them destroyed.

An attitude of *whi*-relating and understanding can be

communicated: we can speak up for less polarisation and more sense of a continuum.

2. *The context of competition*

We also need to recognise that people are impacted not just by specific happenings but much more by the entire collective matrix and milieu in which they exist. Having competition so powerfully embedded in our present economic model is an unquestioned 'given'. While the emphasis on moneymaking success and celebrity status fuels many people's ambitions, arguably it is deeply divisive socially.[50] It can reduce emphasis on the valuing of community life and on giving everyone a voice, a sense of place, dignity, and equal respect. The bias towards reinforcing individualism and inequality may help set up conditions leading to increased social isolation, rootlessness, and a world epidemic of depression.[51]

But most serious of all, the emphasis on competition and separation fixes many of the parameters of a divided world. Arguably, in focusing on asserting 'power over', and disregarding that we're all members of a single species, individualist assumptions help feed the monstrous perversity of war. Organised violence against other human beings does not spring from nowhere: the build-up has to do with

---

[50] Richard Wilkinson and Kate Pickett, *The Spirit Level* (Penguin 2009). See also http://www.equalitytrust.org.uk.

[51] *Depression: A Global Public Health Concern*, developed by Marina Marcus et al., World Health Organisation Department of Mental Health and Substance Abuse, http://www.who.int/mental_health/management/depression/who_paper_depression_wfmh_2012.pdf.

automatically extending a culture of competitive dominance-seeking into the international forum, where disregard of the national pride and collective feelings of other countries is dangerously disregarded. The rights of powerful countries to dictate terms to less powerful ones are simply extensions of attitudes that run through whole societies.

Much changes in our understanding when individualism as a dominant assumption is questioned. However, we are far from being clear as to the alternatives, and about ways to build communities, human connectedness, ethical relations, diversity, and durable peace – even though we may agree that these are increasingly necessary if our species is to have a secure future. We are missing an alternative world view that is based firmly on equality, mutual respect, and celebration of diversity.

Finally, in this section, let's be clear: *individualism* – the cult of survival, competition, self-promotion – is NOT the same as valuing *individuality*. Recognising that we are all distinctive, differ in qualities and tastes, and can offer unique outlooks, suggestions, and solutions is an essential *benefit* to intelligent life. We need to uphold and treasure our differences: any community needs multiple contributions from its individual members. *Celebrating* differences is a sign of ease, of hope, and evidence of *whi*-thinking in action – a sign that we need a social equivalent to genetic differentiation. We can thrive on diversity and multiplicity.

3. *Identification with humanity at large*

Returning to the experiment of the Reds and the Greens, we can see at once the need for more inclusive identifications. Afterwards the participants saw how constricting and narrow-minded a continuing colour identification was, and they resisted even my suggested short re-visiting in the interests of research. So, once achieved, the expansion of vision and wider frame of understanding is far more appealing.

I believe an affiliation with humanity-at-large is already growing rapidly, and that there are more and more of us who consider ourselves first as global citizens, with the relevant 'us' becoming the whole human population. Other identifications – with one's nationality or religious affiliation, for example – become secondary and of less importance.

At the same time, of course, we will also have local affiliations. Human beings need places where they can participate in communal experience and feel a sense of solidarity and membership that comes from this. We have therefore to re-learn localisation and community building – in order to counter individualistic and isolation-increasing tendencies – *at the same time as* keeping an identification with global perspectives that take us far beyond the local concerns.

'Both–and' solutions are often marks of whole intelligence. We need the advantages of *both* the independent and individualistic path *and* a deeper sense of historic rootedness in the long-term development of humanity as a single world-community – or as a species, which through its talent for collective learning, has flourished as no other. In something like the Olympic Games, we can see humanity's various tensions briefly reconciled. Nelson Mandela's insistence on the importance of international sport in world affairs was characteristically *whi*.

Calling for a new welcoming of human difference can be recast as necessary, not only genetically but culturally and interpersonally. We need the sparks of difference, the stimulus of being stretched out of our relational comfort

131

zone, and the opening to other kinds of human meeting and shared possibilities. Within the sense of our being a global community, there are many differences, and potential flash points, where radically different views are held. But these are most often where dialogue is not happening, at least on a sufficient scale.

The sense of potential or actual conflict are the results of turning 'different' into 'dangerous'; and disregarding on the *macro*-scale what we already recognise on the *micro*. Thus, feelings of disregard, of being bullied, of envy, of feeling threatened – if they occur in a children's playground or even in a management team in a large company – elicit insightful and empathic suggestions. Transferred to the field of international diplomacy – where the stakes are far higher – one suspects that such insights get swept away by older, more traditional thinking. Yet departures from the usual moves can break moulds: apologies and acts of contrition, for example, and acceptance of the rules of international justice and other collective agreements, lower tensions. They become the building blocks of peace.

At any one time, there may be overriding reasons for condemning this or that group, and pressure to combat their influence or even to destroy them. But we know that every time human beings do this to one another, not only is a vast amount of extra human suffering added to the planet's stresses, but ultimately it does not work. Dialogue, and we understanding 'their world', and they ours, is the only proven way of creating long-term, sustainable, resilient warm peace. And dialogue begins with good listening, to return us to Malik, with whom we began.

CHAPTER 5

EMBODYING

The Third Exploration

The Third Exploration, into embodying, *takes us into a different realm of human experience. In the previous Exploration, we focused on humanity's differences and on how to bridge them. Here the beginning point is our physical similarity: that biologically we are all members of a single species,* Homo sapiens, *and have common genetic patterning, with body structures and physiological and biochemical systems that operate in similar fashion; yet in living and the treatment of our bodies and in our physical life, there is also striking cultural variation.*

The Exploration begins at a personal, even intimate level – what it means to be embodied, *and how* embodying *emerges as a key dimension of whole intelligence, or* whi. *The realisation of our 'wholeness' as human beings takes us to acknowledging more fully the facts of our physical presence – the actuality of our 'fleshly being', complete with sensations, feelings, and emotions that are rooted in our anatomy, physiology, and biochemistry, and yet also play such a huge role in our lived existence ... in our embodying.*

The Third Exploration 'adds a whole other dimension' – very obviously in this case – to the investigation of whole intelligence. The Exploration follows a series of questions, about knowing ourselves physically and knowing the world through our senses, feelings, and emotional states. The Exploration takes us into radical global implications that follow from humanity becoming more embodied: with a redefined emphasis on our physical nature helping us forge a more inclusive connection between ourselves and the rest of life – LIFE being the core 'value' underlying this dimension. The importance of whi *in enhancing our species' chance of long-term survival also becomes apparent. Realising the full extent of our interdependence with the 'other than human' world extends the Third Exploration into considering some of the most basic and challenging questions facing humanity – and each one of us.*

Questions basic to the Exploration

As significant as it is within whole intelligence (or *whi*), *embodying* is difficult to describe. For some people it is the most difficult of the Explorations to comprehend. There are several reasons for this. *First*, the medium of language is not up to the task. Just as one cannot learn to ride a bicycle by reading a book, however well written, being embodied also requires that the experience comes first. Only when I have experienced embodiment can a description of it make sense and supplement my understanding.

Second, although entering into this 'way of knowing' confers distinct advantages and practical benefits upon those who access a more embodied state, getting there is very challenging for some explorers – it has been for me.

Third, in many parts of the world, those speaking up for

the embodied way of knowing the world are an endangered minority. Human beings of the 21st century, especially those in industrialised countries and urban conditions, live in a culture that seems to care little whether a person is embodied or not; the whole culture is organised around living at several removes from direct, 'hands on' experience.

Fourth, social and commercial pressures are intense, helping to create a climate of gross confusion about the body. The body is big business, the exploitation of fears pervasive, the advertising unceasing and intrusive. Thus, simply through being alive in the present era, we are bound to absorb some of the conflicting trends in circulation.

These four 'obstacles' demonstrate the urgency of engaging with the fact of our bodily life with curiosity – discovering more of this crucial dimension of *whi*.

From the personal to the global, a redefined emphasis on our bodily nature may help us forge a greater, more inclusive connection between ourselves, as 'super-clever beings with animal bodies', and the overall human habitat on which human beings depend – a healthy biosphere able to sustain life on Earth. Some indigenous peoples – those who still live in close communion with animals, trees and plants, and are in touch with changes of seasons and life cycles – have a far greater sensory and bodily engagement with the world than we do. Our 'highly developed', increasingly urban societies do not support this kind of engagement, and we suffer the consequences of the loss – as does the Earth.

First, we have learned to downplay, or even ignore completely, the significance of sensory life and bodily feeling states, and we do not recognise the implication of this diminishment of our sensibilities. Second, we maintain at a distance – and even almost deny the fact – that as a species we exist at the expense of other life forms, many of which we have decimated through either direct killing or the destruction of the habitats in which they live.

I am suggesting, then, that a more caring attitude about the state of the biosphere can only be enhanced by re-owning what we call our 'animal nature' – in other words, a deeper, more committed, marriage with our own physical being. I shall argue that becoming more embodied is thus not just an optional lifestyle choice, but a political, moral, and intelligently sacred act. Whether this is countenanced as a long overdue act of contrition, as the prelude for reconciliation with the planet's beleaguered animal and plant communities – many of which will soon be extinct – or simply as an eye-opening venture into the most intimately known realm of human experienced life, may not matter. There is no single circumscribed agenda.

Patrick's questions

'So what IS embodying?' asks 'Patrick' – who is a composite of several men with whom I have worked and come to know well. By way of an answer, my first impulse is to ask him to notice his breathing, feel his feet on the ground, be aware of how he is holding his head, and notice the feelings or sensations he can detect in his body as he poses the question. However – inevitably – I am drawn back into 'explaining'. This is the usual modality in a society that seems to disown the life of the body; and I don't want to be ungracious.

I reply: 'Embodying is about living fully as a whole body-mind-energy system, which is exquisite in its complex functioning. We think, talk, puzzle things out – and they are important. But *it is through our physical bodies that we actually meet (bump into, take hold of, smell, touch) the physical world around us*'. I pause; Patrick looks thoughtful, and I continue: 'Obviously, life is full of bodies – our own and others. We feed, wash and dress our own every day – and if we are parents of young children, or are carers or nurses, maybe other bodies as well. A vast array of intimate matters are bodily in nature – some are basic and private and go on behind closed doors; others, like eating and drinking, occur in public and are often ritualised.

'Some people have a problematic physical condition, some reduced functioning, a sensory limitation perhaps, or some other restriction of what they can do as a working physical structure: they can't see, hear, smell, or move easily; they may be paralysed; they may be severely injured or sick and are in pain. The full scope of potential body-life is simply not available to them. But embodying refers more to the state of *experiencing the body* than to the state of a person's physical or sensory capacity or incapacity'.

Patrick interrupts me here. He has some physically challenged friends from his army days. Some, he has found, seem actually *more* aware and appreciative of their physical experience and accomplishments than those of us who take our physical life or sensory and motor capabilities for granted. I agree with him that this is likely: friends I know who are visually disadvantaged have revealed how other senses have become acute, so they are able, for example, to judge distances through listening to sounds that most of us with sight do not register. Being more or less embodied, in the sense meant here, is not pre-defined by having particular bodily and sensory qualities and characteristics.

Patrick has become interested; he wants to know more. I start by reminding him of the obvious: like other mammals, we reproduce and pass on DNA, give birth, grow from infants into adults; we age and eventually die, our life cycle over. Along the way, we may be subject to injuries or get sick and – if we are lucky – we can often recover our health and re-claim 'normal' functioning: we have an extraordinary, in-built, capacity for self-repair.

'However', I explain, 'people forget that they are embodied – that they are mortal organisms. Many of us take for granted our daily animal functions: features of existence like breathing, swallowing, sweating, urinating. These remain "out of consciousness" unless or until they either cause some "trouble" of a medical kind, or become sources of a bodily obsession or compulsion – an upsetting "over-attention" which is more common than often realised'.

I explain to Patrick that I do not mean to imply that huge numbers of people are 'abnormal': my interest is not in spotting 'pathology' but rather in general tendencies that are culturally supported and that, through reduced 'body consciousness', also *reduce our access to whole intelligence.* 'We forget sometimes that we are living animals, complete with instinctual reactions, physical needs, emotional feelings, body sensations, gestures, and movements, all of which provide the medium through which we meet the world. They are basic to all experience, to how we react. We can feel the movement of breath – and life – within us. … Or we can pretend otherwise, deny the information-carrying qualities of emotions, scorn ideas of "a knowing body," and simply locate all "knowing" as brain activity.

Many took this position in the past; but in recent years I've noticed a change, with a growing recognition of the importance of embodying – though this knowledge is still patchy, and it is not taken seriously in most of the academic world, for instance'.

∗

Patrick is not satisfied. He's persistent, like a dog with a bone. I like this. He goes back to the term 'embodying', which he finds 'confusing': 'After all, we are all embodied, how can we NOT be?' I reply, 'Of course we are, in the sense of being creatures of bone and flesh, with organs and blood chemistry – but in the specialised sense I am thinking of, No, we are not'.

I explain that being embodied has to do with how people _sense and recognise themselves as alive bodies_, and that in this people vary a great deal – as do cultures. I suggest he and I go on an imaginary trip – transported first to South America, then to Scandinavia. He agrees, so we do some active joint visualising and sharing of images.

In our imaginings, we 'land' first in the centre of an outdoor food market in a tropical country. We are conscious at once of live music in the background, played loudly, and a 'feeling in the air' that dancing could break out at any time. There is a surge of people moving around the market with its various stalls. Altogether, there's a lot of body contact and boisterous conversation, sounds of laughter and raised voices. People are animated as they greet one another, loud as they haggle over prices, and they often hold one another as they exchange intimacies. They carry or wheel away what they have bought.

Then we go to a supermarket in a Scandinavian city. Here the air temperature is cool; people keep their distance, and if there's body contact, it is accidental and may elicit apologies – except between parents and their children or in the rare case of friends meeting unexpectedly. It's a controlled, humanly calibrated, quiet, apparently stress-free physical environment, with piped music softly in the background.

The two locations offer stark contrasts in terms of shoppers' lived experiences and bodily involvement. The supermarket scene fits into a society where people don't expect to bump into others (literally or metaphorically) when shopping, where people commute to work in a car, have sedentary lives, and meet others by appointment. The main physical efforts are to push the trolley to the car outside and to unload it. By contrast, the tropical market permits – in fact, insists upon – a body experience full of sensory stimulus, live contact, physical engagement: there are bags to carry, crowds to push through, noise levels to shout above, smells to sample or avoid.

I detect that Patrick is more interested now. He seems more awake, is standing still and looking me in the eye. We talk about how different cultures and situations have their conventions, limits, and in-built encouragements, and how these affect the way people experience themselves as bodies – embodying the climatic, architectural, and technological traditions and priorities that frame their physical environment.

The conversation moves on to something he recalls I had said in a talk: 'Is it really the case that becoming more embodied "supports vitality and a more vibrant existence"?' 'Ultimately', I reply, 'people must test my various propositions and observations against their own experience. But, yes, I am convinced that deeply relating to ourselves and others *as sensitised bodies*, is a major constituent in living well – fully, expansively, and creatively. Embodied living is a critical dimension of *whi* in relation to the world in which we live'.

The 'lived body' is obviously different from the mechanistic, objectified, or medicalised body. Doctors and nurses may be encouraged to straddle divisions between 'the medical world view' and the patient's 'lived experience', but there's often a gulf between them. Even the meaning of the phrase 'an alive human being' starkly varies: in medical circles the phrase is likely to be used in defining the technical signs of life – often in the context of death and dying; in the language of the lived body, it is more likely to refer to a 'person with a strong life-force, someone full of Life'.

Adopting the medicalised view can encourage dismissal of actual body experiencing – an attitude that stretches across whole professions and has sunk deeply into cultural life, at least in Britain – and acts as an impediment to embodying being understood *as a source of intelligent functioning*. Combining the two paradigms – medical body, lived body – calls for rare competence and sensibility, and perhaps the necessity for professionals to be embodied themselves. Being able to speak both languages is a great talent – one that is found in a significant proportion of doctors and nurses, but not all. It is greatly appreciated by those who are defined as sick, and yet do not want their humanity and 'felt reality' to be diminished. In particular, they do not want to be identified by their ailment or the associated medical speciality – as in 'you are a diabetic'.

I suggest that the more knowing we are 'as beings living bodily', and the stronger our capacity to be embodied, the less likely we are to lose a resilient sense of ourselves in the face of an overwhelming attitude that is medicalised, objectifying, detached, and technical. Such an attitude can appear, in many locations, as the sole mode of thinking about the body, whether referring to its functions or its breakdowns. The sense of existing as a confident, self-experiencing physical being can become eroded in the face of such overwhelming exposure to a paradigm of thought that seems to contradict it.

Anticipating where I think Patrick's thinking is going, I point out that, of course, in many societies, there's no shortage of body-related activities in contemporary life. The Scandinavian shoppers may well visit a gym or attend a yoga class on the way home. Today, in most of the world's big cities, one also finds a variety of sports, exercise machines in gyms, or opportunities to try types of yoga, tai chi, and martial arts, as well as opportunities to sing, run, hike, cycle, dance, swim, receive different kinds of massage therapy, or take part in 'energy work', or in educational approaches such as the Alexander Technique. All these activities are popular, perhaps for the very reason that more people are acknowledging that life is better when they 'inhabit their bodies' more. As Patrick adds, 'They want to be able to restore how they feel when they first come back from vacation'.

However, being embodied in the sense meant here is not simply a matter of taking exercise, breaking patterns of inactive living, and embracing physicality – as vital as all these are for health and general wellbeing. There's something else – more subtle and far-reaching as well. Patrick looks puzzled, so I decide to tell him the story of how many years ago now, I came to realise that I was not embodied – in the sense I am underlining here.

The experience of discovering my lack of knowing came soon after I began in my gestalt therapy training. Two or three days into the course, there was a training exercise. I did not know what to expect. But I was interested and ready. With a background in academic life, I knew that I was taking part in a different kind of education, largely experiential and practice-based. I was willing to park my academic scepticism for the time being, and I knew I needed to judge the course on different criteria.

We were invited to lie down and to relax. The trainer said that we would *hear different emotion-related words*. The suggestion was that we might imagine situations that were evocative and matched the words, and then attend to the *ripples of sensation and feeling* that spread through the body as a result of allowing each word to resonate in our experience.

The first word uttered was *irritated*, and was followed by 2–3 minutes' silence to enable us to 'notice the sensations which arose in our bodies'. Then came the second word, *annoyed*, followed by another silence – that felt a long interval; then *angry* – more silence; and then *full of rage*. As hard as it seems to imagine – now that I am a lot more embodied – I felt no difference at all. I knew I could differentiate subtle degrees of anger in others, but as for having fine-tuned physical responses of the kind being invited … well, there were none to be had.

The exercise continued with about five different emotional continua. With the last series (sex), I noted some changes in my sensations, but with the other series I did not. I remember the thought I had as the exercise came to an end: 'Well, that was a waste of time'. Then came the reporting-in of participants' experiences; it went on for some time. As each person reported the states they had experienced, the differences between the emotions, the variety of sensations around their diaphragm (in particular) which they had discerned – as well as felt changes in their faces, in their chests, in their legs or especially in their bellies – I experienced an increasing sense of deficiency.

I was also mystified. Here was a realm of human experience I assumed I knew about. I thought of myself as an emotionally sensitive person, comfortable with the physical, in good health, and liking my body. How come I simply could not register what others could? In a small group afterwards, I revealed how upset I was. A fellow student (a Canadian ex-monk) was compassionate, but did not flinch from warning me that 'the longest journey was from the head to the heart' – a statement that was prescient but, at the time, unfathomable.

I realised the journey to being embodied was a lot more than feeling my heart beating when I put my hand on my chest. I heard it meant focusing less on my thinking. But the meaning of 'moving from head to heart' remained elusive. When I tried to puzzle out how to make the shift, my fellow students pointed out I was 'staying in my head' in order to resolve it, and that wouldn't work. Over the ensuing months, I had to piece together what these people were talking about. I imagined I stood outside a promised secret garden, but before I could enter, I had to discover how to open the gate.

By stages, I learned to become more conscious of the internal sensations and feelings of my body, by attending in concentrated fashion to different locations in the body and noticing (at first) simple qualities like warm or cool, tense or relaxed. Later, I realised that in 'tuning in' to my body I could also register the overall degree of *aliveness* I felt in various parts of myself, and that it became possible to focus on tensions, stiffness, small aches and pains, and areas of no feeling, as well as the degree of restlessness or peaceful stillness I felt in my chest and gut, and also in my legs and arms.

Once I had grasped more about what embodying entailed, I could begin to see how, in fact, my body was implicated in all aspects of my life and being-in-the-world. Thus, when meeting an old friend unexpectedly, I was seeing him (sight) and listening to him (hearing), hugging him and shaking his hand (touching); and I was also experiencing delight and excitement (feeling the sensations in my chest, diaphragm and belly) and *the entirety of my reactions came together as one whole, unified, bodily-felt, emotionally rich, total experience.*

Recounting my story to Patrick was strange: it was difficult to recapture how I functioned in the years before I had my shock of learning – a bit like remembering what it was like *not* to be able to ride a bicycle.

Patrick asks whether, before I underwent the experience, I would not have felt equally pleased to see my friend. *What was the difference that came from being embodied?* It was a good question. I decided to fill in some more background before answering.

As many coaches or therapists tell me happens for them as well, my own body's responses, when I am with a coaching client, provide significant sources of information. In 'dancing with others', the qualities of what we jointly co-create are reflected in what I physically feel or sense. Perhaps I note a sudden tensing of my arms, or that I am breathing less freely and fully. Practitioners learn to take these changes as possible signs *of the other party's experiencing* – perhaps a subtle distancing from something – whether it's an adverse reaction to something that I have said, or a sudden memory that carries a possible traumatic charge for him or her. The language is awkward here, but it is as if I am *picking up* or *resonating to* something that does not originate in my own bodily experience, but having become part of the co-created dance and shared experience, has physical implications for me too.

Sometimes, to take another example, I can have a feeling of 'weightiness' in the belly which, in the context of what someone might be telling me, seems to confirm that, yes, *this* is a weighty utterance, and it confirms within me a sense of this being important for the speaker too. Likewise, when the owner of a business tells me that he is expanding into a new venture, and I feel a slight shudder in my being, I do not dismiss it – but ask more questions about the research he has done with regard to the new venture, and his decision to go ahead. Becoming more embodied has felt like obtaining access to a vast data-source on which I can draw freely – recognising that I need to check out my 'intuitions', to give them a more usual name.

Patrick brings me back to meeting my old friend. I agree that I would have been equally pleased to meet him, even in the days before I had learned to be embodied. But I would not have registered the *fullness* or *depth of the experience* to the same extent: I probably would have just started talking, ignoring the feelings I was having *as such*, and not allowing myself to feel the full extent of my delight – its particular qualities and depth. Taking the analogy of wine drinking,

I would have gulped down a fine vintage wine instead of savouring its aroma, distinct flavour, and 'finish' or aftertaste.

I suggest to Patrick that knowing one's way around one's feeling states and embodied reactions contributes to becoming more generally sensitive to one's surroundings and others whom one encounters. Thus, when I am with someone I do not know, and am being not entirely open to them, I might be *drawing away* very slightly; with someone else, say, a long-standing friend, I might be *leaning into* the possibility of greater shared intimacy. Direct physicality is part of the whole, and being intelligently responsive to the whole of what I encounter calls for the indispensable dimension of embodying.

In one type of situation, I can still recapture what the state of being far less embodied must have been like. There are times when I sit in an awkward physical position for too long, and don't notice my discomfort till I 'snap out of it' and move. This lack of noticing – this unawareness – is what I must have once taken as normal, unaware of being unaware.

Patrick asks me what I do now, when I wake up from sitting working at my computer for too long. I reply that I'll do a variety of things that many others would also do naturally – especially if they are in touch with themselves in the way I am describing. I'll stand up, stretch, yawn, bend down, shake myself, massage my face, stretch my jaw, do some shoulder rolls and maybe a yoga stretch or two; I may drink some water; and if possible I'll step outside and breathe fresher air, taking in some big in-breaths and extending the breathing out phase further than usual, stretching as I do so. If there is no one around I might also make some voiced sounds to give expression noisily to how I am feeling, and move around more vigorously.

What I notice is that five or so minutes after leaving my desk, I am back, feeling refreshed. Sometimes I also need a few minutes sleep, which is often more difficult to have, as there is no provision (no enabling infrastructure) for the many of us who can refresh ourselves through a short sleep – an example of how the lack of attending to this *whi*-dimension leads to impairments to performance. I remember times when I felt institutionally required to remain at my desk through times when I felt sleepy, and all my effort went into staying awake – nothing else got done. I know that others have had similar experiences.

Finally, in this rapid sweep across the landscape of what it means to be embodied, I point out to Patrick that – as the language suggests – we enjoy our most intense sensual pleasures through our senses. When we are *really* listening into the silence of the woodland, and then to the bird song, or the hum of insects; when we take a few moments *fully* to take in the detailed visual appearance of an ancient and beautifully bound book, drawing on both its tactile qualities and 'antique' smell; when we *consciously* savour an aroma of freshly baked bread; in these moments we are *noticing* in depth – it's a more intense experiencing. The list of possible sensory experiences we can have is inexhaustible … thankfully.

Through bodily movements, too, we derive satisfaction, relief, or some other state, such as a sense of triumph. Physically expressing ourselves – '*bodying forth*'[52] what is

---

[52]   I came across the use of this old-fashioned sounding but useful term, 'bodying forth', in the writings of Georges Wollants, the Flemish author of *Gestalt Therapy: Therapy of the Situation* (Sage, 2012).

within us – is often a liberating process in itself. As often noted, squash courts provide release from accumulated aggressive impulses acquired through a business day. 'Five rhythms dancing'[53] allows for a whole range of emotional releasing, a de-stressing time resulting in feelings of restored balance and energised tranquillity. Or a woman finds a beach – not crowded, but not necessarily deserted either – where the sounds of the breaking waves absorb her loud release of deep-seated fury safely, easily, and effectively in total privacy.

And then there are the manifold erotic pleasures – bearing in mind that 'erotic' applies to the entire range of desires, impulses, and sensual feelings that arise in the context of romantic love, sexual relationships, and our living as sexual beings, and which can suffuse a wide range of felt experiences. Some think of eros as so extensive that it becomes almost synonymous with 'life energy'. Running down sand dunes, or surfing big waves, or simply coming in from the outside freeze and getting under a hot shower have all been described to me as erotic, in the more inclusive meaning of the term. In fact, the capacity for swimming in the sexual stream of thought and feeling can extend to the way a person walks, talks, or presents their ideas – as some have discovered, and even cultivate.

Becoming more sensitised, in other words, is like opening doors to deeper pleasures and richer kinds of satisfaction. This is part of why embodying is so important, and as part of whole intelligence is so central to fulfilled existence.

---

[53] Five rhythms dancing was developed by Gabrielle Roth in the late 1970s. It is a movement meditation practice. The five rhythms are flowing, staccato, chaos, lyrical, and stillness. See www.5rhythms.com.

Restricted, 'lost', and interrupted embodying

Influenced by the 17th-century philosopher and mathematician, René Descartes, the fundamental split between mind and body, consciousness and flesh, has allowed the realm of 'flesh' to be downgraded, its function appearing reduced to that of supporting the workings of the brain – where individual personhood and intelligent functioning are deemed to reside. In reality, of course, the picture is more unified: the body acts as a single, highly complex, anatomical and physiological totality, with many mutually dependent subsystems. Hundreds of interconnections, feedback loops, and biochemical relationships operate in harmony, including concentrations of neurones around the heart and the gut, and linkages between gut flora, emotional reactions, neural networks and brain dysfunctions; all of these interconnections show that any sense of a fundamental split between the brain and the rest of the body is simplistic.

Rejecting dualism is more straightforward and obvious for those who are embodied: they recognise the interdependence between how they are emotionally, how they feel physically, and what they are thinking at the time. If, for instance, they experience strong 'negative emotions' – like feeling intensely angry, frightened, or confused – they can sense the disturbance, as if their whole body equilibrium has been knocked temporarily out of balance.

Being more embodied, one also feels more 'substantial'. As a colleague emphasised, she IS her body; she communicates her experience and who she is through the medium of her physical presence. How she carries herself, the expressions on her face, the sparkle in her eyes, her zest and energy level, and her speed and grace in movement, help define her participation in the world, and in a specific way that is her own.

Being embodied is not a constant state; and any impression – to which I may have contributed – that there is a dichotomy between 'embodied' and 'not embodied' is mistaken. There is a continuum, and where we are along it varies over time and according to context. For many people, the embodied experiences of 'on vacation' and 'in the office' differ markedly, but there are gradations.

I emphasised earlier the pleasurable features of becoming more embodied. But not all embodied reactions are pleasurable, as Patrick raises in the course of another conversation. 'Suppose people have acute pain, or feel they are about to vomit, or they feel extreme fatigue – in these cases, all people want to do is to reduce physical discomfort. At those moments, surely they may prefer NOT to be experiencing their bodies?'

'Yes', I reply, 'heightened sensitivity means that one will also experience sensations that are difficult. But we might not always want to rush to escape the discomfort before we have registered it. Normally, the feeling of wanting to vomit is best dealt with by vomiting, fatigue by resting, extreme thirst by drinking water. People who experience pain have many ways of coping with it; they also have lots of encouragement from the medical profession and pharmaceutical companies to "get rid of the pain". In many cases – especially with acute and prolonged pain – this is judged as an essential step. But many instances of pain are indications that something is not in balance – there may be a health problem; and investigating one's pain or discomfort, if not severe, is a *whi*-response that's often worth making'.

Sometimes in life, people have unwelcome experiences: states of dread, despair or extreme futility, or of feeling humiliated. They may try to 'escape', by resorting to drugs (prescribed or otherwise), or by drinking themselves to oblivion. Patrick took part in heavy drinking in the army, and he knows first hand about people's desensitising themselves. Of course, minor 'tuning out', or 'detaching ourselves' so as not to wallow in feelings, is commonplace – at times we can happily lose ourselves in a movie or get caught up in some body-based activity like strenuous gardening, and we feel much better from doing so.

Likewise, it is common for people to have experiences of hearing or reading about things which are 'too painful' to take in or think about. Stephen, a walker and naturalist, described how, when witnessing destruction by bulldozers of an exquisite natural environment, he had to leave: 'I literally could not look any more, it was heart-breaking'. All of us, even as mature and balanced adults, are likely to have been engulfed in strong emotions at times. Switching off one's feelings can seem a kind of violation, or even an impossible exercise. Yet in certain situations – for instance, with extreme anger that might lead to physical violence – steps are called for to contain, moderate, or at least delay the powerful reactions. A friend of mine, faced with two teenage sons who fought a lot, introduced a punch bag which hung down the stairwell in their house, and fighting between the brothers abruptly ceased, as they 'took it out' on the punch bag.

In relationships and work settings where expressions of (non-violent) anger are accepted, and even valued, raised voices and strong feelings can be almost routine. But for a significant minority, angry feelings – especially accompanied by shouting – may trigger distress and fear reactions. Suppression of angry feelings also has consequences, especially for those very sensitised to other people's anger: they can be disturbed as much by its simmering presence as by its explosive release.

Like all intense and (for some) 'difficult' emotions, anger needs to be explored: the needs that are frustrated, the extent of self-recognising, the alternative means by which displeasure can be expressed, may all lend insight. Also, we should be wary of suggesting that 'all anger is pathological'. I would argue strongly that feelings of anger – such as outrage in the presence of injustice or abuse of the powerless – constitute a healthy fuel to help bring about needed changes in public life.

Simply suppressing emotions or feelings can distort and fragment lived experience. I remember a nurse, Daphne, who worked with children with cancer. She reported: 'At the end of many shifts, I feel like crying, but I don't want to be upset!' She was skilled in changing the subject, or distracting herself by switching on music or checking her phone. While she managed her feelings by suppression and distraction, Daphne came to recognise the downside of this. She not only disallowed the full-on experience of what was affecting her, but in effect she was splitting herself three ways: (1) experiencing intense emotion; (2) holding it back; and (3) concentrating on her phone, all at the same time. She realised this did not allow a corrective, healing, and possibly instructive embodied experience to unfold. Many of us have attempted such divisions of ourselves at times, and have discovered that it takes energy to suppress feelings; tiredness and other physical symptoms often follow, and the opportunity to learn from our emotions is lost.

Telling Patrick about Daphne's experience prompted us to share our experiences of tearfulness, and to note how many people – men more usually than women – have tried to eliminate shedding of tears altogether. Yet tearfulness is a natural body process: it accompanies feelings of grief, disappointment, and other times of being very moved, or in moments of extreme hilarity.

Patrick described how, when he was younger, he had gathered that crying was 'unmanly, childish, and the quickest route to feeling humiliated in front of other boys'. Accordingly, he had learned how to stop himself, by tensing the muscles of his face and 'making an iron face'. It had taken the persistent interest of his long-term girlfriend to encourage him to regain the lost capacity. He was so grateful to her: when his father died, he was then able to cry, and could not imagine how he could have dealt with his grief if he had still been fixated on 'holding back tears'. Their flow intensified his emotions and helped him 'get through the process of grieving in a less disruptive way overall', compared to when his mother had died a few years earlier, when he had suppressed his feelings and become severely depressed for over a year. He also thought there was a generational difference, and that the taboo against men's tears had largely disappeared. I was not so sure.

Part of the way embodying works as a *whi*-dimension, is that a person – or, collectively, a group – can become more skilled in what one might call 'advanced self-maintenance'. Having access to remedies for certain kinds of whole-body disturbance can enhance our capacity to function, and be present in shared situations. For example, sometimes people can feel 'spacey', out of touch or drifting off into vagueness in thinking. To others they may appear 'not fully here', and they can have a 'faraway look'. The simple self-adjustment here, for someone who is experiencing this state, is to feel the ground or the floor under their feet, to wiggle their toes, and to put attention 'fully into the soles of their feet' – noticing the solidity of what they are standing on dispelling any sense of 'floating off'.

People can also desensitise themselves and cut themselves off from noticing smells, colours, flavours, sounds, or sometimes from feeling any emotions at all. Coming back from such semi-shut down states consists in focusing on the immediate environment. This may involve touching different surfaces and noticing how they are different, or looking around and noticing colours and shapes, or listening to ambient noises. We can accompany this sensory immersion with deeper breathing, and eventually sense ourselves in our entirety: thoughts, body sensations, and emotional qualities, along with solidity and body substance, all again available.

If states of cutting out or drifting off persist, or are fixed features of someone's life, usually it is as a function of having an unaddressed or unrecognised trauma in their background. Many who carry severe tensions or recurrent, unexplained, physical pain are traumatised, and they have not recognised it. Traumas – resulting from emotionally charged injuries of any kind, such as losses, humiliations, rejections, failures, or intense disappointments, especially when combined with suddenness and shock – can lead to tense muscles, numbness, or loss of experiencing oneself as an intact body; restlessness, pain, or a surfeit of energy and rapid pulse are other signs. At such times, a person cannot celebrate the life of their body, for in a sense they do not 'fully inhabit' their body any more.

For example, those who have been subjected to brutality or have been in some other life-threatening situation like a car crash – or, as abused children have been terrified and afraid they will die – may cope at the time by freezing, or tensing up against the overwhelming threat, which involves contractions of muscles and body rigidity. Feeling overwhelmed, and being in a situation where one is unable to move, run away, or scream for help, the person's normal processes of responding and integrating what has happened to them are suspended. The natural stages of assimilation and recovery, involving free movement in conditions of safety and trust are therefore not forthcoming, and the terrorising event becomes 'trapped' in the body.

Those who have been traumatised usually need professional care to help them move on. Over the last 30 years, there has been an enormous increase in psychiatric understanding about the dynamics, significance, and treatment of trauma and emotional injuries from the past. Human beings are organised to deal with flux and change – like a river flowing through life. When there are severe life setbacks the repercussions can become stuck in the body – now less a river and more a stagnant pond. With appropriate support, people regularly regain body flexibility and spontaneity, and the ability to relax and let go. As their feelings are acknowledged, their trapped reactions can be bypassed, and people learn again how to relax their tense muscles; they can return to feelings of wellbeing and a sense of full life. The fact that such miraculous developments increasingly can and do occur offers a powerful sense of hope for traumatised communities and individuals.[54]

Extensions of embodying

B y now, many features of embodying, as well as how this crucial dimension of *whi* contributes to human beings' high functioning in the world, should be apparent. If we are able to access the vast data available to us as alive functioning bodies, and can integrate our bodily reactivity to the world, inevitably our engagement with the world around us will be enriched.

As we become more embodied and more self-maintaining, we learn to attune more carefully to our physical and emotional needs, whether for food, sleep, comfort, stimulation, silence, or other missing elements in the totality of our complex and ever-unfolding lifeworld. By more skilfully monitoring our general equilibrium we may notice earlier, for instance, when something does not feel right, or when we may be getting ill.

As Patrick described the journey to becoming more embodied, we 'grow more antennas': we develop more overall awareness of ourselves and heighten our sensitivity to others. Also we become more likely to recognise when we are 'in the wrong place', or have lost energy and enthusiasm; we notice when we are desperate to take a break, or that a sinking feeling in our belly disappears when we move to

---

[54] On trauma, see Bessel van der Kolk, Alexander C. McFarlane and Lars Weisaeth, eds, *Traumatic Stress: The Effects of Overwhelming Experience on Mind, Body, and Society* (Guilford, 1996; 2007).

a different department or renew a particular friendship we had allowed to lapse.

The scope for continued deepening of our embodied nature is unlimited. There are possibilities for recognising better how we become socialised, for instance, by conforming to social trends: the passions for youthful and socially admired appearance, for physical fitness, for giving oneself pleasure, and for displaying and photographing the body. These all suggest a changing consciousness – sometimes, doubtless, out of a longing to be fully embodied and to embrace one's physicality, but perhaps more often about image and identity, with less attention to the fully experienced personal body. As the French writer, Hervé Juvin, points out, fantasy and actuality do not match: the body itself ... 'disappears. It is forbidden to be what it is – tired, dirty, wrinkled, addicted, sweaty, rumbling and panting – and required to be pure image, odourless, without moods, without excretions. The body with its blood and pus, its oozings, its blotches, its wrinkles, no longer has a place in images or words, in fact no longer has a place at all'.[55]

Others find – as Patrick has – that becoming more embodied is associated with extending the boundaries of consciousness into new kinds of knowing and sensibility to the world – often in conjunction with a meditation practice. People engage more with the body, as they become freer from tension, more relaxed in the presence of what formerly have been triggers of stress reactions, and as they learn techniques of breathing and quietening the mind. We can also discover more of what happens to our state of mind as a result of moving, slowly and in full awareness, or by attending to our overall 'felt sense', which helps us recognise and 'listen to' our body's truth.

---

[55] Hervé Juvin, *The Coming of the Body* (Verso, 2010), p. 101.

Part of developing an embodying practice can include expanding our sensory awareness, leading to more acquaintance with what is often referred to as a 'sixth sense'. I am remembering that the chemical engineer I met in my local pub (he featured at the beginning of the book) described how in his work he visited oil installations to check on their safety. Sometimes, although everything seemed in order, he could discern in himself a slight sense of uneasiness that something was amiss, and he had learned to rely on this 'smelling of a rat' phenomenon that he did not understand but had come to trust.

Likewise, Gavin de Becker, in a book about fear, gives many examples of how people 'know things' that do not make rational sense to them at the time.[56] They are picking things up without crediting that they can, or even without believing that the data make logical sense; but they learn to attend to these feelings. He cites a number of cases where people overruled this feeling sense or intuition, regarding it as irrational: they did not act upon a discernible momentary flash of disquiet and tragically suffered as a result. He cites other examples of people who owe their lives to having acting upon sudden premonitions or hunches that, again, were registered as a whole body response. The difference was that the latter group acted upon their hunches, even though to many people – including sometimes themselves – doing so would be considered irrational or superstitious.

In essence, this opening to the extraordinary complexities and wisdom of the body represents an expansion of *how we define the human 'range'*. Instead of simply a mechanistic picture of ourselves-as-bodies, which we hold as some unrefined concept – effectively, as a reduced, specialised, and limited view of our physicality – we can instead enter into

---

[56]   Gavin de Becker, *The Gift of Fear* (Bloomsbury, 1997).

a self-research process into the depths of our experiencing, within a wider understanding of our bodily nature. Our intelligent participation in the world becomes more 'whole'.

*

In many organisational settings, public or private, there is a culture in which embodying might be dismissed at once, perhaps as relating to something that cannot be measured, let alone costed, and that certainly has no relevance other than in the private lives of employees, which are only relevant if they affect absenteeism or declines in performance. Yet this *whi*-dimension can be crucial for a whole organisation. In one large agency, unusual for developing a culture of sensitivity to the collective feelings of the work force, this meant that sensing the changed atmosphere of the plant since the loss of the contract was taken more seriously than it would have been in the past; it was not dismissed as too nebulous for consideration. Connections were then made to unexplained levels of absenteeism and a sharp drop in productivity.

Those who already have begun to live in a more embodied manner – through pursuing yoga or tai chi, for instance – and who understand better than their colleagues the embodying dimension, can help erode patterns of traditional scepticism. Especially when such individuals command respect among their colleagues, they can model unconventional ways to approach work-based problems – including taking seriously one's embodied reactions. The progression of women into more senior management positions may also – in some organisations at least – be shifting workplace culture, with greater recognition of the need to integrate more 'yin'[57] qualities, attitudes and sensibilities into the predominantly 'yang' culture, with its usual hyper-masculine priority of remaining focused on tasks, profits, competitiveness, and market share.

With greater appreciation of a manager's acting as a high-performing 'bodily instrument' – meaning intelligent in a different way – there can be ever more openness to the legitimacy of heightened sensitivity, and more sophisticated understanding of changing trends within the workplace culture. More managers may come to appreciate how work attitudes, employee motivation, and high performance are interconnected. Such workplaces may take seriously aspects relating to the physical and emotional health of their employees, giving real attention to topics such as physical work conditions, opportunities for exercise, work–life balance, provision of healthy snacks, and issues of physical wellbeing and safety.

Leaders who become more embodied find they have new resources with practical benefits. One senior figure, after coaching connected to her embodying, gained confidence in 'speaking forth' as well as 'bodying forth'. She learned that to present bold ideas, she needed to be more 'comfortable

---

[57]   Yin and Yang are ideas that stem from ancient Chinese culture, including Chinese medicine. C.A. Huang defines Yin/Yang as a 'complete concept with dual possibilities, inseparable and constantly striving to complement and unify'. See C.A. Huang, *Essential Tai Ji* (Celestial Arts Press, 1989; Singing Dragon, 2011). Examples of dualities include dark and light, feminine and masculine, being and doing. Each duality is an indivisible whole, in which each of the two qualities 'requires' the opposite to complement it.

in her skin', feel well supported, and breathe differently in order to speak expressively.

Another manager, seriously out of touch with his embodied reality, did not realise how monotonous his voice was or how shallow his breathing; when speaking to his staff he also tended to balance on one leg rather than on two, shifting from one to another. This reduced his sense of balance and physical stability. He learned that these body-based qualities affected his impact; he had only vaguely considered before that the manner of his speaking could heighten or diminish the interest of listeners in what he had to say.

Of course, a more embodied way of public speaking is not some magic extra, guaranteed to improve someone's capacity to lead. Improved ways of speaking are no substitute for clarity of ideas or the building of strong work relationships. Patrick commented how we all know that charismatic leaders can sometimes 'play to emotions', but quickly lose respect and authority if they are judged not to be authentic, or if they prove untrustworthy or do not follow up an exciting vision with quality content and wise decisions.

Even if the language of 'feeling' and 'sensing' almost certainly has to be modified for a business context – substituted perhaps with jargon terms such as 'limbic resonance'[58] and 'interoception'[59] – the scope for more

---

[58] 'Limbic resonance' is defined as 'a symphony of mutual exchange and internal adaptation whereby two mammals become attuned to each other's inner states'. See Thomas Lewis, et al, *A General Theory of Love* (Vintage, 2000), p. 63.

[59] 'Interoception draws on the capacity of the mind to focus awareness on the internal senses of the body'. See Daniel Siegel, *The Mindful Brain: Reflection and Attunement of the Cultivation of Well-Being* (W.W. Norton, 2007), p. 103.

embodying is vast. It may lead to attending to the individual employee's needs – for example the origins and management of stress – or to the situational factors that diminish morale. The understanding that high performance in the workplace derives in part from a more embodied outlook may slowly become accepted, to general human benefit.

Global implications of embodying

At one point in writing this chapter, I was visiting the Spanish city where my three-year-old granddaughter was living. I wrote at the time, 'Her life and world, when not drawing or following cartoons on the iPad, is full of exuberant physical movement, singing, and chattering. Outside, in parks, when not running freely, she is engaged with trees, leaves, stones, puddles after rain; she is chasing birds and looking for frogs in the ponds. Her world is one of intimate physical engagement with the natural world'.

David Abram, describing his small daughter's relationship to her rural surroundings, writes in similar terms, and adds a key point: '… each stone that catches her eye, each bird that swoops or tree that rises up before her is *a ready counterpart to herself*.[60] Each plant or animal evokes qualities 'that she also *senses within herself*'. In other words, young children retain the connection between the natural world and their embodied presence that so many adult humans have lost.

Ian McCallum, a poet and naturalist as well as a practising psychiatrist, also makes a link between embodied life and the non-human world, and suggests that to do so is a contribution

---

[60] David Abram, *Becoming Animal: An Earthly Cosmology* (Vintage, 2011), pp. 40–41.

to our sanity. From his work in Africa, and extensive wilderness experience, he has concluded that as human beings we have 'a deep historical sense of continuity with wild places and the animals that live there'. Moreover, 'to lose one's sense of union with wild places' can lead to 'one of the most overlooked conditions in modern psychiatry – homesickness'.[61]

If the natural world is our 'home', most of us border on homelessness. Living in predominantly urban or suburban conditions, tiny remnants of the 'once wilderness' are corralled into limited spaces and left alone as a token area for 'wildlife': the rest is manicured for the urban taste. Half-detached and emotionally distant, we look at 'the environment' through windows or viewfinders and define it both as a 'thing' and as 'other' – we do not usually think of ourselves as being a living part of it. We have seen how easily we become desensitised or ungrounded – or both. Arguably, we have been educated and socialised to be so.

This sense of 'otherness' appears in stark contrast to small children's boisterous and fascinated participation. Many adults, instead of walking or running in the open air, feeling the contact with uneven ground (or earth), prefer equipment in gyms – we are less likely to 'turn our ankles', get muddy, or experience the vagaries of weather; and we can measure how many calories are being burned off at the same time as watching TV. And – as Patrick comments, 'This is the world as we find it, and we are not going back to when we had to walk everywhere; or go without phones, cars, gyms, and other features of modern existence'.

'So', I reply, 'with more and more technological developments to come, does it mean that human beings will

---

[61]   Ian McCallum, *Ecological Intelligence: Rediscovering Ourselves in Nature* (Fulcrum, 2005), p. 3.

become progressively less and less embodied? Are those who imagine in the future that we will be cross-breeding with robots likely to be right?' Perhaps not. In the urban conditions most of us know best, some might regard being embodied as an optional luxury. But maybe, we pondered, there could be a great rebellion of attitude: a recognition of embodying as a key ingredient in growing our whole intelligence, and leading inevitably to a rapprochement with the natural world, where our embodied status becomes immediately relevant and makes fuller sense.

What it really means to live 'a normal way of life' is emerging as a key question for our time. People are asking fundamental questions about the ways they eat, work, stay healthy, spend money, and affect the biosphere. We may be recognising that with every step we take to a higher-speed, more automated, physically undemanding, and sanitised world, we are diminishing further the need – or perhaps even the ability – to be fully embodied. Touching, smelling, handling, lifting, stretching, and moving across distances by means of our own effort, are all becoming increasingly rare. We can travel to Australia in the sitting position.

The deep questions raised converge on how we relate to the other-than-human world, as much as how we embody ourselves. Also, there's more realisation of how we have been culturally pulled (or pushed) in a particular direction without realising it. For over 300 years, our scientific, technological, and philosophical thinking has endorsed detachment from the rest of 'the natural world'. There has been a threefold effect of (1) the philosophical dualism whereby human beings divide themselves between mind and body, and exclude 'soul' and 'spirit' altogether; (2) the dominating scientific and medical view of the body as a machine; and (3) the shifting technological developments designed to keep us safe and comfortable. Together, they have underwritten our alienation from the rest of the biosphere.

Despite knowing – at least since Darwin – that by evolutionary pedigree we belong to the family of apes, most people feel no intimate connection even with these 'close relatives', much less with 'nature' more generally. Many still have the biblical idea that humans are fundamentally different. They ignore Darwin's own emphasis[62] – later in life and often quietly left out in most references to his work – on our being 'netted together'; his writing of animals as 'our fellow brethren in pain, diseases, death, suffering and famine'; and his view of the whole of nature, including ourselves, being held together by lines of 'mutual love and sympathy'. His belief was that, to be truly civilised, one needed to have a respectful fellow feeling towards the other organisms alive on the planet. In the current linking of the word 'Darwinian' with 'competition', we have lost this other theme of his – our needing to be humane, tolerant, and generous-hearted, and to honour the existence of the other beings in the Earth community. His advocacy of these latter values deserves headlines.

Increasing the distance between human beings and other organisms parallels the 'us' and 'them' theme of the Second Exploration, and helps to legitimise the attitude that 'they' are expendable. As long as animals 'are so unlike us' we can continue to keep them in the appalling conditions of factory farming; hunt them, not from nutritional necessity

---

[62] Charles Darwin, quoted in Donald Worster, *Nature's Economy: A History of Ecological Ideas*, second edition (Cambridge University Press, 1994), pp. 180–82.

but for commercial and narcissistic ends, photographed standing by our kill; kill them illegally (every 18 minutes another rhinoceros is poached[63]); or test our drugs and medical procedures upon them in wholly artificial conditions. A confident characterisation of animals as 'not sentient beings', encourages human beings to live with an untroubled belief that we have total rights over their lives.

Although this is the prevalent worldwide outlook, there are also signs of deeply felt opposition, with shifts in outlook suggestive of a change. There are more challenges to the belief that other animals do not have feelings, and that inter-communication between us and other species is impossible or rudimentary at best. These beliefs continue despite an extraordinary amount of evidence – derived from countless owners of pets, conservationists, and naturalists, as well as from open-minded scientists – which strongly suggests that animals may interact intelligently and purposively with human beings.

What is most irksome to this writer is that the dominant scientific narrative seems still to be one of outright rejection rather than interest or inquiry. Thus, it seems indefensible to me that, for instance, the work of the remarkable Anna Breytenbach[64] – who appears to communicate with animals with striking success – is not scientifically investigated. The evidence of numerous people's senses is dismissed – without looking into it – as 'merely anecdotal', implying that those with direct experiences of communicating with animals are either charlatans or utterly deluded. The assumption that

---

[63] John R. Platt, 'Rhino Poaching: An Extinction Crisis', *Scientific American*, 18 October 2012.

[64] There is no literature on Anna Breytenbach. There is an informative interview on youtube: https://www.youtube.com/watch?v=2JRGJls-_D4 (accessed 29 May 2015). See also her website: http://www.animalspirit.org.

all such phenomena can be 'explained (away) in simple physical terms' thereby remains untested.

Jane Goodall, the distinguished primatologist, ethologist, and ambassador for conservation, stands out in offering some hope of a different understanding. In 'Daring to Admit That We Love', a section of her book *Hope for Animals and Their World*, she describes an encounter with one of the chimpanzees, David Greybeard, whom she had studied over a long period. She describes a moment when, after he had rejected a palm nut she had offered him, and had then taken it, only to drop it, he 'very gently squeezed my hand with his fingers' having looked 'directly into my eyes'. She concludes 'And so we communicated perfectly, he and I, with shared gestures that, surely, predate our human spoken language'. She continues:

> Unfortunately in our materialistic world, where all that counts is the bottom line, human values of love and compassion are too often suppressed. To admit you care about animals, that you feel passionately about them, that you love them, is somehow counterproductive for those in conservation work and science. Emotional involvement with one's subject is considered inappropriate by many scientists: scientific observations should be objective. Anyone who admits to truly caring about, having empathy with, an animal is liable to be written off as sentimental, and their research will be suspect. ... It is this – this link between the human being and the other animals with whom we share Planet Earth, this connection we can establish with another life-form – that for many makes it possible to carry on ... despite the frustrations and setbacks, and sometimes the outright hostility or ridicule of those

who believe that to save any species from extinction is sentimental and a waste of money and resources.[65]

Goodall's plea for a different approach echoes Charles Darwin's view noted above, and describes a fuller and richer picture of human beings' relations to nature: one that – in the terms of this book – is a great deal more *whi*. The more usual distancing and dismissal, by contrast, can be seen for what it is: a 'reduced' narrative by choice, an outlook that is less whole and that's arguably deficient – both in love of and empathy towards other forms of life, and also in scientific curiosity and the pursuit of truth.

I remember the powerful effect on me in 2002 of reading an article by Alan Watson Featherstone,[66] about his work to restore the Caledonian Forest in Scotland. He revealed how the language of human subjective experience has a place, not just for animals most like ourselves, but in writing about whole ecosystems. He wrote, 'Ecological restoration – the practice of *helping to heal* degraded ecosystems – has much to offer in shaping a new human culture which is in balance and harmony with the rest of the planet. At its heart, ecological restoration is *a labour of love*, which necessitates an *intimate knowledge* of the ecosystem being restored'.

I remember noticing and underlining the words I've put in italics. They are indicative of a huge shift. Instead of exploiting

---

[65] Jane Goodall, *Hope for Animals and Their World: How Endangered Species are Being Rescued from the Brink* (Icon Books, 2010), p. 352.

[66] Alan Watson Featherstone, 'Planetary Healing', in *Resurgence*, Issue 211 (2002), pp. 20–21. Italics mine. (See also www.treesforlife.org.uk).

and depersonalising, measuring and dissecting, objectifying and alienating, he suggests an entirely different priority: an attitude towards the rest of nature that is respectful, and the expression of feelings and attitudes that human beings have been invited to negate or disregard as not scientific or even not rational.

Some will argue that any retreat by science from its materialist and mechanistic assumptions will spell doom for humanity, that our greatest hope and best chance of long-term survival is if we 'rely on the science'. And in some contexts, most would agree with the statement. But not all practice of science, not all the emphases, and not all the ways in which science presents itself are necessarily beyond criticism. And what Darwin, Goodall, and Featherstone all agree is that biological understanding does not call for a dogma of ridding oneself of emotion. We do not need to sacrifice sympathetic feelings, including awe, respect, love, and even – remembering William Blake's invitation to 'see a world in a grain of sand and heaven in a wild flower' – a measure of enchantment, of falling under the spell of nature's beauty and bounty, in order to practise scientific inquiry.

Morris Berman has pointed out that 'the view of nature which predominated in the West down to the eve of the scientific revolution was that of an enchanted world. Rocks, trees, rivers, and clouds were all seen as wondrous, alive, and human beings felt at home in this environment. The cosmos, in short, was a place of belonging. A member of this cosmos was not an alienated observer of it but a direct participant in its drama'.[67]

There is no reason for our present-day observing to continue to be 'alienated', no reason for us not to be 'direct participants', simply because we have deeper scientific

---

[67]   Morris Berman, *The Reenchantment of the World* (Cornell University Press, 1981), p. 16.

understanding of the properties of rocks, or the photosynthesis of trees, or the complexity of ecosystems. It is not a reversion to magical thinking or an abandonment of rationality to remain with intact aesthetic sensibilities, or to work with a sense of deep reverence for the miracle of what lies beneath our skin. It's not a repudiation of a scientific outlook to regret, along with Berman, that 'the story of the modern epoch ... is one of progressive *disenchantment*' and a loss of 'psychic wholeness'.

Part of the new questioning comes from a suspicion that the remaining indigenous communities – which the world's dominant forces have squeezed to the very periphery of the lived-in world – may still have memories of a deeper and more wholesome relationship to the land and to animal life. They may enjoy – or now it is perhaps distantly remember in some cases – a deeper felt connection to 'nature' or 'the environment', than most of us reading this do, living in so-called 'advanced societies'. Again, instead of an attitude of inquiry, and respectful interest in 'what they may know that we do not' – and instead of ourselves adopting a stance of being part of a wondrous ecological totality of amazing complexity and connection – we have taken a different cultural and intellectual route.

Rather than cultivating an attitude of deep respect and even love for the natural world, we have collectively tolerated a view that regards the entire Earth as commercially available for material gain, human consumption, and human entertainment – with our dominant thinking and systems endorsing these priorities. The philosopher Martin Heidegger wondered 'what would happen to forests if we categorised trees as lumber', and, of course, many people think in just those terms – witness the catastrophic destruction of tropical and other forests.[68]

---

[68]   I am grateful to Rob Farrands for reminding me of Heidegger's question.

Moreover, those who do have a developed participatory and empathic engagement with other natural beings – of the kind David Abram describes and honours, and which children and indigenous cultures have never lost – easily evoke reactions ranging from mild amusement, to condescension, to outright dismissal. 'Throwbacks to a pre-scientific era' of animistic ideas are regarded as irrational, sentimental, or anthropomorphic. And, as we move from mammals to other vertebrates, and then to invertebrates, and to plants, and then to physical substances (including water, minerals, and oil), the thought of some direct and empathic connection is considered even more ludicrous.

Like chainsaws and bulldozers in a rain forest, ideas and human conceptual templates and belief systems can wreak havoc on natural sensibilities, mock the sensitive, patronise the 'childish view', and continue to insist that, with our mechanical-medical bodies and our taken-for-granted assumptions of an inert and de-subjectified physical world, we should not have 'emotional reactions'. Nor, if we are rational and realistic, should we dare question the power of the technical-rational-commercial model to hold us all in a subjugated trance state.

For humanity to *wake up* to the full magnitude of what our species is destroying would be to break through that trance: it would correspond to shaking ourselves awake, and – yes – would allow our bodies to register the emotions of horror and outrage we have not previously felt or owned.

As conceived here, then, the path of restoring or extending the range of our embodying is not just about enhancing our physical sensitivity or developing ourselves as more refined instruments of situational reading. Embodying has the potential to catapult us into a new era of sustaining human health, and emotional integration. But the *whi*-dimension of becoming more embodied is greater even than this.

The 'biosphere' needs to become more than a concept; the celebration of Life needs to be recognised as a time to be deeply thoughtful. Living, as most of us do, in societies that are increasingly urban, alienated, cynical, and materialist, we can still be stirred by the realities of childbirth and the excitement of a newly born infant, or can feel overwhelmed by the pain of being physically injured, just as we have to face the facts of ageing, illness, decay, and eventual death. We have all the evidence that recognises our continuity with other mammals – and with the natural world.

The valiant efforts at conservation are only the beginning of what is required, faced with the catastrophe of the massive extinction underway. The impulse to preserve Life in all its multitude of forms, noticing its extraordinary beauty and diversity, begins from *recognition that we are joined with, are dependent on, and are part of what is being destroyed*: we depend on the preservation of the biosphere's hospitality to life as much as any other organism. Preservation of other species can also be re-conceived as a *humanitarian* central concern, because our own survival as a species depends on the continuation of the totality of Life. To become more embodied ourselves is to take a necessary first step in our understanding. As animals with extraordinary brainpower and huge untapped potential, we can start applying our gifts and resources to the very task that could lead us away from the path to eco-suicide.

CHAPTER 6

SELF-RECOGNISING

The Fourth Exploration

The self-recognising *function is broad and deep: it's an essential activity and one distinctively human – if other primates and highly intelligent mammals engage in it, they do so without us knowing. Much of the reflecting we do relies on the use of language – in talking to others and ourselves, as we attempt to capture in words many experiences that begin wordless and would otherwise be transitory. In this Fourth Exploration, the range of 'what is recognised' is considerable, yet there are recurring themes, principles, and key ideas. Durable learning and growing more generally into greater whole intelligence depend on this dimension being activated and available.*

The name itself – 'self-recognising' – may be confusing to some. It may seem to imply that the activity is something personal and only individually experienced. However, as we have seen in the previous Explorations, we are so intimately connected with others that such individualisation of experience may be illusory. At any rate, the practice of self-recognising *is evident at every level of human system. Public inquiries, for example, such as retrospective reviews of participation in a war, promote self-recognising at a collective level. Of course, these inquiries may have serious implications for individuals* who made the decisions, but they also reflect how whole groups reacted, or failed to do so intelligently.

Public inquiries and their subsequent reporting are evidence of a country's willingness to recognise itself, including how it has been governed or mis-governed. These inquiries are 'times for introspection', or for 'looking at ourselves in a mirror'. And here is the basis, really, of self-recognising activity: we look back and learn from the past, make new meaning, grieve or celebrate what has happened; and we gain insights that improve future chances or invite saner steps next time.

Another beginning point for the Fourth Exploration – connecting it to earlier themes – is awakening to our living in an era that fragments experience, fills every empty space, and generates a mass of alternative narratives. Tendencies toward multiplying options, tweets, sound bites, and news flashes need to be balanced with coherence, order, and clarity – or we end up in destabilising chaos, stressful overdrive, and crazy-making confusion.

The highlighted value of this whi-dimension is WISDOM. Perhaps never has it been more imperative that human beings listen and learn from each other's insights, viewpoints, and good examples. We need others' wisdom as we seek conscientiously to discover, hold on to, and communicate our own.

Varieties of self-recognising

We can trace *self-recognising*, the fourth dimension of whole intelligence, through a great range of experiences. They include *psychological self-maintenance, learning about oneself, reflecting on how to live a more fruitful and less stressful life*, and *discovering purpose and coherence in one's lived existence*. Our investigative self-noticing – to give it a different label – takes many forms, but they all share a family resemblance.

As members of *Homo sapiens*, we are able to reflect on ourselves – both individually or with others. To varying degrees, we stand back and make sense (if we can) of the world in which we live – our immediate reality and the wider conditions that shape existence. Some people contemplate life and what they are doing here. They learn from mistakes. They may also think of their mortality – the temporary nature of existence. But others will think 'that's depressing, and diverts from living now'. And making this choice itself counts as a form of self-recognising, at least as regarded here.

All of us already engage in self-recognising, even if it does not extend to recognising we are doing it. For some, it happens in long conversations in the pub, or while out walking the hills, or talking to a friend over dinner. Others benefit from writing in a journal at the day's end, or from pursuing long-term psychoanalysis. I know Quakers, Sufis, Anglicans, Zen Buddhists, Muslims, and students of Ibn 'Arabi, all of whom pursue ancient practices that include self-reflection or examination.

Some people are on a private quest, seeking their own answers to 'what it means to be human', while others meditate in conjunction with a yoga class, or follow a spiritual teacher. Some practise 'mindfulness', or simply want to adjust their lives to reach a better equilibrium; some are keen not to drink so much, or they seek a more fulfilling sex life, or want a better relationship with their children or their parents, and a chance to think about these things. Others download on-line courses on how to visualise success, or seek help from a counsellor, or attend an anger-management course 'to save their marriage'. A minority resist altogether: they don't fancy taking time to 'stare at their navels'; such practices are 'not for them'. Yet perhaps they welcome a frank talk with friends occasionally, or they read biographies in order to compare their own lives and thoughts with those they read about. Practices vary, but often there seems a common intention: 'to keep oneself sane in a world which seems mad'. The family of self-recognising is therefore extensive – with wide variations in what it stands for, and how it is valued.

The famous commandment inscribed on the Temple at Delphi, often cited by philosophers and teachers since, was 'Know thyself'. However, 'knowing oneself' is obviously a matter of some complexity: it is often challenging and there is much variation in how we apply the advice to ourselves. And, of course, we might ask whether we *can* recognise ourselves, or whether others make a better job of knowing us than we do ourselves.

Self-recognising is intrinsic to contemporary life. The following are varied examples of active self-recognising:

1. A manager invites comment from staff members about her leadership style, after hearing herself described as 'a natural leader'.
2. After a poor showing, a Formula One team scrutinises what happened in detail, intent on learning what went wrong.
3. A violent offender wants to change his life – he works with a psychologist to learn to spot early warning signs of his anger.
4. A woman walking her dog at dawn ponders a possible career change, and later calls her friend to discuss her ideas.

5. A string quartet listens to a new recording, with a view to refining their interpretation.
6. Two psychotherapists who work together with couples play a tape of a session to their clinical supervisor; they receive feedback about what they could be missing.
7. A person realises that her membership of a political party no longer accords with her values. Both her values and those of the party have changed, and not in the same direction.

We see that self-recognising contributes to all areas of life, from how we relate to our families, to informing the pursuit of high performance, or to how we organise our lives. For many of us, self-recognising is already a regular feature of everyday existence, appearing in annual appraisals, regular meetings of a management group to review the week, or a daily period for quiet reflection or thinking over the day before sleep. Many think about their life direction at the turn of the year, a practice going back to Babylonian times. Self-recognising is obviously no recent invention, and each generation finds its own forms and methods for accomplishing it.

Over a century has passed since psychoanalysis first entered the world in a Viennese consulting room. Since then, countless modifications of Sigmund Freud's ideas have filtered through into a vast range of different psychotherapies, and into counselling and coaching. These methods of personal inquiry through talking to an experienced listener have extended to ever widening groups, and have shed earlier associations – notably, that this form of assisted self-inquiry meant that you were 'disturbed'.

In past epochs, learning about oneself and about how to live well came through contact with respected women or men in the community – figures such as shamans, preachers, healers, or elders. In the present era, many turn to specialist professionals such as therapists, psychiatrists, consultants, and coaches. To be listened to respectfully obviously does not require the involvement of a professional. However, in the contemporary world many people feel overwhelmed by the complexities of life-as-experienced – the speed of technological change, the bewildering number of choices, opportunities, and 'roads not taken' – and have a need to speak freely and unguardedly. Life has become a lot more complicated and many are pressed for time. So assisted self-inquiry has become an expert realm. Such inquiries offer powerful means of garnering insights and fresh realisations to enable people to reach a new sense of equilibrium. Persistent difficulties in relationships and reawakened traumatic memories are often transformed through therapy – at least into more manageable forms.

As with other dimensions of *whi*, personal and public dimensions of self-recognising can overlap. Thus, a reform-minded prison governor may ponder searching questions about how prisoners are rehabilitated, and this may prompt him to re-examine his own values and how they have changed since he became governor – if they have. Coaching that's ostensibly all about work performance can often turn into a wider investigation of life-choices, including perhaps some that were made at the age of seven, or even much earlier.

On the grand scale, initiatives like the South African Truth and Reconciliation Commission (TRC) have displayed self-recognising conducted for a greater purpose, with a huge impact involving hundreds – in this case with beneficial consequences spreading through a country's entire population.[69] The Commission is a conspicuous example of how self-recognising invites more transparency, greater accountability, and capacity to explore human to reality a higher standard of truthfulness.

The TRC experience is a reminder that not all self-recognising is easy. Few people are altogether without blemish or regrets regarding something in their past, the consequences of which may still reverberate in their lives. Acknowledging one's limitations, failures, or moral shortcomings can be an excruciating exercise in itself – one that calls for a particular brand of scrupulous self-honesty. Even more difficult is to negotiate with others involved whose memories of events differ, and who may or may not want to enter into dialogue about what happened. However, when different truths *are* articulated, shared, and reconciled, with an inclusive and agreed narrative, the collective acts of self-recognising and of mutual comprehension can be healing events of the first order.

The word 'self' – as in knowing or recognising one*self* – needs attention: it can consume pages of definition. The contemporary notion is that the self is not a fixture, a 'thing' that can be defined for all time and is unchanging, but is rather

---

[69] Despite many difficulties and criticisms, 'the TRC achieved some notable successes. In an open and transparent process, it compiled a forensic record of apartheid-era human rights abuses that can no longer be denied … its public engagement with South Africa's painful past helped to prevent a return to the political violence of a few years earlier and laid the foundation for a brighter future for all South Africans … The entire process had a cathartic, healing effect that enabled the country to transcend the violence and acrimony of the apartheid years'. See http://overcomingapartheid.msu.edu.

a moving, constantly evolving, and changing life process.

Thus, we saw in the First Exploration how *responding to the situation* calls for flexibility – a range of approaches to meet different contingencies. We saw, for instance, how people can be more directed and focused in emergencies: they organise their 'selves' differently. Likewise, in the Second and Third Explorations there are also changing qualities, life-textures, and varieties of experiencing, whereby individuals reveal themselves as variable rather than fixed beings acting in a predictable fashion.

Emphasising the changeable nature of the self reflects one side of how human beings function. However, we also know that people are not infinitely malleable, and that consistency, stability, and predictability are also important in making life possible and keeping relationships stable. So while the self changes – and needs to be versatile and flexible to engage with the nature of lived existence – we also depend on long-term continuities and outlooks for a sense of rootedness and 'knowing where we stand'. Boats in strong currents and winds need ballast and anchors.

Once again, there is a danger in over-simple dualities. I know for there are aspects of my being that feel like deep roots: I have long-term commitments, strong family connections, and habitual tendencies that 'feel very me'. At the same time, I am inclined to vary a lot from day to day, and according to with whom I am dealing. Somehow, I have to find a balance, so as not to lose myself in dispersing my energies and attentions in too many distractions and departures from the norm; yet I also want to avoid becoming fixed in outlooks and habits that exclude new possibilities and challenges.

I am by no means alone in my balancing act. My conclusion is that all of us have to find equilibrium. Some want to uphold a strong sense of who they are, and what they believe in – in other words, as much constancy as possible; while others can feel almost imprisoned by pressure to be consistent, and may latch on to every opportunity to alter parameters of their existence. As with any such continuum of differences, there are some far along it in one or the other direction, with many in the middle range. Also, people move in their position along the continuum over time – according to changes as they age or acquire new goals in life, for instance with the arrival of new intimate partners.

Applied to human systems, self-recognising is about building collective understanding – perhaps through weighing how our team, division, community, or department matches up against others. There are numerous means by which people realise key facts about themselves or acquire insight: for instance, '360° feedback' can be a powerful force of change in the organisational world. But anything that is eye-opening, or offers us data, or helps us to reconsider our participation in the systems we live within, can be useful.

I recall one organisation where tension existed between what I'll call the Designers and the Makers: it had been a troubling issue for several years. The Designers were engaged in a review of their department and came to recognise how frustrated they felt about this ill feeling between the two groups – it was always the 'same old judo match', as they described it. They had canvassed the possibility of some mediation, or of having a joint meeting with an external consultant. But the Makers were not interested. However, the Designers came to a realisation that they could alter the pattern by changing *unilaterally* their interactions with individual Makers. On a one-to-one basis, they sought out opportunities for friendly contact, and eventually the Makers came under pressure to drop their part in the judo – which slowly they did.

Here was some inventive self-recognising – and also, for the purposes of the book, an example of how an *interrelating* insight combined with a process of *self-recognising* and an act of *experimenting* (see the Fifth Exploration), all in a *response to the situation* of a 'stuck' pattern.

To deepen our self-recognising, a first requirement is often to slow down. Robert realised that he had been planning to take a lengthy break from his very demanding job, yet due to changes in his life unrelated to his work, he had pushed these plans to the side. Several months later he was surprised by his feeling depressed and listless; he put it down to a 'mid-life crisis', forgetting entirely his earlier (accurate) self-recognising that he was depleted, and needed to slow down and take time out – and for longer than a short vacation. At the time I met him, he was over-committed, working long hours, filling every waking moment with intense activities; he was short of sleep and perpetually tired.

Robert is not alone. His 'forgetting to recognise that he had forgotten what he had previously recognised' is characteristic of a great many self-damaging cycles. When we avoid the experience of emptiness that is often associated with fear of feeling depressed, or with being overwhelmed by 'difficult' feelings and realisations, the result can be further loss of self-recognising. So we become harried and hurried, and the prospect of achieving a rounded or balanced life becomes ever more elusive.

Other downward spirals can arise from losing perspective – as can happen in teams or groups, sometimes through preventing some corrective self-recognising exercise from getting underway. 'Loss of connection' or 'loss of the plot' can lead to automaton-like behaviour, 'tuning out' and evident mindlessness – as in 'we just kept going, and going through the motions', sometimes (again) prompted by extreme overload, with no time metaphorically to 'stop and take breath' or recognise 'what's happened to us'. After formal inquiries into calamitous collective mistakes on the part of a public agency, reports can make grim reading: whole systems are revealed as being 'toxic', or 'out of control', or 'completely overwhelmed'. The importance of earlier, built-in, and effective self-recognising is revealed starkly.

Another kind of lost perspective comes about when an individual leader, or some prestigious team, exaggerates their self-importance to the point of no longer being able to look at themselves with detachment. There's a runaway collective narcissistic process whereby those involved will only look at themselves in a distorting mirror that confirms what they believe – the alternative being to consult no mirrors at all.

I remember listening to a revealing interview on the radio. A financial journalist was asking a city headhunter for his reactions to a report about the banking Libor rate fixing scandal. The process by which this dishonest practice became established and then taken as understood in many banks – as a means of increasing profits for their bank, and for senior bank employees themselves through adding to their bonus – was itself a staggering failure of appropriate oversight. My attention was caught, however, by a revealing comment by the city headhunter being interviewed. He was talking about the emails that proved that there had been collusion: 'I must confess I was shocked by those emails, not by the fact that there was collusion but by the fact anyone was that stupid. These emails are kept for years, the banks try really quite hard to keep them for as long as possible ... and they had your name on them and they still chose to put in clear admissions of collusion and wrongdoing. That level of incompetence is amazing'.

I sensed a far more serious brand of incompetence and lack of *whi* – the failure of those taking part in the scam to recognise that illegal and unethical actions have consequences: litigation, vast fines for the banks, damage to their reputation, loss of international confidence. The real 'stupidity' was not that they got caught out by not deleting incriminating emails, but that they acted in a 'get-rich-quick and don't think through the consequences' frame of mind. Failure to recognise our interdependence and interconnectedness is often a form of woeful ignorance that breeds hubristic self-delusion. That people in responsible positions do not access their understanding of human organisation, or have never been educated to think contextually, or do not comprehend that scams and unethical practices do harm to collective wellbeing, is very dangerous and supports the argument of this book: that we need an altogether different conception of intelligent behaviour, including a capacity for *self-recognising*.

The task of honest looking may call for ruffling feathers, unsettling an equilibrium, stirring things up. Yet colluding with corruption or cheap advantage-seeking leaves a bad taste, even if we try to forget what we have allowed to pass unchallenged. Speaking up may not be easy. Whistleblowers and others exposing fraudulent practices can suffer as a result of doing so; but at least they do not have to live subsequently with a sense of their cowardice or complicity in greed and avarice, unattractive features in what it means to be human.

Affected as we are by what is happening around us, part of self-recognising is noticing the pressures on us to think and behave in certain ways. At a personal level, we can be swept into arriving at a particular group or family decision that – if we stopped long enough to notice – we know we would oppose. Self-recognising often arrives too late. This Exploration is about promoting 'during the event' consciousness, rather than waking up only afterwards to what we truly want or believe are values worth preserving.

To sum up, self-recognising activities are as varied as the human beings engaged in them. Self-recognising can be portrayed as 'waking up', in contrast to 'sleep-walking through life'. Many advantages accrue and people recognise the benefits. In big organisations, individuals may start the process on their own – and only subsequently do the workforce or members as a whole catch up.

An obstacle, as we have seen, is that human beings can be proficient in the psychological equivalent of double bookkeeping or sustaining awesome levels of self-delusion and deception. As Saul Bellow reminds us, 'A great deal of intelligence can be invested in ignorance when the need for illusion is deep'. However, the most common limiting factors are ignoring our natural rhythms and our need to take time out to reflect, or the need simply to rest and gather ourselves for the next phase of intense activity. In many settings, especially work ones, little value – *if any* – is placed on staying quiet and allowing time for thinking and sharing of experiences, let alone sitting with 'not knowing', withdrawing into emptiness, and allowing insights and new possibilities to arise from within the 'creative void'. Much self-recognising comes to be labelled 'unproductive', or regarded as a luxury, rather than as an essential feature of sensible living.

When more *whi* is manifested, of course, absence of opportunities for regular self-recognising is itself more likely to be recognised – and rather than a downward spiralling, we find one that is upward and brings long-term advantage.

Personal inquiry

An immersion in one particular form of self-recognising came in my very first encounter with the discipline I later studied, gestalt therapy. I arrived at the introductory event with a friend and colleague called Peter, a skilled college teacher. We were invited, with about a dozen or so others, to pair up and take part in an exercise of making 'present awareness statements'. This sounded trivial and not very challenging, but we were curious enough to continue.

What were we noticing around us; to what were we attending? When thoughts took us somewhere else, we were just to come back to observing, and reporting what we noticed: things we could see or hear or touch. The instruction was to begin each report with: '*Now I am aware of* ...' and to report the first thing that came to us. We had five minutes each to do this, repetitively, speaking without long pauses between successive reports.

I soon realised this trivial-seeming task was not so easy. I noticed how my attention divided. While focusing on something – like the sunlight coming through the window, or Peter's facial expression, or the carved ceiling – I was also trying to hold and develop 'ideas', probably trying to figure out what this was all about. I probably had other thoughts running too, like 'Why is Peter so much more fluent than me?' After five minutes or so of attempting to comply with the instruction, I was registering frustration but also curiosity. Given how my mind spun off in different directions, I found the task damnably difficult!

It struck me as an unusual but not altogether mad idea to investigate 'live experience' in this way. At the same time, I was thrown by what was happening. It was reporting my stream of consciousness *as it happened* – or as soon as possible after – that troubled me. There was a skill required here which I did not have, nor did the task fit with anything I knew about or had come across before. It wasn't free association, nor was it classical 'introspection' as employed by a 19th-century school of psychology.[70] This was something different – real but strange. I was embarrassed

---

[70] I had encountered both of these in undergraduate psychology classes: 'free association' as described by Carl Jung, and 'classical introspection' as practised by Edward Titchener and others in the early era of psychology's striving to define itself as a science. A good introduction to the history, arguments, and confusions that existed around how possible or impossible it was to examine the workings of one's own mind, is available in Edwin G. Boring's 'History of Introspection', available at http://psyc405.stasson.org/ Boring.pdf. Gestalt therapy includes 'phenomenological reporting' as part of what the therapist and client investigate together in dialogue, often spoken of as 'working with awareness'. Some kind of self-reporting, and monitoring of one's thoughts and feelings, is more or less inevitable in many spheres of human life, and especially in therapy and counselling.

that I found it difficult, and inevitably, along with all my other self-referential musings, this made staying with the practice even more difficult.

The first exercise was followed by something that appeared even stranger. We were asked to complete sentences beginning: '*What I am NOT aware of is ...*'. This at first struck me as nonsensical – something out of *Alice in Wonderland*. How could I be aware of 'something of which I was not aware'? I could retreat into the safer territory of scepticism: at the very least, the instruction should have made clear that, of course, it was still an awareness, but simply one accessed in a different manner.

Continuing to oblige the instructor by trying out the exercise, both Peter and I discovered something surprising: the task brought to the fore other concerns – or happenings, or people – in our lives at the time. These were physically *absent*, yet were also obviously *present* for us in a different meaning of 'being present': they did not need to be searched for, but were ready at once. Moreover, some of these remembered people or situations carried emotional punch: I thought of my children, for instance, who were in the UK, and whom I was missing. Not surprising, I thought, that they were immediately available without my having to consciously search for them: I was thinking about them frequently. Later, in a group discussion, we recognised that often 'what arises from nowhere' has already been tugging for attention on the fringes of consciousness, even though we have been ignoring it. In a sense, the exercise 'gave permission' to attend to the peripheral and excluded matters of our lives.

Next, in this mind-blowing sequence, came another bizarre notion. Now the statement to preface each report was: '*I choose to be aware of ...*'. How, I asked, could I possibly be responsible for random awarenesses that arose within me, over which I had no control? However, I accepted that 'everything in my head' was closeted with me, and this exercise brought it home to me: I was choosing, whether 'consciously' or not, to focus on *this* while cutting out *that*. I was allocating attention in directions that revealed themselves. I began to grasp that I really was 'creating my own reality', at least a lot more than I had realised. In 20 minutes I had grasped an existentialist idea that had long remained opaque.

The above experience – an exercise in mindfulness long before the term became popularised – alerted me to a basic type of self-recognising, which subsequently I was to think of as *registering one's present experience*. To register is to notice, to bring focus to something, or to bring something 'to the foreground of attention' as a 'figure' – often against a diffuse background of miscellaneous sensory stimulation, vague thoughts, associations. Many teachers and writers have described this procession of mental activity – the sub-vocal conversations, must-do lists, memories from the past, and rehearsals of things we want to say to someone. And usually passes unnoticed for what it is – our 'stream of consciousness'.

However, whether through meditation, mindfulness training, or gestalt awareness practices, a new skill can be learned: that of finding a steadier 'observation point' – a place from which to 'watch the procession go by'. Again, as many others can substantiate, meditating in this way proves a hard practice to maintain, and rather than emphasising any 'state to be reached', the task is more usually thought of as 'bringing back one's attention' from being carried along in the stream without spotting that this is happening, and making the return to sitting on the bank of the stream as often as we can. The act of *registering*, as I am calling it here, corresponds to this act of focusing on the moving point of our experiencing, rather than 'getting lost in our thoughts', and no longer being 'aware of our awareness'.

In the field of contemporary neuroscience – itself in the midst of revolutionary developments – the act of registering has been identified as of enormous importance, not only for our immediate mental condition, but with longer-term implications as well, especially for young people. As Dan Siegel explains, '… the power to direct our attention has within it the power to shape our brain's firing patterns, as well as to shape the architecture of the brain itself'.[71]

Self-recognising includes the above kind of basic attending to immediate experiences, and also to the need – metaphorically speaking – for other kinds of 'standing back'. We need to take note, witness, and realise what has been preoccupying us; what in our environment fascinates us; what we feel drawn towards; or 'what's bugging us' or is 'alarming'. We may wake up to a long-term discomfort or an emerging new interest, or – more disturbingly – a realisation of how we 'have been running on automatic'. The mere act of registering our 'state of self' can bring us up short. The immediate thoughts and feelings we get in touch with are often tips of icebergs. Discovering the early-life foundations for them, which lie below the surface, can be a lifetime's quest.

Self-recognising is *not* about indulging in bouts of self-criticism: this dimension of *whi* is promoting constructive, non-judgemental, detached, and curious inquiry. Indeed,

---

[71]   Siegel, *Mindsight*, p. 39.

one thing some of us can become curious about is the extent of our crushing self-criticism. I remember explaining to Pamela, a sportswoman who was highly critical of the team she was coaching, that self-recognising was not an exercise of self-flagellation – or of flagellating others for not doing their own. Of course, there are times when taking a critical look at something we have done that we should not have done is a necessary step; but the overwhelming finding, throughout my career as a therapist and latterly as a coach, has been that people's capacity for 'self-punishment' and 'self put-downs' is often enlarged to proportions way beyond anything that is reasonable, just, or loving towards oneself.

In speaking of Pamela, I am shifting attention to what follows on from *registering* – namely, the need to *investigate*. The woman I mentioned who walked her dog and contemplated a career change had *registered* her dissatisfaction with what she was doing, and was now set on *investigating* her next steps – in this case by calling her friend in order to talk about it. So Pamela (I suggested) might also investigate how her own punitive bias originated, beginning by asking: 'Where and when was this standard of perfection established?' This is one useful route for many people: to go to the historical roots. But often it is equally relevant and significant to investigate what's happening now: 'How often do I criticise myself? Is it a pattern that I want to change? Can I learn to be less punitive without lowering my standards?' These are matters for inquiry, and for Pamela would include whether her team's decline in performance may have been partly a result of her sustained critical stance towards them – a disturbing thought for her.

Investigating is also what the Formula One team were doing with a vengeance – and with a timer. The registering of failure may have prompted some inquest into what went wrong, but their emphasis will have moved swiftly on to the fine details of maximising performance; the string quartet listening to a recording needed to become focused, to inquire, and to tease out the subtleties of technique and musical interpretation.

When, in the awareness exercise I described, I registered the fact that I was missing my children the realisation hit me hard. My investigation was to re-think some of my professional commitments, and in today's terms, my 'work–life balance'.

Often in self-recognising, people discover influences pulling in different directions – some feel ripped in two. Catherine, a woman in her forties, had already pursued a therapy training, including a lot of self-recognising. She described how, before she began, there had been a 'part of her' – which she called 'the choice of health' – that was keen on the idea of exploring her inner world and relationships; but this had been offset by 'absolute terror' of the 'beast in [her] cellar', which others would discover and which she imagined would destroy her as well as others.

She realised that other people had similar fantasies, and it kept them away from engaging in *any* therapy, counselling, or coaching, or from taking part in personal development groups. Beasts in cellars, monsters, inner terrorists, sadistic rapists, or cruel bitches seem to stalk the private lives of many well-functioning and successful adults, apparently lurking in the wings of their imaginations, ready to come out and wreck lives. Catherine remarked that 'If only people realised it was not like that'. Now that she had experience of therapy, she felt so vastly more relaxed and altogether lighter with no such conflict 'raging inside her' any more. Opening the 'door to the cellar' in therapy had been far, far easier than she imagined from a distance.

Self-recognising reveals many 'splits' of kinds that we know about, even if we are lucky not to be riven ourselves. There are straightforward conflicts, such as 'I want to play tennis but I'm supposed to finish this repair job first' or 'Shall I follow my hunch, or do the "rational" thing?' And there are other long-term tensions like Catherine described, between 'parts of herself' – her 'bossy', 'jokey', 'religious', and 'dishonest' selves all capable of making appearances.

Very profound dilemmas can cleave a person's lifeworld in two: for example, people born into a gendered body that does not fit their experience of themselves, and thinking of undergoing gender reassignment, or senior figures in a political party struggling with whether to resign or not, being so much at odds with the majority view in the party.

In all such cases of inner conflict, the possibility exists for *heightening* the difference between the two 'sides' to the argument, rather than letting them continue in their confusing, to and fro inner wrestling match. To sharpen the differences and set the two positions further apart may seem paradoxical at first, but invariably this seems to throw new light on the issues at stake.

One man I know well writes dialogues, like a play, between imaginary advocates for each point of view that is jostling for prominence in his life; others, in more embodied style, move between two bodily positions – 'standing up I'm resigning', 'sitting down I'm staying in the job' – and they experience the contrast in an embodied way. Others move between two positions on a sofa, and have an argument between their selves – and some speak it out loud. The point is to hear fully from one position, then from the other, rather than flit between them second by second. This way, the 'case for' and the 'case against' are both more fully articulated, and 'truth' often emerges spontaneously.

Heightening differentiation in this way is usually a precursor of *integration*. To 'integrate' means to combine things to make a whole. In the examples above, the integration derives from either a clear understanding of which option feels most true – often with an embodying-type check. Alternatively sometimes a third position comes into focus which combines elements of the two different possible ways forward, perhaps in a creative compromise: 'I'll do a temporary repair and still get to tennis'; or 'I'll write an article explaining my unease in the party and hold resignation as a step if I don't get a favourable response'. Via heightened differentiation, what starts as a disabling confusion arrives at a point where 'things fall into place, and make sense'.

Dan Siegel emphasises how important integration is in the working of the brain. There are many different parts to the brain, and the flow of energy and information between the parts is necessary to create harmony and stability: 'Impaired integration results in chaos and/or rigidity'.[72] However, in the case of past trauma, the levels of confusion, chaos, and instability reveal divisions of a different order. They can be disorienting to the point that to bring about integration normally requires specialist help. Sometimes the self-recognising we most need is to realise that we cannot 'handle this on our own', and 'even my best friend doesn't really understand why I'm like this'; or, indeed, that 'I have taken this fear (or depression, or outbursts of destructive rage, or…) for granted for far too long!'

---

[72]   Siegel, *Pocket Guide to Interpersonal Neurobiology*, 4-4.

Reading a therapy case study,[73] I notice the writer concludes with a summary of one woman's journey in therapy – what she had to learn on the way. The young woman (20 years old) had grown up deeply enmeshed in the dynamics of a traumatised immigrant family, and she had been regularly beaten by her father. She was suicidal and felt that 'things had fallen apart'. The integration she found through therapy meant learning '…to slowly believe in and value her experience, to accept a less grandiose reality of her and others' strengths and limitations, to embrace the legitimacy and normality of the full range of her negative emotions and to accept her conflict of loyalties'.

These kinds of learnings, whether achieved through therapy or not, are powerful steps towards a more integrated sense of a 'true self' rather than a 'false self'. The case study captures a part of the overall purpose of investigating and integrating: '… so as not to repeat, in the next generation, the patterns of denial and abuse she had endured herself'.

Self-recognising as protection

There are wider implications of 'self-recognising': in order for us to know our own values, needs, fears, aspirations, and 'inner truth', sometimes we need to insulate ourselves from what's impinging on us. A barrage of societal, political, and commercial messages assail most people every day: pressures to consume, to conform, and to

---

[73] E. Virginia Demos, 'Intergenerational Violence and the Family Myth', in *Lost in Transmission: Studies of Trauma Across Generations*, ed. M. Gerard Fromm (Karnac, 2012), pp. 131–47. Quotations are from p. 146.

make sense of the world and life in ways that are dominant in the culture at large – through advertising, news media, government propaganda, and social conventions. Given these powerful influences, we need to recognise how easily we can slip into swallowing whole great slices of pre-packaged 'mental food' without critical attention, and this may be as damaging to our overall wellbeing as, in real eating, would be a diet exclusively of fast food, never tested for its flavour or its capacity to nourish us.

In an interconnected world, we are influenced by prevalent thinking and by others, and we, in turn, influence others; in small ways, we constantly export our view of the world – including our prejudices. Arguably, then, we have a simple human duty to self-recognise what we feed into the world – by noticing what we are exporting. I am not suggesting this as some dampening and inhibiting moral absolute: we cannot avoid influencing others by communicating who we are and what we believe. At the same time, actually noticing what we remark casually, and when and how often we say it, can sometimes be a sobering experience – as well as a socially responsible practice.

The moral argument for self-recognising is obvious in the case, say, of medical specialists. If they don't know that they don't know something, they are hazards to others. Similarly, team members working on major projects who do not realise how 'high maintenance' they are regarded by their colleagues, may endanger both the project and others' wellbeing. All of us have 'blind spots': we may be overly assertive, or hesitant at the wrong time, or prejudiced towards certain types of people in ways we barely notice except after the event, or through feedback from others.

∗

In talking with Rita, a deeply thinking senior manager, we agreed that the integrity of each person's conscience affected the quality of collective life. Collective trends and 'group-think' often trump individual inputs and the views of minorities; but corruption of systems still rests ultimately on individual complicity.

Rita and I agreed that each person's act of acknowledging the truth with integrity, or each management committee's owning of and correcting departures from humanitarian values, are contributions that *strengthen* the systems involved, at least in the long term, as well as benefitting the individuals most involved. Long-term benefits flow from openness and transparent decision making, and from leaders admitting mistakes and fallibility: they gather force, like new streams of influence entering a larger stream. There is a discernible relaxation in the system when the incomprehensible is explained, when overdue apologies are given, or when the truth of an unexplained mystery finally comes out. A collective release of tension occurs, which may be registered as an embodied shift.

In the short term, messengers with bad news, critics of a system – family, organisational, or communal – may not be welcomed. As Albert Einstein pointed out, 'Few people are capable of expressing with equanimity opinions which differ from the prejudices of their social environment. Most people are even incapable of forming such opinions'.[74] This may be too pessimistic: while some choose the path of

---

[74] Albert Einstein, *The Philosophy of Albert Einstein* (1879–1955) http://www.plainview3d.com/Strategy_inspiration.html.

'keeping their mouth shut', others are beginning to realise that 'they have to speak out' to question a general practice that 'has gone on too long'. The only way to alter the balance of forces in favour of more truth-speaking, is by naming, legitimising, and rewarding procedures of self-recognising. This dimension of *whi* needs to be taken up as a sign of organisational maturity and systemic health.

I often ask, when running a group event, whether someone's expressed reaction to what is happening in the group is shared or is unique to that individual. I have found, almost invariably, that what one person experiences is also experienced by others, even if others have not talked about it. Some member sounds an alert, or expresses some discomfort about what is happening. He or she acts as a 'canary in the mine', giving expression to something, a strand or theme, which is shared but not previously aired or noticed. A group's recognising its collective limitations can be a profound gift, opening doors to rich conversations and deep sharing. The more threads individual members contribute, the more compelling the tapestry that's woven. It becomes an act of collective self-recognising.

The much talked-about ideal of the 'learning organisation' is a reference to how self-recognising can occur at the level of a large system. Again, the shared activity relies on the members taking part. They not only carry the system within their own 'life-space' and bodies (see Chapter 5), but also are the essential generators of insight: each at times can be the canary. Each system-holder has views of its possible future. And it is often lone voices which sound alarms, or define the exact issues to be faced.

*

Authoritarian leaders and oppressive governments often discourage self-recognising on a collective basis. An awake, politically curious, question-asking population or assertive workforce is experienced as a threat. Moves to greater transparency come from the grassroots, not generally from those in power.

As a fundamental human priority at significant times, self-recognising has survival value. Coming to terms with 'what we are like' may be the saving of a business. Waking up to early-warning signs of disaffection in a small community is preferable to postponing action till it's too late. Recognising ourselves and our actions is not an act of self-indulgence – rather it is a check on whether we are acting in a competent and intelligent manner, or whether we have become distracted or lost the plot, need a rest, or are not in the right state of mind to undertake a given task. It's about ensuring quality control. We gain more degrees of freedom in the ways we operate in the world – sometimes at the cost of having to deal with more feeling and more difficult truths. But, overall, our views of ourselves and our lives are expanded.

In an organisation, there is sometimes a long-term problem of someone being 'unawake'. They are not grasping what everyone else realises about them – for instance, that they are self-obsessed, or constantly telling the same stories, or always complaining about their misfortune. Being 'woken up' can be a painful experience for them, and one that often evokes discomfort and unsettlement – and the possibility of a shame reaction. Fear of triggering distress can lead to others wanting to preserve the person's sense of dignity, and colluding in not 'shaking them awake'. Others may say, 'They have to do it themselves and in their own time'. And, of course, they may well not.

For all the difficulties encountered sometimes in bringing difficult matters to a person's or a group's attention, we need to remember that human beings have a developed capacity for integrating experiences and making meaning out of them, placing them in a context and weaving them into a narrative with which they can live. Delivering difficult messages is a necessary task, and needs an exquisite deftness and sense of timing, and deep respect for the fact that the person is already doing his or her best. When difficult feedback is made with gentleness and candour, most people receiving it are thankful – if not instantaneously.

We all – individuals and groups alike – need to know our own limitations: each of us has perceptual censors – not taking in what we don't want to – and old habitual tendencies and weaknesses that can reappear in conditions that call them out. Sharing stories and our narratives provides a versatile vehicle for 'discovering who we are' and for receiving input from others. As already noted, to be 'received' by others – who listen to our experience in a welcoming and open frame of mind, offers powerful reinforcement for self-recognition, with often the story-telling being healing in itself. Of course, there is a discipline to doing this as well: listeners to people's accounts can be tempted to direct the speaker along lines of their own interests. And anything akin to cross-questioning, advice giving, or interrupting with one's own ideas, can undermine the sharing process. What does seem effective, though, is for listeners to report on how they have been emotionally affected – what, in particular, they 'responded to' or 'were impacted by'.[75]

*

In the practice of self-recognising, we are 'called back' to remember what we stand for, or perhaps to realise how fuzzy we are about our most important values or 'sense of ultimate purpose'.

Although some will draw back from the very idea, as if they have been scalded, something approximating a spiritual life may be one of the most effective ways by which people can recognise and stabilise themselves and nurture a sense of direction. Integrating what's happening in our lives is often about *finding a greater context of meaning* in which we can locate our thoughts and life-events. In reaching this more inclusive view or bigger picture of our existence, many seem to experience a sense of release – and of 'things falling into place'. Seeing the totality of our lives can bring us up short: we may realise the extraordinary fact that we exist at all, and also remember that we are mortal. For some, this perspective can induce a despairing sense of futility, while others report a sense of urgency, linked to awe and wonder – perhaps through acknowledging their fragility and tiny status in the vastness of the universe, at the same time as recognising the miracle of their temporary presence on Earth.

Another great way of making meaning and an overall sense of continuity may be through highlighting love as an

---

[75] This has been developed as a highly effective procedure by the Relational Center of Los Angeles, and has spread to other parts of the growing Relational Movement. See http://www.therelationalmovement. org.

extraordinary force that acts throughout the world. Here there is an immediate problem, given the over-use of and confusion around the word 'love'. I am referring to Eros in all its forms: the different kinds of affection and bonding that exist between human beings, and between humans and animals such as dogs and horses. More generally, I am speaking of love as the basis of the ultimately irrepressible humanitarian impulse of kindness, which manifests again and again, even in times of bitter division, hideous cruelty, and release of *Thanatos*.[76] Conceived in this way, as a procreative and generative force in the world, love is also the polar opposite to fear: love approaches, fear holds back. Love is evident in mitigating the suffering of others; in engaging passionately to safeguard the beauty and wonder of the planet's vulnerable biosphere; in protecting the innocence of children; and in bringing music, dance, and laughter into the lives of the downcast and deeply fatigued.

For many across the world, of course, experiences of 'humility in the cosmos', or of being part of the web of Life, or of love as a powerful agent for good, are allied to a religious conception such as 'divine purpose'. However, even for those with no religious affiliation or metaphysical inclinations,

---

[76] Thanatos is Sigmund Freud's term for the 'death drive', the urge to destruction, self-destruction; the counter to the life-giving and replenishing of Eros. The place of kindness was memorably recognised by Aung San Suu Kyi on the occasion of her accepting, in 2012, the Nobel Peace Prize awarded to her in 1991. Alluding to her long period of house arrest and confinement, she said: 'Of the sweets of adversity, and let me say that these are not numerous, I have found the sweetest, the most precious of all, is the lesson I learnt on the value of kindness. Every kindness I received, small or big, convinced me that there could never be enough of it in our world. To be kind is to respond with sensitivity and human warmth to the hopes and needs of others. Even the briefest touch of kindness can lighten a heavy heart. Kindness can change the lives of people'.

there can still be something like exaltation as they reflect on their deepest values or regard the unfolding of their life, which can appear 'oddly purposeful-seeming' in the course it has taken.

To imagine any kind of mysterious organising of our lives, with some direction other than what we have determined ourselves, is likely to be dismissed by those who locate themselves on the higher and safer ground of (assumed) scientific certainty and associated materialistic beliefs. Yet others – many others, I have found – are unhappy to discard altogether a spiritual outlook. They may feel uncomfortable with the apparent certainties of religious institutions but do not wish to reject altogether the experiences and insights buried within these ancient traditions. Many practise entering into a frame of mind that is 'unknowing' – opening themselves to more numinous and wordless experiences, for instance through meditation or being deeply embodied; others prize what they describe as 'coming home to themselves'. Attempting to verbalise the indescribable is to call on our inner poets; once grasped and condensed into words, these introspective, meditative, and reflective states can sound banal. However difficult to capture, such states of thought and feeling are highly prized by those who access them: they can inspire states of reverence for life and gratitude for multiple 'gifts from the universe' or for 'acts of grace'; or they can be stepping-stones to 'letting go of ego', to 'non-duality', or 'reflecting on Divine Purpose'.

I suggest that the particular words, images, and concepts people draw upon may be far less significant than the experiences themselves. Encountering one's existence, or recognising oneself in ways that seem more truthful, or altering the course of one's life after a period of contemplation will be labelled as 'spiritual' or as 'religious' by some, while others will speak the very different language of neural integration and brain function. Ultimately, our choice of language and outlook is a deeply felt and private matter.[77] However, because these experiences relate to the whole of Life, to questions of morality and responsibility, and to our most profound sense of ourselves as conscious animals, we may all be tempted to suggest we have found '*the* way', or that our truth is better than someone else's truth, and that our tradition is sacred whereas another's is not.

I suggest that here is a need for collective self-recognising and growth of *whi,* on the part of all humanity – a further step in our social evolution. We need to acknowledge with respect and forbearance human beings' vast variation in how we approach and think about the whole of our lives and the mysteries – or astronomical unknowns – of existence. Increased awareness of the entirety of our lives seems to be part of conscious dying, and – I suspect, for an increasing number – more conscious living as well.

Developmental self-recognising

People enrich or deepen their self-recognising in a multitude of ways: for example, they draw or paint images, or 'connect to themselves' through music, dance, or drama. However, perhaps story-telling provides the most versatile means. The telling of one's story – the first person account – gathers together facts, feelings, and

---

[77] Atheists who describe themselves as 'non-believers' are on very shaky ground. They often hold sceptical beliefs with a fervour that others might regard as 'religious' in kind; and they can seem just as unquestioning of their beliefs as fundamentalist religious people.

reflections on experience, all in one creation. It is part of the search of the big picture of one's life.[78] In organisational and communal terms, it is the dominant narrative, which is passed on to newcomers.

As part of making sense of our journey, we sometimes need to look back. Many have little interest in thinking about their childhood – quite understandably, given the demands of their lives as adults. However, sometimes there is no option: some shocking event or disturbance – an unexpected illness, the death of a much-loved parent, a career closed down – will often force people to stop and confront who or what they have become. They have been swimming along, as it were, in the ongoing river of existence, and suddenly find themselves sitting on the bank instead, noticing its current, or the distance travelled, or the fact that they stopped just in time before the falls. Questions arise with new urgency: 'What do I stand for? Where am I going? What's my true calling?' These are characteristic of many a 'mid-life crisis' – which people can have at any stage of life.

What has struck me – as witness to many such crises – is how powerful and durable are people's long-term interests, or personal passions. Most of us know someone who started off in one direction and 'found their true path' later. Noticing where someone's attention is repeatedly drawn, or where our private longings lie, or 'what we are meant to do' becomes key in direction-finding for the future.

Often it is in our early experiences of life that our personal interests and priorities originate. But that does not mean that the path between then and now is straight, obvious, and always clear. We develop, change, and many of us have

---

[78]   I recommend Geoff Mead's book, *Coming Home to Story* (Vala publishing, 2013), for a powerful insight into how story-telling is part of self-recognising.

steered a winding course. All sense of direction may be lost – and then the trail is re-found. I've chosen an example from my own experience: my lifelong interest in war and peace, which has also been part of the 'fuel' for writing this book.[79]

My earliest conscious memory was a moment of war. I was just under three years old. Someone was holding me and pointing upwards. Planes flew overhead in steady progression, trailing gliders behind them. As an adult I realised this memory had to be of D-Day itself, when parachutists and extra supplies were ferried in gliders across the English Channel as part of the invasion force.

Through much of my life I have felt moved, tearful, and a tingling down my back whenever D-Day and the invasion of Normandy has been mentioned, let alone depicted in documentaries. I am now certain that I was permanently affected by the extraordinary emotions funnelled into that day. One can imagine the high pitch of excitement, edge-of-seat anticipation on 6 June 1944; by mid-morning, the BBC had broadcast the news that the long-awaited invasion had begun at dawn. It must have been like waiting outside a hospital's operating theatre for news of someone undergoing life or death surgery. All across southern England families were watching the skies and listening to the radio in varying states of anticipation, anxiety, and excitement.

I have travelled my path of post-war integration in fits and starts. While my D-Day experience stands out, the whole of

---

[79] Parts of what follows first appeared in Malcolm Parlett, 'The Impact of War', *British Gestalt Journal*, 23/1 (2014), pp. 5–12. Reprinted with permisson of the editor.

my early life was dominated by the fact and presence of the war – it framed my young existence, as it did that of countless others. I realise now that I escaped lightly, compared to many children around the world, then and now: I witnessed no violent death, and experienced no overwhelming terror. Unlike friends in other countries, I have no memories of being under occupation, or of forced parental separation, or traumatic train rides to safer destinations; I received no sweets from occupying German soldiers, nor took part in wild celebrations when American troops arrived. But there's no question that 'The War' was all around me. By the time it ended in Europe, I was four years old and attending my first school: the war was my 'normal'.

I have other assorted memories of the war, though none carries the same charge as that of D-Day. But references to the war were inescapable – others of my generation report the same. As I got older, I began to piece together the jigsaw of what the war entailed. I remember how I would devour anything about the war I could. TV programmes, films, and picture books added to my impressions, way beyond anything I had myself experienced, of course, but getting fed into the slowly growing jigsaw picture. At a *Readers Digest* level, the war was chopped into digestible episodes that became the narratives in constant circulation: that Britain had fought alone at first; 'we' survived Dunkirk against the odds; 'the Few' in their Spitfires saw off the Luftwaffe; 'back-room boys (and girls)' were part of the success; and Churchill inspired the nation.

When my serious reading of war history began to take off, in my twenties, I realised how childishly simple and incomplete was the picture I held. I am not sure that many of my generation in Britain really grasped until well into adulthood that the real attrition of the German army was accomplished on the eastern front by Soviet forces, not through the heroics of Normandy and the Battle of the Bulge; or that the Blitz was not just a British experience but was replicated in several European countries – where, unlike in Britain, it was followed by massive military invasion as well.

Slowly, I began to fill in gaps and could assimilate discordant history. I started to ask more fundamental questions. I wondered, for example, in what ways the British had really been the victors. A couple of decades after the war the German economy was soaring ahead of Britain's; and by the war's end the United States had replaced Britain as the dominant superpower, with Britain effectively bankrupt: it was only in 2006 that Britain made its final payment on its post-war loan from the USA.

Self-recognising, as underlined already, takes many different forms, and the process of 'updating ourselves' is just one of them – but one that's significant. Integration of the past and present is not a steady, organised process of historical research – at least as I have observed it in both my own and others' experiences.

In updating our pictures from the past, we all know the confusions that arise: how easy it is to fall backwards into an outlook or behaviour pattern we thought we had long ago abandoned. In later years I sometimes found myself slipping back into old simplicities with regard to the war. For instance, around 12 years ago I was visiting the German city of Würzburg to attend a conference. This was many years after I had first learned about the area bombing of Dresden, with the arguments about whether or not it was an atrocity: given the 15 square miles of firestorm that resulted, along with 25,000 deaths, two months before the end of the war, I think it was.

What I had not realised, however, was that Würzburg – another ancient and beautiful city – experienced a similar bombing and ensuing obliteration by fire, on the night following the destruction of Dresden. When I was gently informed by my German host that this had happened, I could note my mixed reactions: they included an automatic pull to defend the RAF's action, along with more up-to-date feelings of sorrow, guilt, and shame – the latter somehow compounded by hearing how the citizens had painstakingly built an exact replica of the medieval centre as it had been before the raid.

In other words, as time passed, and I looked at an ever-widening vista, I was slowly extricating myself from a particular way of thinking and feeling, and letting go of beliefs, outlooks, and perspectives on war with which I had grown up. I was also registering that new interests were landing, as new layers on top of the old.

The move that I needed to make was parallel to moving from self-*pity* to self-*compassion* – a distinction drawn by Frank Staemmler, a German psychotherapist. Self-*pity* – 'characterised by a paramount preoccupation with one's *own* suffering' – is ultimately a dead end, while self-*compassion* – 'realising that [one's] own problems do not differ from those of others' leads to engaging 'with our fellow human beings in the same way we share our talents, joys and successes' – and opens us to contact and the world.[80]

---

[80] Frank-M. Staemmler, 'Self-Esteem, Compassion, and Self-Compassion: From Individualism to Connectedness', *British Gestalt Journal*, 21/2 (2012), pp. 19–28.

Out of my expanding view, I noticed an increasing interest in war-related trauma, which I have progressively realised is vast in scale – beyond imagination. Those in active combat undergo threats to their own lives; they witness the violent deaths and ghastly injuries of their comrades; and they may have to cut themselves off from the otherwise unbearable feelings about those they have themselves killed – not just 'enemy soldiers' but also civilians, including children. In modern war, more civilians than military are killed; and each person violently killed has a circle of people who loved them. The trauma load is spread thickly over whole populations, and it affects subsequent generations.

I was also recognising that my own experiences in war had had a much bigger effect on me than I had realised before, even if they were not of the severity of the experiences of other young children and adults – in fact all who have been plunged into the chaos and carnage of direct violent warfare, experiencing its anguish and terror, its injuries, deaths, and destroyed homes, and all the rage, grief, and hopelessness which follow in the wake of shooting, shelling, and bombing. The consequences for those affected, including in their becoming parents in a traumatised state themselves, cannot help but affect their children who have developing brains which are at their 'most malleable and most sensitive to experience – both good and bad – early in life'.[81]

The final stage in my war-related journey – the *release,* or moving on phase, continues. The impact of my D-Day experience has far less personal urgency: even my interest in following current wars on the international stage has reduced. At the same time, my horror at the swathe of invisible damage

---

[81]   Bruce Perry and Maia Szalavitz, *The Boy Who Was Raised as a Dog* (Basic Books, 2006), p. 38.

left by war in the long-term experiences of families and young children, continues to grow – along with a deep anger and revulsion that war and violent conflict continue in the 21st century – as if humanity has learned nothing.

＊

In conclusion, we can see that self-recognising engages deeply with some of the most sensitive, deeply rooted features of human existence, as well as being of general usefulness as a kind of ongoing monitoring of our lives, energies, directions, and levels of performance. The last section of this chapter describes a journey of progressively making sense of the past. It suggests a possible new kind of human activity, which communities could pursue more assiduously and deliberately. I suspect that in the sphere of academic history, what I am about to suggest is not uncommon.

The idea was triggered by remembering a powerful process with a troubled training group, which had been disturbed by a constantly changing membership and unstable leadership. Frankly, it was a mess, as members of the group acknowledged. We decided on a way to proceed. We went back to the very beginnings, and traced exactly the stages it had gone through: 'Janet and Dirk arrived then, but there was that woman who came once and didn't stay … Then Iris left, and it was the re-scheduled weekend'. It went on like that. The process was one of sifting through what had happened, without judgement, just neutrally acknowledging what had taken place – stopping where necessary to revisit the feelings that had arisen at the time, and which now, regarded in hindsight, had lost most of the charge they had originally carried.

The exercise, which took about two hours in all, turned out to be transformative: the group got up to date; it had recognised its history, and had a shared narrative of what had happened. It became the basis for the group's moving on. It was an exercise in sophisticated self-recognising which we had co-created.

My proposal is that such recapitulations might be tried more often. They could happen in small or large groups, especially when there has been a troubled past. An organisation's rethinking of its present direction could reconstitute its history as the first stage of the process: noticing how styles of leadership and organisational fads from the past may still have subterranean effects in the present-day, long after the organisation's stated functions have moved on. Long-term conflicts, old resentments, and past sorrows need not be re-worked at length, only briefly visited along the way back to present conditions and today's actuality. This is very different from what commonly happens, when background narratives and history receive scant attention, often because what was once explosive is still considered too dangerous to touch. Keeping the past sealed off from cool-headed present consideration, however, allows it more power to influence the future, not less.

Truth and Reconciliation procedures – of which there have now been a number tried across the world – perform the same function as that experienced by the group described above. There is a revisiting of the past, and an opportunity to learn from it. The overall emphasis is on settling the past as well as it can be, and consigning the past to history – very different from carrying the past into the present with all the loose ends and residual feelings of hurt and loss not being recognised but still being carried by those with loyalties to the past, but now on an even bigger scale.

I am wondering if there is not a need to retrace some of the most basic assumptions in the societies and systems in which we live. Humanity as a whole needs to find some common narratives as to how we have inherited the kind of world we have at the moment. If we are to reinvent ourselves as a species, which will be necessary if we are to learn how to live together and also to protect the lives of those who come after us, perhaps this is the agenda for self-recognising that we need the most. A common narrative can only come about in the present, and the story of humanity's development through the age of modernity could show us how we still carry the burdens of past ways of thinking and managing our world.

In this suggestion, I am already moving to the Fifth (and final) Exploration, of *experimenting*.

CHAPTER 7

EXPERIMENTING
The Fifth Exploration

We live in an overflowing global marketplace. New ideas, fresh thinking, social and technological innovations are flooding the world – trending, chaotic, turbulent, and life altering. For a great many of us, it's an exciting and stimulating time, rather in the manner of a long ski-run, sailing close-hauled in a strong wind, or perhaps playing in an orchestra with a world premiere to challenge us. For others, though, living in the present era is not like this at all: it's a bewildering exercise in staying afloat, a world in which forced change is decided by unknown others, and where life seems full of relentless pressure, stress, or the demands of 'simply getting by'. Whether stimulated or overwhelmed, human beings are encountering novelty and changing attitudes at an unparalleled rate – and the very ways we live are being transformed in shape and substance.

Experimenting, as a distinctive human feature and mode of human experience, is therefore already deeply familiar to us. The dominant economic model makes sure of this. The pursuit of growth, the pressure for ever-increasing consumer choice, and the need to develop new products and services are all pivotal to present political and economic assumptions – even though they are part of a system that is widely recognised as unsustainable and inequitable. In fact, the further evolution of our fundamental economic model will ultimately rest on developments from new ideas and smaller-scale experiments, many of which, such as local currencies and exchange systems without money, may already exist. In other words, we already know the Experimenting dimension in a myriad of forms: one could almost call this an Age of Experimenting – and arguably, we need more, not less. However, the experiments we may need more of are not necessarily the kinds that attract enthusiasm in present economic conditions.

Critical to the Fifth Exploration, and to appreciating this dimension of whole intelligence, is realising how we tend to be energised by novelty – recognising the creative inspiration that often accompanies experimenting. Yet human beings are also creatures of habit. For all the attraction we can feel for new developments, there is also a strong magnetic pull back to the known and habitual.

This fundamental tension leads us to explore, for instance, how political attitudes at both ends of the left–right spectrum can lead to so much sterile – and arguably unintelligent – debate, often displaying the opposite of an open and inquiring experimental attitude on both sides of the aisle. But even in the political domain there are signs of more fluidity, as greater public knowledge is communicated via social media and the world wide web.

Experimenting represents a means of learning and extending the known, of upturning assumptions, and of making deliberate changes in systems and procedures and in ways of looking and understanding. The freshness and unpredictability can be playful – indeed, it's the pleasures of experimenting that underlie all sport and games, with PLAY being the defining value of the Fifth Exploration.

What is experimenting?

When people comment that a team leader or work colleague is 'always open to new ideas', or 'she likes to stop and ask questions' or 'he's always up for scrapping a plan if something better appears', they are commenting on someone who is manifesting this dimension of whole intelligence, and is displaying a sophisticated attitude to matters of innovating, changing course, staying the same, and, if necessary, going back to something that has been rejected before. Experimenting is not an optional skill that's added on to life; it is a universal feature of everyday existence. Every time we follow an idea or proposal without a near-certain outcome, we are experimenting.

Some commuters, driving the same route over and over, may divert to introduce novelty and or find a possibly better route home. Others will repeatedly take the same route unless forced to change through a route diversion. They may then be surprised at how much they like the new route; or, alternatively, they may feel so 'loyal' to their old route home that they return to it as soon as possible, confirmed in their preference for staying with the familiar. Whatever the various alternatives – switching, staying the same, being dragged into the new – there are benefits, possible hazards, or disappointments. A natural 'diverter', for instance, can end up going miles out of their way; a natural 'sticker' can add 10 minutes to their route repetitively and unknowingly.

A personal education in experimenting is built into ordinary maturing. When we do something for the first time – like going to college, becoming a parent, or turning up on the first day of work in new employment – we are stepping into the unknown, which for most people carries a *frisson* of anxiety or excitement. We are engaging with strangeness that may surprise or stretch us – may feel immediately comfortable or unpleasantly challenging. Encountering the unknown happens all through life, right up to our dying. The last words of a good friend of mine, a physics professor and lifelong experimentalist, were: 'This is a strange experience'. As his wife commented later: 'An experimentalist taking note to the very, very end'.

In other words, experimenting is not just a creative exercise, a trying out of possibility, or playful departure from a norm; it is a key feature of human existence *all the time*. Arguably, every conversation, at least those that are not robotic or scripted, is an improvisation – an experiment – invented in and for the moment. Willingness to experiment, to try things out, to see what works, is a powerful catalyst, orientation, and stimulant for effective personal and group change – a key constituent in all kinds of 'action research'.[82] Experimenting also offers something like a personal practice, stance, and attitude.

As with the other dimensions of *whi*, experimenting is evident in all domains of life. People add pleasure and

---

[82] The term 'action research' was coined by Kurt Lewin in 1944, and has spawned a massive body of work. Present-day usage of the term is broad: '… action research is about working towards practical outcomes, and also about creating new forms of understanding, since action without reflection and understanding is blind, just as theory without action is meaningless'. See the Editors' Introduction, in Peter Reason and Hilary Bradbury, eds, *Handbook of Action Research: Participative Inquiry and Practice*, 1st edition (Sage, 2001), p. 2.

variety to their lives by experimenting – trying new cuisines for example; experimentation with technology can result in innovative new tools such as electric cars; and continuing experiment finds new solutions to old problems – for example, new gene therapy in the treatment of cancer. This quest for novel solutions and fresh directions is evident across all age groups – it's part of our heritage and promise, and a key factor in our aliveness and wish to participate.

Among young children, experimenting is constant and exuberant: playing with, chewing, handling, 'locking on' to something that fascinates – and discovering consequences, for example, that if you use a toy bus like a hammer, the wheel breaks. This exploratory impulse in children can be turned off only by the interventions of 'grown-ups' who wish to direct, corral, or channel this vibrant natural force into some adult-preferred direction.

Not surprisingly, passionate inquisitiveness declines with age, as formal education imposes its hierarchy of what's important, and as progressively we decide 'we know stuff'. Among the elderly, experimenting is more measured, though more and more the age factor seems immaterial: there are instances of octogenarians going back to study, or entering marathons, or making a first film. Less adventurous ones may nevertheless still experiment – as in trying new ways to manage physical tasks without strain. At the same time, the stereotype of experimenting falling away with age may be justified in part: 'sclerotic' is often an adjective of choice when younger people's ideas get crushed by establishment committees – on which younger people rarely sit; and some believe that scientific shibboleths are abandoned only when an entire generation of scientists pass away – which is sometimes rather long to wait. In some communities, 'change proceeds funeral by funeral', as I heard recently. A reader of this chapter commented that she had felt 'locked in' till both her 'paternal and maternal grandmothers died'.

At whatever age, the scope of our renewing, our inventiveness, our flirting with novelty provides stimulus, the thrill of possibility, and is part of the 'spice of life'; it is a natural state, or accompaniment to being fully alive, creative, and high functioning. As a wider activity drawing on the human urge to innovate and extend boundaries, it can also breed disturbing questions. Many experiments are serious or even deadly – military or medical ones, in particular – and raise troubling ethical questions.

The spirit of experimenting, as it first appealed to me, is reflected in statements such as the following:

1. 'Let's find out about it by trying it out and seeing what happens.'
2. 'Let's think of a whole range of policy options rather than having just two.'
3. 'I want us to take note of what we are doing here, and ask ourselves why we continue to do it this way?'
4. 'Stay with the uncertainty before rushing to a solution.'
5. 'What is essential to hold on to here, and what needs to change?'
6. 'The consequences of doing this could be enormous. I need to know more before we decide.'

These statements reveal that experimenting can serve as catalyst, method, and stimulant for effective personal and group change: we take initiatives and question what is possible. It presents a stance of inquiry and open-mindedness, rather than either rushing to conclusions or stumbling into ill-considered innovations. In practical terms, experimenting is often about incremental change, about practical inquiry, based on Kurt Lewin's belief that we learn most about something through trying to change it.[83]

Despite enjoying what's novel or 'not tried before', human beings often are confused about their attitudes to changing the familiar – there's a whole range of ambivalent attitudes. The confusion is revealed in our varied choice of terms. Thus, we sometimes talk about changes in positive, even glowing terms: *births*, *openings*, *new frontiers*, and *vistas opening*. Or, a very negative gloss can be put on what seems roughly the same order of change. A scheme might then be described as *rocking the boat*, a *recipe for chaos*, or *unnecessary tinkering*, or may be dismissed as *change for change's sake*.

Similar contrasts show up when speaking of change NOT happening – this, too, excites comment and contradiction. On the one hand, lack of action can be lambasted as *stuckness* or *paralysis*, or as evidence of *dinosaurs* being in charge, or of *dead wood* in the leadership. But at other times or in different contexts, we can find ourselves making statements extolling the resistance to change: there is talk of how important is *maintaining stability*, *holding the line*, or *upholding the tradition*.

---

[83] See, for instance, William Passmore, 'Action Research in the Workplace: the Socio-technical Perspective', in *Handbook of Action Research*, pp. 38–47.

What is clear is that, while we are attracted to excitement and new vistas – to fresh faces and ideas – most of us are also creatures of habit. We are conservative (with a small 'c'), wanting high levels of familiarity and structure, and feeling the need to know where we stand. It underlines the significance of experimenting as a skilful human enterprise that is problematic, often emotionally charged, while also being central to lived existence. Arguably, it needs a good injection of increased understanding, which brings us to *whi*.

In fact, the tension I've mentioned between the urge to change and the urge to stay the same is a powerful one. The experience may be one of 'a wildly stormy strait, like the Straits of Magellan, where two fierce and opposing currents meet'.[84] We are caught between the current sweeping us toward the future and its new possibilities, and the opposing current tugging us back to the familiar patterns of the past.

Without doubt, along with the numerous attractions of change – novelty, fresh energy, spring-like new possibilities and openings – there can be difficult consequences. We may have regrets for what is disappearing or nostalgia for the previous; we need to come to terms with discarding something in which we have invested much; or we may be frustrated by others' stubborn resistance to making a change at all.

When we are at the point of realising that our thoughts, work methods, or ideas have been superseded, disproved, or 'holed below the water line', we have no choice but to wave them off, grieve, and let go. It can be a stretch. In addition – with a move to a new location, for example –

---

[84] Borrowing an image from D.H. Lawrence, *Kangaroo* (Cambridge University Press, 1994), Chapter 9.

there is novelty and 'getting used to it' required, even as we are working through the missing of what was there before.

In the early days of thinking about experimenting, I had a colleague who challenged me whenever I expressed uncritical appreciation of innovation, how exciting it was to break new ground, or how encountering something not tried before provoked new aliveness. She thought I was neglecting equally important priorities, such as sustaining good habits, upholding strong commitments, continuity and predictability, and the need for steady maintenance of things that matter over time – like families, consistent management, preserving local traditions, and building a business. I had to admit to a bias in favour of adventure, change, and novelty, but I also acknowledged how much I admired and appreciated those who sustained long-term commitments, steadily built families and careers, and lived regular lives over long periods. I realised that my own record – like most people's I suspect – was somewhat mixed, with some definite continuities and also several lurches sideways.

The more I investigated, and the more I talked with my colleague, the more I realised that, in a sense, we were both asserting a need for balance. To experiment with greater *whi* requires a perspective that honours the familiar *as well as* having a welcoming readiness to encounter the unfamiliar. As revealed in many different spheres of human action, performance and effectiveness require core stability and new thinking at the same time. Indeed, experimenting cannot be opting for the unusual every time – not least because it would no longer be an experiment if 'unusualness' became 'the usual'. 'Change for change's sake' can sometimes become a toxic habit – as many whose work arrangements have been repeatedly re-organised can attest.

The *whi*-quality required is *discernment*.[85] This involves weighing familiar with unfamiliar – the hoped for benefits with the probable costs of unsettlement. Experimenting with discernment calls for more finely tuned discriminations between the two poles, tolerating neither too much sameness nor too much difference from the usual. Sometimes a work-team, a teacher, or a business leader needs to lean towards destabilising the *status quo*, and at other times there is satisfaction in a feeling of 'coming home' to the trusted features of our known ways. There is also an obvious place for establishing 'good habits' as desired and chosen regularities that are life sustaining – for example, early morning stretches, remembering to turn off lights, and allocating domestic responsibilities. In this respect – especially for the sustainability agenda – the world needs *more* habits of the right kind, and children brought up without developing them often realise later in life the advantages that accrue from establishing habits.

Sometimes the need for order, regulation, and machine-like predictability needs to be ruffled up by some introduced novelty, refreshment, or wildness. Otherwise the fire and spirit of an organisation, or long-term relationship, can disappear. On the other hand, some situations need the reverse – to *reduce* unfamiliarity, not to stir things up. Changes can still be experimental in the sense meant here:

---

[85] I am grateful to Archie Roberts for discussion of discernment in particular.

they can break a run of instability by offering something that is necessary and stable, but has become unexpected. For a traumatised child, for instance, to introduce safe boundaries and continuity is often the required change. And people in shock need steadying, containing structures, and no new demands. On a less serious scale, those in repeatedly destabilised working conditions often crave a period of stable and predictable routines – to 'catch up with themselves' or sometimes to allow finely tuned long-term organisational changes to become apparent in ways that had been impossible when major reorganisations were landing on them in swift succession.

Commanders in a military operation have to pause to practise discernment, and to find a balance. Thus, assessing tactical options following a reverse, they may have difficult choices. There is the need both to avoid becoming risk-averse and to resist feeling pressured to return immediately to a standard off-the-shelf solution – to remain open to the possibility of doing something truly novel. At the same time, embarking on an untried solution – especially when the consequences can be dire if it does not work – may be hazardous, even when the facts on the ground may suggest it's a good idea. For sure, they must never lean into believing they can *never* try today what was not successful yesterday. The same kinds of dilemma might well apply to a management team thinking about introducing a new scheme of working, especially after a former change had not worked well.

It is necessary to enforce and strictly maintain standardised practices in systems that involve high levels of technology and where huge dangers can result from system malfunctioning as a result of human errors. People

– in these instances often designated 'personnel' (a 'lesser person'?) – may be natural experimenters, but on an oil-rig, for example, or in air traffic control centres, or nuclear power stations, uniform practice is necessary for safety. In such situations, experiments that unsettle procedures or cut corners can lead to catastrophes.[86] At the same time, when there is an extreme emergency, with events not anticipated, perhaps only a bold experiment can save the day. In the catastrophic conditions of the World Trade Center in New York on 11 September 2001, experimenting with breaking safety regulations saved many people's lives.

Looking even more widely across fields of human activity, there are numerous delicate balances to find between preserving and adventuring – literally so, for instance, in the case of opening up an unexplored wilderness for either scientific study or for ecotourism. The balancing extends into longer-term discernment. When an experiment is undertaken with an interconnected, context-sensitive outlook, it is never 'just an experiment' in isolation, but helps create conditions for later ones. Thus, for example, pushing the limits regarding the amount of violence portrayed on television in the direction of, say, permitting more blood to be shown, alters the criteria of acceptability for all later producers. In this case, what perhaps needs to be discerned is whether the field needs to be refreshed at all – and, if so, to what degree, for what purpose, and in whose interests?

---

[86] At the time of writing, a major air crash is being reported: it seems the aircraft *did not have permission to fly a particular route*. Because of this earlier decision, when they requested permission to fly on a course to avoid a storm, they could not, as another flight was already allocated to that flight path. If proven, it was clearly a dangerous departure from the normal: an experiment without sufficient discernment.

Discernment is not easily acquired or taught. Yet this intelligent appraisal of likely consequences, ethical dimensions, and motives for proposing a change, seems more and more necessary in an era of frequent and massive change, often with what appears to be a surprising lack of forethought. Experiments are often carried out in a rush, blindly, or with insufficient foresight – notably so in the case of the Bush/Blair instigated war on Iraq in 2003.

The Fifth Exploration, or *whi*-dimension, is therefore about our engagement with what is often depicted as 'the change process', in which experimenting invariably plays a part.

Links and continuities between experimenting and the other *whi*-dimensions are many and various. Thus, there may be an appeal to an *embodied* reaction in questions like 'How do we truly feel about going ahead? Are our hearts really in this? What's your gut feeling? Do you sense it's a winner?' Likewise, there are connections with *interrelating*, reflected in such statements as 'Let's put the plan to everyone and see what they say', or 'What about asking them over? That would be a real step to getting to know them'. And another link, to *self-recognising*, might be 'I realise I always put a damper on your suggestions to alter the procedure'. But perhaps the biggest overlap is with *responding to the situation*, where any situation as first encountered calls for an element of experimenting. Responding in a particularly experimental way might be indicated when the response to a situation is to question established patterns or to encourage the possibility of exploring 'business as *un*usual'.

I indicated earlier that the 'underlying value' of the dimension of experimenting is 'Play'. Children's spontaneous playing, sports of all kinds, adult card games like bridge or poker are all about operating in some field that is continually newly formed, with elements of uncertainty. Games that are foregone conclusions are no longer 'at the edge': in sporting contests, evenly matched sides make for the most exciting occasions.

Experimenting can evoke an attitude of playfulness, dispelling the tendency to take oneself and the ways of the world too seriously – at least, *all* the time. Much recreation, play, and art is designed to draw upon this kind of human exuberance – so obvious and accessible in the young and ever young. Two of the most enjoyable (and productive) periods of work I had were when my colleagues and I allowed humour and hilarity full scope – these qualities being conspicuously absent in other departments in the organisation. More generally, I've noticed that a capacity to laugh and question orthodoxy can infuse much needed life-blood to organisations that have existed too long on a diet of formal reports, sterile language, and routine thinking.

Many organisations veto expression of mockery and frivolity altogether in order to preserve a culture of seriousness, and sometimes their leaders' sense of importance; this tends to force those who question, and step outside the organisation's 'usual mode', into a position of a suppressed minority. It is not surprising that authoritarian regimes are often harsh towards cartoonists and others who puncture pomposity.

Radical thinkers, innovators, progressive reformers, prophets, inventors, social critics, *avant-garde* artists and writers – all active experimenters, in the sense meant here – are by no means always popular or welcomed, and the more questioning and radical their contribution, the harder it is for non-experimenting others to notice and listen to them. They can often be dismissed as peripheral or irrelevant. Experimenting that questions common belief systems and widely accepted practices requires courage and readiness to be criticised or ridiculed.

Improvisation and the present moment

Keith Johnstone, the author of a classic book on improvisation and the theatre,[87] wrote that 'At school any spontaneous act was likely to get me into trouble. I learned never to act on impulse, and that whatever came into mind first should be rejected in favour of better ideas. I learned that my imagination wasn't "good enough"'. I remember that I was much affected reading Johnstone's words. Not only do I like to improvise and act for sheer pleasure, but I have long recognised that, in writing, first drafts are full of life which can be lost in second, worked-over ones.[88] Luckily for his many readers, Johnstone survived the discouragement, and went on to become a master-improviser, a director at the Royal Court Theatre in London, and teacher of this active form of experimenting.

Debbie Carroll, a garden designer, whom I interviewed at length, was even more pointed about how the experimenting attitude had been devalued at school: 'Education is not about

---

[87] Keith Johnstone, *Impro: Improvisation and the Theatre* (Methuen, 1981).

[88] For a discussion of how this happens, I recommend Barbara Turner-Vesselago's book, *Writing Without a Parachute: The Art of Freefall* (Vala Publishing, 2013).

developing our intuitive capacity, following a thread; [it's not about] asking "How can I make this better?"'. Instead, in school, she explained, the capacity to engage with what was as yet undiscovered or *not yet realised* – but still had the *potential* to come about – was 'knocked out of people'. Her comments rang true for me. Experimenting is all about 'bringing forth' what's not yet realised, and is thus a crucial – even defining – quality of creative thought; it contributes to a particular professional attitude, one of remaining open to change, learning, and new discovery.

If Debbie Carroll's comment on how we educate the young was true – and I thought it broadly was – how could this be? How could our extraordinary human power to *invent*, to *imagine* something different from what's in front of us, and to *explore* the unknown, be other than valued during the formative years of development? The answer is presumably that the predominant task of formal education is to inform young people about what is already known, and preferably known for sure. The fundamental orientation is therefore to the past. The idea of plunging into the *unknown, the unsure, the realm of the uncertain,* or *what could be in the future* represents the antithesis of the usual agenda.

In a similar spirit of valuing improvising, of welcoming spontaneous and uninhibited invention, I recall a product manager, whom I'll call Brian, who encouraged his young team 'to throw ideas around' without inhibition: later they could 'apply a more rigorous criterion for seeing whether proposals were useful or not'. But for an hour or so, he wanted them to 'take risks, use their imaginations, and to think in terms of "business-as-*un*usual"' – the phrase which sums up a key quality of this dimension. Brian discovered that some of his team found it difficult to let go, and to interrupt their usual censoring and vetting, and well-developed capacities for strangling ideas at birth. We decided it was not surprising, given present-day technological imperatives – including the dominance of technical rationality, as described in Chapter Three – that qualities of being rational, logical, predictable, and consistent are valued so much more highly than being spontaneous, impulsive, original, and improvisational.

On another occasion, Brian tried expressing to his team more about 'the present moment'. He reminded them that it was 'now, at *this* moment', when proposed changes could be implemented. He stressed that given that the past is unchangeable by definition – 'it's gone, it's over, it's done' – and that whatever is being talked about for the future is at the moment only something proposed as a plan, possibility, or conjecture, *the present* becomes the only time when a change can be made that is certifiably real.

Obviously there are limits in practical terms to immediate implementation of, say, a whole plan for a big event. But the questions can invite a way of framing reality, 'What can we do *now*?' or 'Given that we are moving in Direction A, what concrete step can we take *at once*, in this meeting, "Yes, NOW!" that sets us on the path towards A?'. This is different from saying, for instance, that 'We will do something about the problem at the next meeting'. Too often, the latter can be a way for indefinite postponement: the time may never be so ripe again.[89] I have known a number of people who felt

---

[89] A successful organisational consultant, Peter Hawkins, suggests that people need to make an actual commitment to a plan – an embodied act – rather than end a meeting with just a verbal agreement or proposal that is not backed up with the equivalent of an actual signature on a piece of paper. *Personal communication.*

a strong impulse to take up an offered opportunity but who did not 'seize the moment' and spent years in nursing their regret instead.

I realise that emphasising the advantages of the present moment can suggest a general advocacy or encouragement to 'follow one's impulse'. What feels right at a particular moment can represent a spontaneous and brilliant flash of inspiration, but equally, with hindsight some actions can be seen as ungrounded foolish whimsy. In extreme situations, such a case may even trip over into being unethical or criminal, a kind of pathological experiment. In short, *now* – sometimes referred to as the eternal present – is when aspirations, prospects, and ideas actually materialise or fail to do so. Now is where it happens, or does not. This realisation is part of this *whi*-dimension. Fostering an experimenting attitude calls for entering more fully into the present moment. This happens in an obvious way with theatre improvisation, or in playing jazz, or simply in circumstances of 'going live'. One discovers the energy, enjoyment, and sense of danger that often accompany spontaneous expression and in-the-moment creativity. 'Living in the now' is a mark of our full aliveness.

Debbie Carroll, collaborating with Mark Rendell, another garden designer, told me more about how they had realised there was a growing interest, among both care providers and garden designers, in creating 'dementia care gardens', or spaces around care homes for residents with dementia.

Carroll and Rendell, however, noticed that 'all these gardens are being built, with many of them going on to become unused'. They explained that it 'felt like a really important dimension for us to have a look at. If the gardens aren't being used, what's missing? What part of the process is not being engaged with?' One immediately senses the two of them embracing an experimental attitude – fuelled by curiosity; and, if the gardens are not being used, this itself is an example of an innovation that had not taken off. On both counts, I was interested.

Originally (they told me) they had planned to investigate what kinds of gardens would be most suitable for residents. But their project unfolded in unexpected directions. Over the course of a year, their consultation shifted into investigating the whole way in which care homes approached 'the outside': how the staff of the care homes thought about and used – or ignored, or hardly ever used – their gardens or grounds as a resource for their residents. Revealingly, their project was self-funded. In most funded inquiries, there has to be an exact plan as to how the investigation proceeds. They explained: 'We weren't sponsored by anyone, so we had the freedom to make mistakes'. They were able to re-tune what they did in a spirit of open-ended inquiry, rather than proceed with an investigation that had been pre-designed, which no longer was relevant in light of what they were discovering.[90]

---

[90] Earlier in my career, I was instrumental in developing the methodology called 'Illuminative Evaluation'. Part of the procedure involves continuously refining the nature of the investigation in the light of what is being uncovered: we called this 'progressive focusing'. Debbie Carroll and Mark Rendell drew on this illuminative approach. See Malcolm Parlett and Garry Dearden, eds, *Introduction to Illuminative Evaluation: Studies in Higher Education* (Pacific Soundings Press, 1977). Debbie Carroll and Mark Rendell are preparing a book on their research, *Why Don't We Go Into the Garden?*

Care home residents might not use the garden, but Carroll and Rendell realised this 'wasn't just about the garden: we had to find out from within the culture of these places where the resistances were … often based on fears about using outside space'. They began to 'notice patterns' – for instance they discovered 'that most of the chairs in the lounges were not looking on to the garden, they were looking at the TV screen inside'. They took this as evidence of the 'value placed on the outside space: the direction of the chairs showed us it was not the garden' that was valued. In one care home, when they asked the reason for 'keeping the seats facing inwards', the reply was 'that the cleaners would not like them being changed'.

Alighting on the theme of seating patterns, they suggested an experimental change to a household manager: 'Would you mind just doing an experiment for a short period and change the layout of the room – moving the chairs around into groups that focused on the outside, and just capture any evidence or changes that you notice as a result of doing that?' The staff member agreed to try it, and the experiment had a profound effect: 'An email arrived 48 hours later stating that within an hour or two positive changes were detected'; the residents were engaging with the outside space, 'getting up and going towards what they were looking at'. They commented: 'This was an experiment that cost nothing. It was about just reframing something, having a go, trying something afresh. And this home was OK about that'. A disturbing but not perhaps surprising fact was that it took two enterprising and inquisitive outsiders – specialists in garden design – to prise open a settled set of assumptions and practices that defined basic living conditions of the residents: effectively, for those in most of the care homes, there 'was no outside'.

The two garden designers experimented in a variety of other ways. They stressed they were not researchers from 'the realm of academia' and while being 'professionals from [their] own particular sector' they remarked how they sometimes felt like 'innocents abroad'. In other words, they were also experimenting with their roles, and widening their angle of view. They realised they had 'bright open minds', and were also extending the boundaries of what garden designers usually did. Operating outside their field they said they could more easily 'ask stupid questions: "Why have you done it like that?" "Well we've always done it like that". "But it's not working"'. They explained they weren't being 'provocative in a negative way, it was really just the innocent question, because we didn't know'.

In terms of this Fifth Exploration, Debbie Carroll and Mark Rendell were underlining, for me, the fundamental sequence of what might be called 'natural, or unforced, experimenting' as a dimension of whole intelligence: following up curiosity, pursuing an open-ended investigation, asking simple questions that stimulated new thought, and extending the boundaries of the known. For them, such experimenting was the 'opposite of stagnation or just filling the comfort zone'.

Almost inevitably, such experimenters are energisers: my impression was that Carroll and Rendell were also stimulating curiosity and interest in experimental change among the staff of the 17 homes they visited as part of their study. Their keenness to question 'what was normal' became contagious and inspiring. The key question: 'What if you try …?', seemed to heighten awareness, and wake people up to the fact that 'usual practice' could be altered. They reported that in several care homes the staff wanted to develop this action research model more generally for their own organisation: there had been a 'knock-on effect with carers [the staff] ... starting to look at their residents afresh. It built value back into their role. Because they were having to observe them [the behaviour of residents], they had to operate [in two modes] simultaneously – subjectively doing the work but objectively watching what they did at the same time. They realised how much they did'.

The more that these two enterprising figures told me about their work, the more horrified I was by what they had uncovered about prevalent institutional patterns. To single out the staff of dementia care homes would be unfair to those who work there; many are unsung heroes, poorly paid, and working under trying conditions. Yet, in exploring this dimension of whole intelligence, there are profound questions about *what stops or discourages a great many people – maybe from all occupational categories – from experimenting.* What closes off people's natural curiosity and creativity? What stops people from questioning procedures that are manifestly wasteful or limiting, or have become stale from years of unquestioned passive adherence?

The spirit of inquiry and freshness of outlook is like a flame – it can be snuffed out and it will weaken if deprived of oxygen. In one organisation, an instruction from management to comply exactly with procedures they had specified, led to a shift in attitude: staff ceased to question assertively 'what doesn't work'; they just 'switched off'. People need strong encouragement and clear permission to think in innovative ways, and they need to regard themselves as equal partners in a shared enterprise. Hierarchical systems can fail to foster an attitude of experiment and licence to innovate and question.

Experimenting can easily lead to 'not following the rules', and this may be dangerous – as noted earlier. But there are also 'rules' which are imagined rather than real; or are in manifest need of being challenged. Debbie Carroll – who before studying garden design was a senior manager in a high street store – said that back then, when she 'had a bright idea' for the store, there was always a phase of resistance; but if she persevered, 'it pretty much always came out right in the end'. She paused, then added: 'But I can honestly say it is a hard way to do things in a world expecting you to follow the rules'. The pressure – she was suggesting – is always to conform.

One major inhibitor of experimenting in the dementia care homes was 'health and safety' regulation. Thus an enterprising activity co-ordinator in one care home arranged for a basket of wet clothes to appear from the laundry, whereupon she invited the residents to help her put them on the line – an activity familiar to the generation 'that would have hung washing outside more', and was an example of 'engaging with the outside space in a way that mirrored normality'. Evidently, a number of residents loved engaging in this. However, in another care home, the same idea did not get off the ground: 'No, we can't do that, there's a ligature risk'. Our intrepid experimenters wanted to follow up this remark: '"Well, hang on, we need to have a conversation about this, what's this about? Are you risk-assessing the item or risk-assessing the people who might use the item? What might not be good for Flossie could be very good for Mavis and Bill". But [the staff] decided that because it's not good for Flossie, it's not good for anyone else. That's anti-experimentation'.

Carroll and Rendell agreed that experimenting often calls for some challenging of existing culture. In places like care homes, where being 'safe' and 'prudent' are elevated above all other criteria, the managers and others in supervisory roles would, first, have to agree to a cultural change, and second, need to communicate very energetically that questioning assumptions and standard operating procedures was a valued part of everyone's job description. Of course, in cultures unused to changes, in which the emphasis is on continuity and reliability of care for their vulnerable patients, it is hardly surprising that Carroll and Rendell had difficulty in finding homes that were prepared for bracing change.

Ordered sequences, conventions, and common procedures constitute much of 'ordinary life'. Unsettling them can often seem impossible, even when there is agreement that they are dysfunctional or outmoded. One can almost say that people, or whole systems, behave as if addicted to 'normal practice'. Of course, habits and established customs do not denote addiction: preferring a particular daily newspaper or engaging in small rituals before going to bed are benign enough – even if not always welcome to others affected by them.

One begins to think of *addictive* levels of habit on hearing terms such as *having to, feeling compelled to*, or *giving into the craving for* something – whether it is for a cigarette, alcoholic drink, playing a computer game, sex, or an injection of heroin. Fixations and obsessions can become deeply grooved, to the point where the rest of life is organised around them.

It is easy for addictions and addicts to be righteously condemned by others. Yet few of us – if any – avoid states that border on being addictive: watching sport, clicking on the news, playing golf, checking mails, soap operas, computer games, can all 'take over'. Being utterly in love – transfixed by a desire for being with one's beloved – is a well-known addictive pattern. Even being in the grip of a novel that we cannot put down has some of the same restriction of options and compulsion as an addictive state, albeit temporary. Each ingrained habit that borders on addictive represents a reduction of possibility, with automatic behaviour and limitation of experience substituting for a full range of options within a flexible and varied life.

Many people have an experimental attitude; the impulse to come up with new solutions or find new experiences is irrepressible. In the present era, there are attempts to dislodge dominant patterns of thought and everyday practice: especially energy use in affluent countries. Others are choosing to step away from dominant conventions, in a spirit of protest: they give up altogether watching TV, or they let their front garden return to its natural state.

There is no sharp distinction between experimenting and protesting – for instance, against injustice, inequality, or abuse of power. Both focus on taken-for-granted issues and communal thinking; both open doors to inventive ideas that are not mainstream. Experimenting can enhance cultural variation, as can complexity. They can both set a cultural precedent, with questioning in one domain stimulating more questioning in others. Equally, a traditional and unchanging culture that deliberately stifles major reforms can set another kind of precedent that is hard to escape. This is evident when considering the near impossibility – short of some cultural convulsion or outright rebellion – of major changes in long-established national institutions.

Would-be experimenters should not underestimate the addictive-like attachment to the *status quo*, and the levels of threat that can be experienced in any undoing of what is well known.

The 'discomfort zone'

At this point I am remembering Walter, a retired policeman, who like most of us had some deeply held conservative tendencies. As we well know, sometimes those on the political left are just as conservative in their own way as any on the right.

Walter recognised that one of his 'strong views' acted as a line of defence against unwanted and unsettling change. His daughter, Suzy, a woman in her forties and a mother of three, had recently left her husband, Brian. Walter 'felt neutral' about his son-in-law: 'I came to respect Brian more as I saw him manage the kids …'. What was a whole lot more disturbing for Walter was Suzy's deciding to live with a woman. Her announcement that she was lesbian had shaken Walter; and for a time he floundered.

Our ability to experiment, as Walter came himself to recognise, includes noticing when to break patterns which have become set, or have never been questioned before. His view of homosexuality was grooved so deeply as to appear unchangeable, but turned out not to be. 'I could not fathom it, something surely we were not made for … That's what I thought. But then when Suzy got together with her friend, I had to weigh what mattered most: holding on to my beliefs that it was unnatural and wrong, or moving on and giving her my love and support – after all, her happiness matters so much to me'. When Suzy and Brian decided to continue to share parenting, and were amicable together, he had other ironclad assumptions to soften up. He had not entirely relinquished his critical views about 'couples splitting up'. His perplexity did not stop there: after 18 months, Suzy and her woman partner decided they wanted to marry, and if he wanted to be present at the wedding, he had to change some more, concerning his attitudes to gay marriage.

Often, ways of thinking and operating tend to continue in an automatic and unexamined fashion until there is a stimulus to change, like a 'kick up the behind' as Walter described it: 'That's what I needed … to force me to think about what really mattered to me'. Two other factors helped – both taking him to familiar thoughts. One was to think about how his late wife would have responded. At times when he wanted to put distance between his daughter and himself, he realised that his wife would have drawn closer to her daughter at a time of upheaval. The other was an absolute core value that had always been their way: 'We stay together as a family and never turn on each other' – this being the most decisive stabiliser.

We can easily revert to habitual responses, especially in times of uncertainty, falling back into ruts of old thinking and fixed attitudes that we rely upon like favourite but worn-out shoes: we like their comfortable fit, even with the holes in them. But Walter realised that the costs of so doing would have been too high – so he acquired some new shoes. His most deeply held values decreed that he had to do this, and he surprised Suzy – and himself even more.

Experimenting, in engaging with the unfamiliar, often means crossing a boundary: we enter into a 'discomfort zone'. Discomfiture can be mild and inconsequential, but at times is severe, sometimes devastating. With experimenting, some degree of uncomfortable self-consciousness or 'loss of face' is almost guaranteed at some stage.

Take any act of live performance: whether it is spontaneous or rehearsed, however large or small the audience. Performers will likely experience raised arousal ahead of the event: they may be excited by the thrill of what they are going to do, or feel stage fright, tensing up through fear of 'drying up'. Regular actors, speech-givers, and stand-ups, as well as professional sportsmen or women know they need a scent of danger, of living at the edge, if their performance is to reach the heights.

Within the greater context of experimenting – for example, as pursued by creative artists or sports professionals – experiences of failure, especially the conspicuous variety, can result in strong reactions, often almost forbidden to reveal. Performers can learn to survive defeats and losses, and to 'come back' after being humiliated, or savagely criticised in newspapers, or after falling foul of critics or the sports-going public. But it is never easy. Reports are frequent – of 'shattering blows', collapses of confidence, runs of poor performances, or experiences of being trapped in some 'downward spiral', rather than lifted into the opposite cycle of 'success breeding success'.

There are many prescribed antidotes to feelings of sinking or losing creative confidence, or skills suddenly found inaccessible. Individualistic thinking tends to dominate in the manner of giving advice, with references to having 'sufficient character' to weather the storm and come back. In my own experience, and that of those with whom I've worked, ego strength and self-confidence can fluctuate, though some people are a lot more resilient, and fortunate, in 'coming back', compared to others.

Recovery from 'blocking' – as the loss of flow and grace is also called – may call for professional help. Failing that, there are steps people can take on their own, drawing on the other *whi*-dimensions. For instance, through *interrelating*, people can receive reassurances and affirmations from others who know them long-term, and who blow on the dying fire and find an ember: soon, forgotten strengths and previous triumphs crackle into life. Sometimes, in an act of co-created *self-recognising*, simply hearing others describe their own experiences and how they survived them intact can be the spark that relights the fire.

Embodying can also be a crucial support, through allowing (preferably with informed help) feelings of collapse to be registered in full, before any remedial regeneration of confidence is attempted. Many have reported that only when they 'fully collapsed' did signs of revival begin to appear, spontaneous regeneration following from permitting oneself a more deeply felt experience. If feelings of great deficiency persist, however, there is likely to be a need to explore early life issues, and professional therapeutic support is recommended.

Experimenting itself can be brought into play, so to speak, to support itself: this can also break a pattern of floundering. I once suggested an experiment to a woman who, at the beginning of an all-day meeting, announced she had been 'trapped in a depression' for weeks. I suggested she might like to consider having a day off: a few hours 'vacation away from her depression'. I pointedly said she could return to feeling depressed at the end of the day if she wished, but at least she could have a day free from 'feeling trapped'. She agreed to the experiment. At the end of the class – during which she had thought of herself as being on vacation, and had thrown herself into taking part – she was clear she did not want her depression back, and she could say goodbye to it: for how long I never found out.

In doing anything for the first time – whether breaking new ground or dispensing with old habits – there is a similar living in the moment and going to an edge. At such times, anyone can feel exposed and vulnerable, especially if they judge their new behaviour harshly, or keep repeating that they do not like 'the way they have been'. Such self-assessments are often wild exaggerations of their 'imperfection', and are obvious forms of diminishing one's confidence.

The felt experience of shame and loss of a sense of wellbeing increases in situations where we have insufficient support and reassurance from others, are stuck in some long-term pattern of shaky self-belief, or both. Being insensitively criticised can crush many a new artist's hope and confidence. Unwanted public exposure can be excruciating for some emerging young performers. Responsible, *whi*-accessible educators and trainers learn to notice signs of embarrassment and shame in first performers and other beginners; they offer reassurance, often by recounting how they've 'been there' themselves – generally a reassuring message if one thinks one is alone in experiencing something unpleasant.

Julia Cameron[91] remarks how, as a teacher, she saw many talented younger artists 'daunted early and unfairly by their inability to conform to a norm that was not their own'. She has a call to academics and other 'taller trees': 'let us not allow our darker critical powers unfettered play upon the seedling artists in our midst'. When a young novelist, Ted, submitted his first novel, it was turned down by an agent, who commented, 'I can't tell you how to fix it. I suggest pitching it out'. Ted did not write again for seven years. After Julia Cameron helped him 'unblock', he became a successful writer and filmmaker. She writes that he 'had to refeel and mourn the wounding he had endured as a young writer' and 'a page at a time, a day at a time, he had to slowly build strength'.

However commonly experienced they are, shame reactions around experimenting are rarely talked about: the syndrome is uncomfortable for many – perhaps for most or all of us. There might be general advantage if shame reactions were acknowledged as normal human phenomena – albeit uncomfortable ones. For some of us it can seem, on a painfulness scale, somewhere around the level of stubbing one's toe or experiencing mild toothache, while for others of us, shame reactions can be like excruciating physical pain or a 'total meltdown'. To encourage this key dimension of whole intelligence, understanding and communicating

[91]   Julia Cameron, *The Artist's Way: A Course in Discovering and Recovering your Creative Self* (Pan Books, 1995) pp. 232–4.

the dynamics of shame seem essential. What are the main points to get across?

In summary form, I suggest the following:

FIRST, it needs to be understood that feelings of shame and embarrassment arise frequently, probably universally. First attempts at doing something of importance to us, or any breaking away from the already known, always entails a measure of uncertainty and, for the less experienced, some inevitable discomfort. A cluster of body reactions can ensue: blushing, feelings of 'awkwardness', and a pronounced sense of isolation: many of us have felt 'At this moment I do not belong among the community of the competent'. Some people may feel acutely embarrassed and just want to disappear into a hole in the ground, which they wish would magically appear and swallow them up.

SECOND, people may attempt to suppress or hide what they are feeling. Sensitive handling by others – which may include 'not making a big thing of it' or just recognising it empathically and signalling this understanding – can help to avoid this. People easily become 'ashamed of their shame', thinking they are lone sufferers. Of course, they are not. Here's another reason, metaphorically, to throw open windows and ventilate the topic: to detoxify it.

THIRD, at low levels, feelings of embarrassment or shame can be tolerated, perhaps supported by breathing and grounding – as discussed in the *Embodying* Exploration. *The feelings soon dissolve, especially in a safe setting with supportive others present.* In these circumstances shame and the fear of it do not hamper the experimenting: they just need 'handling'.

FOURTH, often in a group setting – family, sports team, or work social life – someone may get teased, and not showing they are uncomfortable, get teased again. In even less hospitable settings, showing vulnerability to taunts simply provokes more of them. Especially those who have been mocked or teased long-term may attempt to *encase themselves in a hard carapace of apparent indifference.* If this becomes a fixed attitude or mode of being, it may result in the person – or perhaps a whole group – coming over as 'shameless'. Such protective armouring often disguises an even greater degree of shame – one that's never to be admitted, unless, eventually, to a particularly empathic and trusted confidant. In the process of protecting ourselves, we may lose access to essential qualities of humility or capacity to show our vulnerability. Needless to say, the pursuit of others' discomfort and deliberate mocking of them is a signal failure of empathy: it is disrespectful and a mark of incompetent, non-*whi* interrelating – as well as very often a preventive move to protect the perpetrator's own shame from ever being exposed.

FIFTH, for many people who, in the past, have been abused, bullied, mocked, punished, humiliated, neglected, or publicly attacked, their experience of shame at what happened was often traumatic. During or immediately after the original event, they felt so exposed, raw, self-conscious, and alone with their embarrassment, sense of deficiency, or lowered self-esteem that subsequently they never spoke about it. *They simply curtail any participation afterwards in any activity they imagine might lead to a repetition of the event.* In effect, they create a 'no-go area' in their private world, which now they avoid going near to at any cost. Thus, *any* suggestion they hear that gets close – or *could* get close – to approaching their no-go area is resisted. One can imagine, therefore, that *even in discussing the possibility* of 'throwing ideas around' or 'deliberately upturning conventions', or 'dismantling habits', that a proportion of those invited to take part will immediately reject the idea.

SIXTH, given the human propensity for shaming, and how easy shame is to rekindle, attention to any proposed experimenting activity needs to include *the nature of the context in which it is to be conducted.* Having any fixed assumption shaken, or jettisoning what we've always done before, is inevitably unsettling: it requires taking a risk. *Is the surrounding context one in which risks can be taken safely?* And are there safeguards to mitigate the likelihood of extreme shame reactions becoming triggered? If an outlook commensurate with whole intelligence is to become more common in the province of experimenting, these are questions to address.

More generally, I am speculating that shame is a largely invisible residue that accumulates in people's lives – and is *mostly hidden away.* Airing the topic in general terms can be a first step. A general reluctance to embrace novelty and its inherent uncertainty is likely to be connected with the presence of multiple no-go areas that have never been addressed. If someone's personal world has one or more significant areas of acute sensitivity – or no-go areas as I have called them here – then their life is likely to be oriented towards survival and avoidance of threats rather than towards open-minded curiosity and playfulness, and readiness for greater risk-taking. Such closing-downs are tragic pointers to how human capacities are lost – not just for those afflicted, but for the wider community.

Effects of experimenting

Important questions about the quality of experiments remain: How worthwhile are they? What needs are they satisfying? What values do they express? And are the expected consequences likely to be beneficial or harmful, in the short, medium, and long term?

Terrible crimes – not least by sexual abusers and predators – have been fuelled by desires for thrills, or the compulsion to cross boundaries, in which the consequences for their victims do not feature. Experiments with highly addictive drugs are self-destructive – and stopping using them may require the far more difficult experiment of recovery from addiction. Political experiments can be prohibitively expensive and wasteful of vast amounts of public money. Sometimes, too, the wish to innovate – and be seen to be doing so – leads to unnecessary tinkering, producing yet more unwanted objects, initiatives, leaflets, or other ephemera. Like anything else, change itself can become addictive. Many industries – notoriously car manufacturing, software development, and communications – are built on the principles of planned obsolescence and of creating a climate of perpetual need for the latest version. This mass 'addiction' draws in legions of us.

Seen from the point of view of sustainability, the pattern is absurd, of course – and anti-*whi* on every count. It conspicuously fails to respond to the situation we face, and we fail collectively to self-recognise the ways we are held in thrall, and do not foresee the long-term consequences. Our embodied truth is also often over-ridden in our tendencies for greed and grab.

At the same time, the experimental drive is a powerful agent of global change, and massive accelerator of our human social evolution. Increasing humanity's total capacity for self-recognising in line with our experimenting might result in more discrimination – more discernment – in what experiments are most beneficial, and which ones could diminish rather than enhance our whole intelligence.

Without question, some experiments open human beings to new learning, significant discoveries, and radical shifts in their outlook: they add to our civilisation and are truly 'steps into the unknown'. To grasp the power of experimenting globally, we can learn from monumental events that took place in the lifetimes of many people still alive: namely, the first human explorations beyond the planet's atmosphere.

As in all the best experiments, the first astronauts and cosmonauts in the 1960s and 70s were stepping into the unknown. There was, of course, extensive preparation – rehearsals and simulations with the astronauts' safety a prime consideration. They had a good idea of what would happen and of the various points of risk and challenge. But for all the preparation, there was still a sense of living at the cutting edge, with many steps calling for the direct, live, and embodied participation of human beings willing to take the risks.

They went with a whole series of tasks and investigations to be done. They went with their own expectations of what their journeys would be like, and what was expected of them as seen from the perspective of mission control back on Earth. What had not been anticipated, however, were the powerful effects on those who – in our terms here – were the experimenter-participants themselves.[92]

Time and time again, these early travellers in space reported being shaken. 'The view of Earth takes your breath away … you see subtleties and nuances in the view … It is endlessly fulfilling', reported Joseph Allen (who went on two shuttle missions in 1982 and 1984). A 'tiny pea, pretty and blue', 'so wonderful from up here, so peaceful', 'fragile', 'vulnerable', 'beautiful' – are some of the words they used to describe how they saw the Earth from a distance. New realisations came to them, along with cautionary thoughts: 'You looked down and you could see how incredibly thin the Earth's atmosphere is and realise that if we pollute it, we all breathe it together, and if we are so dumb as to start a thermonuclear war, we all go together; there is no lifeboat, and everybody is in it together' (Don Lind, a specialist on Spacelab 3).

Ed Gibson (a member of the Skylab 4 crew in 1973–74, in orbit for 84 days), described that, after being in space, 'you are able to really picture the physical universe … It is not a concept anymore … You see how diminutive your life and concerns are compared to other things in the universe. Your life and concerns are important to *you*, of course. But you can see that a lot of the things you worry about don't make much difference in an overall sense. The result is that you enjoy the life that is before you … It allows you to have inner peace'.

---

[92]   The quotations from astronauts that follow have been collected from a variety of sources. The theme of the Earth's beauty and vulnerability in the writings of astronauts (and earlier thinkers) is well documented on http://www.spacequotations.com/earth.html. See also Michael Collins, *Carrying the Fire: An Astronaut's Journeys* (Farrar, Straus and Giroux, 1974) and Frank White, *The Overview Effect: Space Exploration and Human Evolution* (Houghton Mifflin, 1987).

Returning to Earth, others reported other profound shifts in outlook: Edgar Mitchell (Apollo 14) wrote that 'We went to the moon as technicians, we returned as humanitarians'; Alexei Leonov (Voskhod 2, and the first man to 'walk in space') thought the earth 'must be defended like a holy relic'. Some had fantasies of taking political leaders into space so they could realise for themselves how, seen from afar, their preoccupations and disputes were 'petty'. Edwin ('Jake') Garn, an astronaut and US Republican Senator, reported 'a changing and softening in my attitudes' as a result of his six days in space: '... we really are all travelling together [on Spaceship Earth], so there ought to be more equality of opportunity around the Earth'.[93] Nothing reveals more the power of doing things in different ways to change perspective. Admittedly, 'the experiment' in this case was vast in scope and scale, but even smaller experiments result in re-framings and unanticipated outcomes.

The author and aviator, Anne Morrow Lindbergh,[94] wrote in 1969, after the first moon landing: 'No one, it has been said, will ever look at the Moon in the same way again ... we may have taken *another step into adulthood*. We can see planet Earth with detachment, with tenderness, with some shame and pity, but at last also with love' (italics added). Lindbergh's phrase, 'another step into adulthood', describes the change well. What happened to the explorers into space was not just an intellectual shift or cognitive change but something greater altogether – a transformation that embraced emotions and perspectives, values and life priorities.

---

[93] White, *The Overview Effect*, p. 271. Jake Garn travelled on the sixteenth flight of NASA's Space Shuttle Program in April 1985.

[94] Anne Morrow Lindbergh, *Earth Shine* (Harcourt, 1969), p. 44.

*

The global steps that now need to be taken, half a century later, are of course very different. But there is similarity in terms of significance, and in a sense of possibility – new departures for human beings on Earth, once again daring to attempt what has often been considered impossible or unrealistic. Just as space travel was once a wild dream, then became a serious possibility and finally an actuality, so there is a similar progression now, regarding the sweeping changes already underway in humanity's overall view of itself.

Who are the equivalent planetary explorers today? There are so many – thousands who are reaching out towards a vision of a fundamentally different future: peace-makers and trust builders, working at the frontiers of inter-ethnic prejudice; environmentalists and radical industrialists making serious attempts to think 'outside the box' regarding sustainability; alternative economists and thinkers questioning 'money' and drawing attention to the flimsiness of some of our routine economic assumptions; and historians who are crossing barriers to write history from multiple points of view, rather than donning a single set of cultural blinkers.

These are only a tiny sample. Paul Hawken points to a parallel with what happened during the 18th and 19th centuries: 'The Industrial Revolution went un-named for more than a century – in part because its developments did not fit conventional categories but also because no one could define what was taking place, even though it was evident everywhere'.[95]

---

[95]   Paul Hawken, *Blessed Unrest*, (Viking, 2007), p. 242.

Just as the early space explorations opened a new phase in the social evolution of humanity, so do all the developments now happening, cumulatively taken together, represent a vast and shifting picture – one that extends radically some of the key developments in perspective from that earlier season of profound change. The changes are not all in the same direction. Nevertheless, Keith Kahn-Harris, a sociologist, has aptly identified 'A trend, a direction, an idea-virus, a meme, a source of energy that can be traced through a large number of spaces and projects. It is also *a way of thinking and acting: an agility, an adaptability, a refusal to accept the world as it is, a refusal to get stuck into fixed patterns of thought*'[96] (my italics). To me, this sounds very similar to the *experimenting* dimension of *whi*.

---

[96] Keith Kahn-Harris, quoted by Paul Mason, *Why it's Kicking Off Everywhere: The New Global Revolutions* (Verso, 2012), p. 66.

CHAPTER 8

RETURNING TO BASE

After the five Explorations, it's time to return to base. Such occasions are for reflection, for making sense of the journeys travelled. The five previous chapters occupy central place in the book and need to speak for themselves; this chapter looks at the way these five Explorations fit together, and returns to themes raised at the book's beginning.

My hope is that the various Explorations will have chimed with readers' experiences of life and the world, and revealed the diverse qualities of whole intelligence. The personal integrations and points of resonance will differ for each person. Readers' own conclusions are the most important outcomes. My own concluding thoughts are something extra – akin to artists explaining their work. This said, readers are entitled to hear my own reflections at the end of the book, and how I see the various parts fitting together as a whole.

In this chapter there are four sections: The first section is about integrating the five Explorations that we have explored in the preceding five chapters. In Section 2, I move to framing them in the context of 'whole intelligence' and the 'whole' argument of the book. Sections 3 and 4 point to two major directions in which the ideas of Future Sense can make sense of the future.

1. The five Explorations and how they work together

The five Explorations provide perspectives on living in the contemporary world. They summarise human potentialities in ways that seem to speak to people: neither obscure and hidden in mists, nor formatted and formulated to the point that dulls the appetite. They are intended to be generative ideas – inviting readers' further inquiries and ways of applying them.

Future Sense builds on the discoveries of many people, and the ideas will already be familiar to consultants, coaches, therapists, and others engaged with human beings and our personal and working lives. Even if terminology and imagery differ, the five *whi*-dimensions are recognisable in management training circles, in leadership development, in the mental health professions, and in the arts. They offer a possible common language to assist in cross-disciplinary conversations. Though they originated from my own practice, and made sense to me alone at the beginning, others since have reported finding them useful as taken-for-granted forms of 'procedural' knowledge,[97] and as a stimulus for thinking about their methods of practice from new angles.

In a musical analogy, the five Explorations are like five different instruments in a quintet. Each has enabling

---

[97] Procedural knowledge is the knowledge that is drawn upon in the accomplishment of a task, which is mostly 'implicit' rather than 'explicit' – more 'knowing how' than 'knowing what'.

functions towards the others. While each is distinctive in its own right, their joining together is what matters most.

The Explorations can foster a different kind of sense making for all kinds of human occurrences – especially in problem situations where it's difficult to fathom where to start. I am recalling an example of a complex situation from earlier in my career, which has stayed with me. Working with the five Explorations together enabled a whole system to change. I was working with a particular therapy training group of about 20 members. The group had existed for two years and was regarded as 'difficult'. My co-worker Judith Hemming and I were not their regular trainers, so when we met them, we were able to stand back and regard the group's culture afresh.

First, we invited them to do some *self-recognising*: 'Tell us about this group. What's it like to be part of it?' To begin with, they were diffident and not very forthcoming. Further encouragement resulted in members speaking out. Some said the group was 'blaming' or 'unsafe'. One woman described the culture as 'toxic' and another – a woman from Northern Ireland – had a strong *embodied* reaction of feeling afraid: she said that she had 'lived in Derry with a permanent threat of bombs and shooting and had never felt as scared' as she did in this group.

Our impression was that the group's *interrelating* was 'ungenerous' – and we shifted our focus. Over the course of a day, Judith and I were able to identify a number of ways in which the culture was maintained – for instance, by the way they spoke to each other. They did not look directly at one another when speaking; they reacted super-swiftly to anything said to them by someone else in the group, as if expecting attack; and they rarely, if ever, said anything to one another that signalled appreciation, agreement, or understanding of what another person had said. While holding on to the issue of their *interrelating*, we were also set on discovering more about how they regarded the whole *situation to which they were responding* – and we noticed that they were operating in a very habitual and *non-experimental* fashion.

Judith and I shared with the group some of our observations, based in part on our own *self-recognising* – our feelings, thoughts, and *embodied* reactions as they arose for us, sitting with the members of the group in the field we were jointly sharing. We were not setting out to identify the 'underlying cause' of the malaise: rather than any question of *why*, we kept returning to elucidating *how* they were *responding to the situation* of being in the group and how they *related* to one another.

As the two leaders, we also wanted to model ways of communicating and *relating together* that differed from the group's habitual patterns: an *experiment* in itself. Thus, we openly shared observations, listened carefully to one another, checked meanings, and voiced areas of agreement between us. Slowly, members began to *recognise* how their corridors of communication in the group had become narrower and narrower. They realised they were *interrelating* in a 'set' manner, and differently from how they were in other *situations* of their lives. They registered *embodied states* of discomfort and confusion. They woke up to having lost their capacity to be spontaneous together, playful *experimenting* having long fallen out of the group's allowable repertoire.

Next, we confronted them with how individually they might be contributing to the culture they claimed to dislike:

an invitation to *self-recognise* in a novel way. And some – just a few individuals to start with – realised unprompted that they could help change the pattern (*respond differently to the shared situation*). Even if they were not sure how, they were at least ready to *experiment*.

Moving further into a teaching mode, we pointed out how they could communicate differently – for instance, by allowing a pause after someone spoke to them, permitting the utterance to 'land' rather than instantly reacting to it, and by sharing their feelings in the present with greater openness. Here one can see the interweaving of the dimensions. However, their learning was neither easy nor instant – the patterns were deeply entrenched. We suggested that in order to act boldly in defiance of established patterns, certain *embodied* changes might prove helpful: feeling the support of the floor, breathing more deeply, and sometimes standing up to speak, perhaps with a friend alongside with a hand on their back.

With some group members leading the way – for instance, by *experimenting* with maintaining eye contact with someone they were addressing, and giving space to others to speak or listen without interruption – others began to follow. A consequence was that others acknowledged the group was becoming less of a dangerous place in which to participate: the hurdle of taking the risk to relate differently did not seem so high. The group were discovering that, while it was not altogether safe to take risks, they had to take risks in order to feel safe!

In a way that would be tedious to elaborate, all of the dimensions interacted, each enabling others to become active in turn. Just as all five dimensions had been compromised in the emergence of the group's problem that had seemed to them unalterable, so now they all needed reinstating – or finding for the first time in this group – in order for a transformation to happen.

In this example, we were not really looking at five separate changes, but to a single, complex unfolding, step by step. Here a mini-community that had been operating like a dysfunctional family moved towards demonstrating greater whole intelligence. Any of the five *whi*-dimensions can offer an entry point or relevant inquiry in achieving a total system shift, for each dimension points to specific behaviours and priorities that can become catalysts in the emergence of the others. Given how interdependent they are, the others are automatically enhanced. The process becomes cumulative and self-reinforcing – trust breeding trust, courage to depart from a norm inspiring others to do so as well. An enabling, virtuous cycle replaces one that was disabling and vicious.

A powerful extra comes about when all five dimensions of whole intelligence are conspicuously evident at the same time. There is a sense of major discovery, or operating on a different plane. When people, simultaneously, (1) are in touch both with their own needs in relation to the overall situation and also with 'what the situation requires of them' – and these are in alignment; (2) are engaging together with others, maintaining eye-contact, and 'following the dance of the between'; (3) are breathing fully and freely 'bodying forth' what they are experiencing, through body-positioning, gesturing, and possibly physical touch; (4) are letting go of feeling self-conscious, while also are not 'losing all sense of themselves' in some dissociated manner; and (5) are creatively adjusting to whatever is happening as the present unfolds, moving continuously between 'breaking new ground' and drawing on the solidity of what they know from past experience, something comes into existence that is almost beyond words, but is intensely felt.

According to the circumstances, these times of _whi_-convergence can be celebratory, satisfying, full-bodied, and redolent of how life ought to be. Or, in a time of devastating grief or horror, the feeling may be of an underlying resilient solidarity which is soul-stirring and silently known. In all such moments of congruence there is a deeply felt satisfaction; something emerges that is powerful and vibrant, that feels 'true' and affects one's whole being. Remembering such times fuels this work for me. I suspect it corresponds to what others describe as 'flow', as 'a higher state of consciousness', or as the presence of 'grace'. At such times, the whole is obviously more than the sum of five separate parts – a coming together or synergy that seems rich, fulsome, and intensely real.

2. 'Whole intelligence' – also signifying an 'intelligence of the whole'

With the Explorations, I remind the reader of my original intention to offer five different clusters of skills, attitudes, understandings, and practical insights, and to present them as _sub-divisions of whole intelligence_. We can remain frustrated with the apparent impossibility of defining _whi_, or we can accept – as I have done myself – that grasping the nature of whole intelligence is not achieved by struggling to pin it down conceptually: it will forever prove elusive. Coming up with a definitive list of what it refers to is not possible. Best is to affirm that whole intelligence is known through appreciating it in action, and is the kind of concept that serves a function – of 'pointing us in the right direction'.

Whole intelligence needs, therefore, to be understood aesthetically and ethically more than conceptually. On these criteria, human beings seem able to register times when whole intelligence is evident. An analogy might be that of the experienced surfer, who can look at waves and spot one that's exactly right – but is unable to describe such a wave with exactitude, or even what makes it 'right'. Between surfers, however, there is likely to be resonant recognition, a deeply felt appreciative reaction that's shared.

Likewise, with regard to whole intelligence, there is a 'rightness' that is widely endorsed. An understanding and recognition can echo round the world when, for instance, a species is brought back from near extinction; or when a peace treaty is signed and holds; or when a building of brilliant architectural design opens its doors; or when a great scientific breakthrough occurs; or when a girl – who has been shot to silence her – talks to the United Nations.[98] These occasions – all impressively 'world class' and each revealing human beings' capacity to act creatively and effectively – can inspire

---

[98] Malala Yousafzai (b. 1997) was shot in the head by the Pakistani Taliban in October 2012, for speaking about the right of girls to be educated. She survived the shooting and, on 13 July 2013, she addressed the UN General Assembly. In 2014 she was awarded the Nobel Peace Prize jointly with Kailash Satyarthi, another activist and peaceful protestor against exploitation of children.

many millions. These are times when humanity feels pride in itself – recognising human strengths, and glimpses of what's humanly achievable. When Nelson Mandela died, there was a powerful recognition of what he evoked and represented, and this was shared worldwide. Lots of attempts were made to describe his qualities: for me at the time, as I was writing about the five Explorations, I thought of his manifesting each of the five *whi*-dimensions to a high and moving degree.

The Explorations provide five distinctive routes to greater whole intelligence. Yet there are parallels between them – and these are worth noting. In each case, with deepening familiarity and facility with the dimension in question, an *expanded point of view comes into existence*. It is equivalent to standing in a higher place and thus being able to see further: from this vantage point we may notice where we have come from, or realise that there was something we could not see from down there where we were, but now, from up here, we can. This extension of outlook, offering a new and more extensive vista, can yield practical benefits – such as more choice, a chance to re-think, greater confidence, or increased peace of mind.

The path of this broadening process of development, and greater claim to *whi*, is perhaps most easy to see in the case of Walter who appeared in Chapter 7. Walter, you will recall, was the retired policeman who was jolted into new behaviour by his daughter's diverging from his expectations in her personal life. He felt almost forced by circumstances to *experiment* with thinking differently – for instance, about marriage between members of the same sex – and also to *respond* and *relate* differently, and to deal with the *embodied* turbulence arising within his bodily felt emotional states. The movement he went through was of opening to a broader and more inclusive outlook, framing his circumstances in more congenial, more tolerant, and less divided ways.

All sorts of different paths of thought could have got in the way of Walter's change: accusations of sacrificing his principles, of selling out, compromising his beliefs, or going soft. But the costs of listening to these voices would have kept him locked into what he later could recognise was a 'narrow' and 'cramped' mode, confined in a box in which he would be saying 'this is how I am and this is how I will stay'. Walter came to recognise how stubborn, self-damaging, and relationally disastrous such a stance would have been for him. Instead, he allowed the mini-crisis to flow through his existence. He did not rush to his doctor for sedatives to suppress his feelings; nor did he suddenly switch allegiances and rush to condemn all those who continued to hold opinions similar to those he had held before. Instead, he simply opened up to embrace a new phase of life and renewed his love for his daughter – and demonstrated whole intelligence in practice.

Walter's move was to free himself from prejudices; Jane – the painter at the outset of the book – was able to expand into a form of painting she had long avoided; Stig and Inger, work colleagues in different consulting firms, were able to transcend the 'obstacles' of staying friends rather than be tangled up by them. All involved acts of choosing greater wholeness in being alive, and a broader vista.

In the preceding chapters, there are many kinds of fixedness and boxed thinking which I've highlighted as inimical to the emergence and energy of *whi*. In each of the five Explorations we've noted how traps and limitations can easily arise – leading people and groups away from a broader conception and freed-up outlook: they interfere with the emergence of *whi*.

Revisiting the engineer's question with which the book began – 'what stops us from acting intelligently?' – we could now approach an answer. We could point to the numerous ways in which whole intelligence gets undermined, lost, or has never been learnt. In fact, the whole realm of non-*whi* could fill another book.

My own wish, however, is to avoid creating another dichotomy: talking of *whi* and non-*whi* can itself be counter-productive. We would join the 'good or bad', 'on or off' school of categorical thinking, and be contradicting a repeated theme in the preceding five chapters. I have emphasised that it is most realistic to think of a continuum. People occupy different points along the continuum at different points in their lives, and these may change if political, economic, or interpersonal conditions change drastically. Thus, people can demonstrate *whi* in some contexts, and then absence of *whi* in other contexts.[99] If there are plenty of enabling factors, or if the prevailing climate is 'set' in ways to support the emergence of *whi*, then whole intelligence is more accessible and likely.

---

[99]   In other words, we need to be less free with the abstract nouns and fixed categories and concentrate more on verbs and variability. That, of course, is evident in my penchant for participles, for 'experimenting' rather than 'experimentation', 'embodying' rather than 'embodiment' – an invitation to think of our constantly being in the process of evolving, shifting focus, growing, even growing up some more as adults.

In promoting *whi* responses, however, we also have to pay attention to opposing forces and obstacles – to both enabling and disabling infrastructures. If the new management of a company pushes for wholly different values than existed before, or a young child falls out with her new stepparent, the chances are that emergence of *whi* may be more problematic. Most of us attempt to hold to certain core beliefs and habits with a change in circumstances, but this may be prodigiously difficult in some instances – say, for a young child in relation to a dominant stepparent.

Similarly, an understanding of peace-making needs to include the underlying motives for war, paying attention to history, the background fears and grievances of the combatants, and – more generally – the attractions of warfare to many young men. As Chris Hedges, who has experienced being in several wars, describes so vividly, 'Even with its destruction and carnage it gives us what we long for in life. It can give us purpose, meaning, a reason for living … war is an enticing elixir. It gives us resolve, a cause. It allows us to be noble'.[100] These are crucial factors in the genesis of war.

Reinforcing peaceful global conditions is a rational necessity in a time of global crisis, and it is set back with every new step taken towards militarism, steps to re-armament, and increases in defence budgets. While the world is grooved to 'think war', there's an obvious need as a world community to start 'thinking peace', more experimentally – which means building an infrastructure which supports it. The lack of any serious government priority more consciously to reach out to other cultures and countries in order to accelerate the growth of 'warm peace',

---

[100] Chris Hedges, *War is a Force that Gives us Meaning* (Anchor Books, 2003), p. 3.

through increased trust-building and active cooperation, is an example of the all-too-familiar shortfall in *whi*-responsive action.

3. Educating for the future

Future Sense invites us to think fundamentally about schooling, the transmission of what we know, and the preparation of young people for living in conditions of complexity, rapid changes, and manifold uncertainties. It is worth asking whether present modes of educating are the best way for young people to discover their individual strengths and interests; to gain self-respect and confidence; to realise what they do not know and yet are interested in knowing; and to discover both the ways by which they resist learning, and also how they can 'learn how to learn'.

The five Explorations have immediate relevance here: they can be regarded as offering learning principles, and as such may be of direct relevance in institutions devoted to learning. However, I realise they may conflict with long-standing and deeply entrenched assumptions about education – with trench-warfare likely between those who might change and those who will uphold the current thinking. I am reluctant to join the battle, yet neither can I skirt the war-zone altogether. So here are some ideas.

In the educating of young people, *self-recognising* of talents and keen directions is of key significance. *Responding to the situation* – where the situation may include experience of school or university life, of compulsory education (to a certain age), and of living within the force field of parental expectations – is often a central preoccupation in a young person's life, as are the challenges of *interrelating* with peers and relevant adults. They are forced continuously, too, to cope with novelty, not knowing, and encountering the unfamiliar and often difficult; and to deal with the inevitable shame experiences that accompany *experimenting*.

Most conspicuously, current models of education leave out the *embodying* function, or push it to the periphery of education. Present policy seems increasingly to diminish bodily priorities – abandoning exercise and playing outside in favour of more desk-bound activities conducted indoors – thereby restricting opportunities for children and young people to raise their voices, sing and shout, and express themselves in gesture, vigorous movement, and physical play. The youngest also go without being safely touched and held. From a developmental standpoint, these are serious omissions. A decision to elevate cognitive learning so far over, say, physical agility can only have originated in the minds of those who are themselves disembodied – as described in this book.

I wonder, however, if what is required in serving the next generations is a questioning of even greater scope – about *whether it is right to regard educating as an activity set apart, and considered on its own.*

If the current educational system did not exist, and we were starting afresh, what kinds of experience would we want for our children and grandchildren? Others have shown how much thinking about educating future adults was laid down in the 19th century, long before the technological, economic, social, and sexual revolutions of the last decades.[101] These revolutions have brought about a world with very different needs from the one in which the 19th-century educational framework was created. Future society needs thoughtful, well informed, psychologically mature, and sensibly grounded leadership, skill in collaboration, effective communication, and a highly developed capacity to handle complexity and changes. Lacking these – in a world full of upheaval and uncertainty – we could end up with even more corrupt systems, bullying by egomaniac leaders, and continued resort to violence and oppression.

There is also a need to instate 'wholeness' as a priority. In fields of scientific and academic study, reductionism and specialised studies have carried the most weight in the last century: holism and attempts to integrate across disciplines have had a harder time in proving their value. Likewise, in government, joined up thinking has been given lip service, but the whole system has been inclined to develop different spheres of policy within separate departments.

To compensate for the trend – at least partially – there are institutes and think-tanks where the dialogue is interdisciplinary, with 'bringing together' and 'teasing apart' both being given priority. These must surely point the direction that education, in its broadest sense, must go. Otherwise the old warning against 'knowing more and more about less and less' will go unheeded. Already, specialisation is academically rewarded to the point that generalists and those who cross disciplinary boundaries have become a rarer breed – despite their gifts for rendering academic thinking relevant to government and to the public.

---

[101] See, for instance, Ken Robinson, *Creative Schools: The Grassroots Revolution That's Transforming Education* (Viking, 2015).

Attending to wholes and not just to parts has value in another respect. The models we make of reality can be dualistic and fragmenting: the province of splits, opposites, and divisions. Think, for instance, of overriding divisions such as that between *academic* and *non-academic* approaches, between *subjective* and *objective* knowing, or between *bodily* and *mental* experience – and the relative loadings of value placed on these. *Hard* data are contrasted with *soft* data – and receive automatic higher status.

The conclusion is that with each attempt to order, pin down, label, and demarcate we also lose something: we simplify reality and get trapped by our divided ways of thought – often ending up 'taking sides', whereby simple divisions become chasms. The need to bridge divisive, simplistic, and partisan thinking is obvious – but how can such a 'renaissance' come about, if not in the ways we educate and shape a vision for the future?

The need to cross boundaries and shed divided thought patterns offers the possibility of a radical realignment. Perhaps we need to draw together features of education, therapy, personal development, group-life, and community development in a single kind of exploratory activity that would appeal to newly emerging members of our global community, as they tackle the developmental challenges of their age. It could entail a new kind of assisted self-exploration, inquiry, and exposure to the culture's richness – using multiple methods of inquiry, on-line learning, and building on the strengths and naturally emerging interests and values of the young person. Such multi-disciplinary, multi-method, personal inquiry opportunities might overlap with fields such as social ecology, consciousness-raising, and engagement with existential, spiritual, philosophical, and political issues as they impact their lives, families, and peer-groups. They would also make conscious the implicit, taken-for-granted, underground, and invisible organisers of people's thinking – which help fashion how they perceive and make sense of the world and describe reality.

In short, beginning from three bases: (1) appreciating the five Explorations; (2) the importance of 'wholes' in a time of fragmenting knowledge; and (3) the idea that *whi* is not a fixed given but is something to cultivate, we are naturally taken into thinking afresh, setting aside the strangled notions of much contemporary debate.

4. An activism of being and becoming

In *Future Sense*, we have explored five expressions of whole intelligence: they qualify to be central to human existence, and can help re-make the world. They point to how, as global citizens, we can function with more competence, creativity, and authenticity – both individually and jointly with others. The Explorations are not optional add-ons, or simply one person's pet ideas, or irrelevant matters to consign to the dusty libraries of general thought. They are of critical significance now.

People are consumed by the agendas of their lives, and stay inside the small worlds of their villages, intimate circles, or commercially cultivated obsessions. Many defend against the flow of change and have not grasped that the global emergency is already here. To varying degrees, we are all skilled in pushing world affairs and crises to the boundaries of our lives at times, and in holding news at arms length, simply for the sake of engaging with immediate life.

At the same time, in the background of our consciousness – or, as we say, 'at the back of our minds' – we know that enormous dangers stand and glower at us. One is the further destabilising of the climate and biosphere of Earth – a real and urgent danger that human beings will destroy the habitat on which all forms of life depend. The other is allowing violent conflict to spread like cancer through the body of organised humanity, remembering that we have assembled and proliferated the most lethal armoury of all time. A third danger is tied up with one of the greatest of high promises: the internet, with its capacity for spreading good news and the pursuit of whole intelligence, has also the dangers through social media of being a vehicle for organised violence, sex abuse, and acts of profound vindictiveness.

In personal terms, there are numerous consequences of living with these scenarios of horror. Allowing the thoughts room, so to speak, can simply trigger distress – so we deny them any room; but they can eat into full wellbeing, perhaps registered at an embodied level in depressed feelings or deep tiredness that lingers. Some feel overwhelmed and powerless, but their lives bulge with crammed-in activity – 'if enough's going on, I distract myself'. Others assume a cynical kind of detachment combined with gallows humour. Many of us do not speak about the big issues at all. Superficiality reigns. That this is a momentous point in world history and in our social evolution can seem not to be the case, amidst the plethora of diversions with which we distract ourselves.

Again, though – as members of our species who are currently alive – I suspect many of us register at some level the responsibility we carry. After all, we are inheritors from thousands of preceding generations; we received life and cultural knowledge from our ancestors; and we are the links to those who will come after – the young and the unborn – who have at least as much right to a lifetime's existence on Earth as we have received ourselves, and a right to the hope for a future beyond their own generation. We recognise at some level that indifference to the fate of later generations is inexcusable: denying to our successors what we have ourselves received constituting an obscene dereliction of duty. So we have a job to do.

Paradoxically, facing the collected global dilemmas is part of what can stimulate our hope for the world and lend direction to our lives. We exist at a time of revolutionary rethinking of the whole of human life – and we are caught in the excitement of new possibilities. The book's title makes reference to a 'world that's waking up'. While some are still asleep or repeatedly pressing the 'snooze' button, others yawn and rub their eyes: they sense that 'business-as-usual' thinking is no longer reliable, but neither do they want to face the full facts – the equivalent, on waking, of being ushered into a cold shower. However, a growing number of people, still a minority, are already wide awake, and have been up since before dawn. They recognise that it is not sleep, but more a state of collective trance that afflicts so many of the world's population. *Future Sense* is one contribution among countless other projects, books, innovations, and specialised campaigns. Once we learn to spot the signs, we notice the awakening everywhere. The currents flowing through the Explorations already run strongly elsewhere.

Paul Hawken, quoted in Chapter 7, referred to an 'unnamed revolution', in which some are championing new outlooks and new uses of existing technology; others respond to unjust situations, or force new transparency on the dealings of unaccountable power elites; still others are quietly getting on with transforming un-ecological practices locally step by step. There are humanity's collective 'self-recognisers' – thinkers and writers[102] like Naomi Klein, Thomas Piketty, Scilla Elworthy, and Nira Yuval-Davis – helping to re-frame our understandings of human life and its overall organisation. Here is where humanity's infrastructures, and the extent to which they are enabling or disabling, are being comprehensively re-examined. One of the most important, visible, timely, and generative developments is the revolution in breaking out of deeply held assumptions relating to gender. This releases extra human energy and wisdom, more *whi*, which has been curtailed for too long in half the world's population and consequently has led to a lack of overall balance generally for all human beings.

Just as adolescents are jolted into adult attitudes by realising that former child responses have no longer a place in their lives, so human beings are being confronted with an equivalent necessity, to 'move on' collectively speaking from detrimental habits. Egocentric self-pity, blinkered complacency, stuck attitudes, and ignorant prejudices are all under fire. Collectively we are seeing shifts of public attitude and newly prevalent ideas; questioning of taken-for-granted thinking in organisations; and a dawning recognition that

---

[102] Naomi Klein, *This Changes Everything: Capitalism vs. the Climate* (Simon and Schuster, 2014); Thomas Piketty, *Capital in the Twenty-First Century* (Harvard University Press, 2014); Scilla Elworthy, *Pioneering the Possible: Awakened Leadership for a World that Works (Sacred Activism)* (North Atlantic Books, 2014); Nira Yuval-Davis, *The Politics of Belonging: Intersectional Contestations* (Sage Publications, 2012).

many of our economic, political, and relational assumptions are outmoded.

There is a new spirit of life, excitement, and emergent enterprise that accompanies the developmental shifts that are in process of unfolding. I notice some correspondence with the stage in therapy or coaching when a client, or a group, makes a key shift in their thinking and awareness: that moment when the penny drops and they realise they are not stuck with 'how they've always been'. They can open to an expanded sense of themselves and of the fullness of life. It is invariably a time of hope and of surging energy.

Of course, there are forces of reaction – those who want at any cost to preserve privileges and to obstruct any who advocate change. Sometimes these seem so powerful that attempts at rethinking and experimenting can be sidelined at source. Naomi Klein points to an example of blind adherence to the *status quo* when she writes that 'changing the earth's climate in ways that will be chaotic and disastrous is easier to accept than the prospect of changing the fundamental, growth-based, profit-seeking logic of capitalism'.[103]

There are different ways in which a revolutionary turnaround in thought and political thinking could come about – for example, through a sudden global catastrophe of disaster movie proportions. In other scenarios, what seems likely to catalyse significant change is unprecedented public participation and pressure on powerful elites from below. We can be sure that intelligent evolutionary developments are unlikely to be government-led, because governments, increasingly allied to mega-corporations, form part of the power structures which dominate global life. They are buttressed by institutional assumptions, precedents, and

---

[103] Naomi Klein, *This Changes Everything*, p. 89.

deeply grooved thinking, and continue with illusions that are not supportable long-term: for instance, that we can have an expanding economy, with increases in population and finite planetary resources, and can also sustain the biosphere as humanly habitable; or, in another realm, that we are all safer if armed to the teeth and increasing our military expenditure.

To summarise: *Future Sense* is grounded in the idea that human life and conditions of living are not unalterable. Human beings have in-built potential strengths that are not unknown to them: they are simply under-cultivated. Often missing are the enabling conditions that help to draw them out – but these can be built. Moreover, we are in charge of our selves, lives, and fates; the assertion of world citizenry who *are* waking up can be an irresistible force for changing the core assumptions by which human beings live.

Some words of Mikhail Gorbachev underline the ultimate message of this book.

> The task is simple. Get down to the basics, understand that global problems are not foreign to us. They are our problems. We are all touched by them, and touched by them not any less than we are by ordinary, everyday things. And it is we, each one of us, who not only can understand these problems, but can also do something significant to overcome them.[104]

---

[104] Mikhail Gorbachev, Introduction to Ervin Laszlo, *You Can Change the World: The Global Citizen's Handbook for Living on the Planet* (SelectBooks Inc., 2003), p. xii. This also contains an excellent chapter by Masami Saionji, titled 'You Can Change Yourself'.

'Overcoming' global problems by 'doing something significant' is more difficult than Gorbachev implies. Yet the intention and his basic premise – that the two realms of world affairs and our personal lives are interlinked – is indeed the central theme and emphasis of this book.

In addition to the frequent references in earlier chapters, there are two ways to reconsider 'activism'. One relates to *capitalising on interests and passions*; the other to a longer-term *building of enabling infrastructures.*

When it comes to influencing what happens in the world, people can report feeling a disjunction between their own actions – like recycling or signing on-line petitions – and the scale of the world's issues. Their efforts seem pathetically minimal. Others retain a general sense of anxiety or concern, but seem unable to commit themselves to some particular project or social action.

However, there are also numerous examples of people ready to pick up responsibility – remembering that this often refers to 'ability to respond'. In one powerful account, Elizabeth Claire Alberts[105] talks of her strong feelings about the killing of whales, provoked by reading Peter Heller's *The Whale Warriors*. It was reading 'fact after fact that startled me awake', she writes. She wanted immediately to volunteer on the ships that were out there, intercepting the Japanese factory ships. But she could not jump the line of applicants

---

[105] Elizabeth Claire Alberts, 'Leaping Aboard: On Shore Volunteer Work with Sea Shepherd', in *Stories of the Great Turning*, ed. Peter Reason and Melanie Newman (Vala Publishing Cooperative, 2013).

who also wanted to do this. Also she was employed as a university teacher and was finishing a Ph.D.

Once alerted, and recognising the need in her to do something about the whales, but thwarted in her first response, she ended up being an onshore organiser of fund-raising events – to very great effect. Another response, which she might have made but didn't, would have been to withdraw altogether, her hopes of going to sea once dashed. But she realised that not responding at all was not possible for her, so strong was her *embodied* reaction to the needless killing of whales, which she *recognised* in herself; she realised she had a passionate desire to *respond to the situation* by volunteering and working extraordinarily hard. As a successful fundraiser and organiser, she was also constantly *experimenting* and *interrelating* with others. Yet all she did – very successfully in terms of fundraising – rested on her initial, very powerful emotional reaction when reading Heller's book.

I have included Elizabeth Claire Alberts' experience as a reminder: namely, that our *embodied* reactions, if *self-recognised*, can be important signposts to what we are energised to do: often to *experiment* with something different from the main direction of our lives. In most cases, the passions that serve as the 'rocket fuel' for our *responding* or *interrelating* choices derive from events in childhood – whether injurious or benign. However, because the general pressure of society is 'to grow up', and also not to be embodied, many would-be passionate activists may end up suppressing, or ignoring, the very initial impulse that might otherwise be propelling them forwards, ready to pick up the Gorbachev challenge.

*

Perhaps I go even further than Gorbachev, in suggesting a direct linkage between global and personal. I believe that inevitably we are involved in the state of society and the world, and cannot NOT be.

The groundwork for this claim has been explored in previous chapters. Each person is a 'live node' in the overall network of interlinked human beings, and thus becomes a joint contributor to the collective 'sea of thought' in which we all swim. As such, we have a sphere of influence – especially with those who swim close to us. Just as we are affected by others, so also do we affect them: we may think we do not, but this is illusory.

However, I have slowly come to appreciate again how 'over-individualised' my thinking has been: a struggle I wrote about in Chapter 4. Let me explain the change I have gone through – for it bears relevance to picking up what I am calling Gorbachev's challenge. My years working as a therapist with a large practice revealed to me the extent and depth of other people's suffering. I was not usually working with the most distressed and psychologically disoriented patients, but immersion in the mental health field revealed that to speak of an 'epidemic' of depression and anxiety was justified.

While – understandably perhaps, in historical terms – the focus of the psychotherapy professional community has been on individual suffering, and the disfigurement of lives and wellbeing on a personal and family scale, I found I was constantly drawn back to a bigger picture. Obviously, most therapists do acknowledge the 'external' social, political, and economic conditions that affect individuals, but most tend to see these – as do many members of the Western world – as fundamentally peripheral to the personal or 'internal' world of personality and self-experience. To return to the analogy of swimming, they see people in the sea who swim strongly, and others who do not and who need inflatable supports; in extreme cases some are terrified of being in the sea. They regard a therapist's or social worker's task as being to help them swim more strongly, or to prescribe the equivalent of inflatable supports, or to treat their phobia.

With this view, the fact that mental health problems are increasing every decade leads to inevitable calls for extra services, more sessions of short-term therapy offered, and yet more drugs to be administered, in order to handle the growing scale of the problem. Staying with the image of swimmers, more may need help from lifeguards, with better surveillance to keep down the number who might drown.

However, the course of my own thinking has developed otherwise. Increasingly, I regard human beings as being like sea creatures of a different (imaginary) kind: organisms that are continuously immersed, creatures soaked full-time in the taken-for-granted assumptions, models, languages, and powerful images that the sea of thought contains. These creatures have semi-permeable membranes, taking in nourishment from the medium in which they are steeped. They are capable of keeping some sense of separateness from the sea around them, but it is not easy: no way can they reliably keep out all that is toxic or unhelpful to their survival.

Thinking along these lines, and bearing in mind the mental health 'epidemic', has led me to realise more clearly than before that instead of focusing on individual swimmers' problems – their 'illness' or even their 'lack of *whi'* – the emphasis should rather be on the pollution and presence of toxins in the sea in which they swim. Paying attention to society's living conditions – the sheer difficulties for many in managing economically, or feeling overwhelmed and confused by the totality of their social and technological environment – can lead to people being classified as 'mentally ill', which locates the problem with the swimmers, rather than with the water quality and the polluters.

I realised that a comparable shift in outlook has occurred regarding the 'obesity problem'. There's recognition that explaining the increasing incidence of obesity by reference to dietary ignorance or people's foolhardiness, or lack of 'self control', or some other personal shortfall is misguided. Instead, health and food experts acknowledge that the issue is equally a product of food-providing systems, manufacturers and their commercial policies, and, ultimately, of powerful economic interests tied up with promoting additives – sugar, in particular.

If the 'obesity problem' is as much political, social, and ethical as it is personal, so also may be the prevalence of depression and other types of mental ill health: there are many morale-lowering conditions in the surroundings – the equivalent of 'food additives' in the sea of thought. The image of creatures in the sea of everyday thought is a powerful one, at least for me. It also points to a second way in which we can respond to Gorbachev's challenge.

We can be influential in changing the general thinking in circulation. We can commit to advancing the cause of whole intelligence – and the presence of *whi*-attitudes and the perspectives of the five Explorations. Again, this is not an invitation to ascend a psychological hierarchy or to strive after becoming 'a better person', or a superhero – it's not a 'motivational call' in the conventional sense. There is to be no cult, no heroes, no sign-ups, no preaching. I'm proposing something far less programmatic and far more practical: the strengthening of infrastructures that can enable others and ourselves to function with more whole intelligence. Every act of questioning foolishness, of pioneering alternatives, of challenging hubristic illusions, and of educating the young in ways that lead to different norms, may be providing a critical input which reverberates more widely – and could have an effect on the course of history.

Here and earlier in the book, I am suggesting that individualism as an ideology is outmoded and dangerous. But I was careful earlier to underline that our *individuality* was to be prized. Each of us has a unique history, background, and range of skills; so each of us, through our exploring, participating, and taking action, can impact the world – and can do so in a way which is unique to each of us. This does not mean acting alone, or in isolation: but that when working together, or being together, whatever we personally bring to the collaboration or other occasion will not be identical to anybody else's input – even if, from the outside, it may appear so. The diversity of human beings is an immense resource, providing different perspectives and needed variation.

On a bigger scale, that we are inevitably implicated in world affairs is not a new idea. When Gandhi said 'Be the change you want to see in the world', he indicated that he was thinking along similar lines. As many wisdom teachers have pointed out, the way to a greater state of peace in the world around us is to live more peacefully ourselves. But this raises a question: even if we 'live peacefully', what is the guarantee that this affects events far off?

Recent studies have shown the extent to which we influence others, even unintentionally. For instance, obesity and smoking occur in clusters, and are in some sense 'contagious'.[106] We also know experientially how strongly we can sometimes feel part of a community, a family, a football crowd, or group of mourners, and how it seems plausible that we share a common 'mindfield'[107] – even if the scientific validation of this phenomenon is some distance away. On the basis of all my own observations and conjectures, our connectivity seems a powerful phenomenon, in which 'contagion effects' are confirmed over and over: clinically, we can observe numerous ways in which people influence others – especially those in their inner circles. Just as we are affected, so also do we affect others; *and we are doing so all the time.*

The implications are profound and obvious: acting in more embodied, responsive, relational, conscious, and experimental ways, we are likely to support others to do so too; similarly, if we act in unintelligent, destructive, or deliberately offensive ways, we create conditions in which others are more likely to follow suit – an occurrence all

---

[106] Nicholas A. Christakis and James H. Fowler, 'Social contagion Theory: Examining Dynamic Social Networks and Human Behavior', *Statistics in Medicine* 32/4 (2013)10. Available at http://www.ncbi.nlm. nih.gov/pmc/articles/PMC3830455/.

[107] Ian McCullum's book, *Ecological Intelligence: Rediscovering Ourselves in Nature* (Fulcrum, 2008), is an excellent accompaniment to this book. In it, among many other ideas, he develops the case for there being a mindfield – as a 'field of information in which conscious and unconscious mental activities, signals, and directions interact and influence each other' (p. 115).

too evident in some anonymous internet communications. Offering what we have discovered, value, and know about, is therefore another way we can contribute to the general awakening of the world.

We are all implicated – *either* in sustaining the present manner in which the human world operates, *or* in acting to transform it. Revolutionary levels of change begin with us. The five Explorations together serve as a serious and thoughtful agenda for change-makers – promoting small changes that are doable and cumulative, and which can help restore the quality of the cultural sea of thought in which humanity exists. We begin with the most local reality we have: ourselves as explorers and as exponents of *whi*.

POSTSCRIPT
AND APPRECIATIONS

In 2007, I met a gifted and revered Norwegian gestalt therapist called Bjørg Tofte – to whom this book is dedicated. We fell in love and imagined our future together. These hopes shattered when she was diagnosed with inoperable pancreatic cancer. She died ten months later.

During our nearly four years together, we shared ideas and writing. I had been trying to revive a long-standing project – that of writing this book. Several previous attempts had collapsed. Bjørg was intrigued: she read some of the unpublished material and encouraged me to continue. Her illness then intervened, and writing stopped.

One day about three weeks before she died, she asked about my future plans. I was too upset to think about them. But I surprised myself by 'bodying forth' an answer. Without any intention formulated in advance, I heard myself telling her: 'I will write the book, publish it, and dedicate it to you'. She looked pleased and thanked me. We did not speak of it again.

Several months after the funeral, I began registering the enormity of what I had promised to do. Even at the moment of committing myself, I had a fleeting sense of the scale of the challenge. I was conscious of my history of difficulties in attempting to write this book in the past. I knew there was no escape this time: I would have to 'work through my resistance' – excavate the buried obstacles and confront whatever was stopping me.

To tell the story of uncovering the basis for my fears would take another book. Needless to say, they lay in the dynamics of my family, and in my silencing myself as a child – evidently I did not speak until I was three. I found myself confronted with what in gestalt we call the *impasse*: in my case, deep fears of revealing publicly my personal ideas and passionately held beliefs, *and* an unbreakable commitment to write and publish this book, which was full of them.

I realised I had to draw upon the very resources I was writing about. Maybe I came up with the Explorations because there was crucial learning in them for me. At any rate, all five have been prominent in the journey to completion. And with each Exploration, key individuals and groups appeared in my life to offer support and encouragement to continue. I want to thank them here.

In *responding to the situation* – engaging with the practicalities of book writing – I have been supported by many different readers, critics, and discussants. Very particular thanks to Hugh Pidgeon, Sally Croft, Emily Skye, Alan Allport, Gordon Wheeler, Gill Caradoc-Davies, and Peter Reason for their significant input, wisdom, and encouragement to continue. David Mann, Arch Roberts, Andy Birtwell, Leanne O'Shea, Sandra Figgess, Gabe Phillips, Judy Ryde, Liz Savage, Deb Uhlman, Peter Hawkins, Ruth Finar, Sue Congram, Mark Nicolson, Nelly Uhlenkott, Piers Parlett, Jo O'Brien, Michael O'Brien, Sally Birtwell, Caroline Warhurst and Mark Stevens have all listened to me reading or have read chapters themselves – and given useful and welcome feedback; and thanks to valued fellow members of the BGJ Writing Support Groups for their ongoing encouragement and feedback. None of the foregoing bears any responsibility for any shortcomings or inaccuracies that readers may find.

By way of detailed editorial support, I have been lucky: very special thanks to Laura Macy, my creative and indefatigable copy editor. Thanks, too, to Tess Bird and Tina Leonard for their timely inputs. Thanks to Carola Soltau for her internet searching. Hilary Hosier's prompt and accurate transcribing has been essential; big thanks to her. And to Simon Dawson, who has rescued me computing-wise on so many occasions, my warm appreciation. For design help, my thanks to Piers Parlett and also to Kim Freeman.

In terms of *interrelating*, my need to feel connected has been mainly met by those just listed. But I also want to appreciate here members of my extended family who have had a major role in willing me on to finish, and been very understanding that I have so often disappeared while staying with them in order to continue to write. My gratitude goes to the O'Brien family, Jo, Eugene, Michael and Emma in California; to Piers Parlett, Carolina Moncada and Laura Isabela in Madrid; Rosemary, Mike, Melissa, Harry, and Matilda Hoggett in Cornwall; Joy Parlett in Bristol; Sally Croft in Totnes; Beth and Warren Robin in Hertfordshire; and Tone Thingbø, Philip and Isak Mlonyeni in Oslo.

Friends, too, have been highly supportive: special thanks to Sharon Berbower, Aksel Toft, Virginia Allport, Hassa and Eli Gabrielle Borchsenius, Grete Hauge, Rosie Hill, Rob and Bridget Farrands, Elizabeth Adeline, Wendy Chadwick-Sykes, Sandy Elstob-Johnson, Jacqui Lichtenstern, Marigold Farmer, Jane Williams, and Barbara and David Manzi-Fe for sustaining my spirits and being in my life.

My long-term professional community has also been a supportive presence in the background, and I would particularly like to mention those whose ideas have influenced me the most: Gordon Wheeler, Sally Denham-Vaughan, Mark Fairfield,

Philip Lichtenberg, Georges Wollants, Frank-M. Staemmler, Lynne Jacobs, Margherita Spagnuolo-Lobb, and the late Edwin Nevis; and thanks to Ty Francis, Joe Melnick, Des Kennedy, Nancy Amendt-Lyon, Ansel Woldt, Christine Stevens, Marie-Anne Chidiac, Sonia Nevis, Robert Lee, Brian O'Neill, Neil Harris, Rob Farrands, Mike Turton, Helen Kennedy, and Seán Gaffney and many others for their expressed interest and professional comradeship over many years.

In the longer term, my men's group also played an important part in the book's pre-history, before the group wound up on the death of John Crook: he, along with Peter Tatham, Peter Hawkins, and Peter Reason, were present at the beginning of my long journey with these ideas, and I learned so much from them. Also in the pre-history of the book, other people encouraged me and kept the fire alight. I remember with thanks Peter McCowen, Mel Bucholtz, Tunde Horvath, Peter Philippson, Trevor Bentley, Judith Hemming, the late Dan Rosenblatt, Talia Levine Bar-Yoseph, Nancy Lunney Wheeler, Faye Page, and members of the EAGT writers' conferences (in Sicily, Spain, and Greece).

In terms of staying *embodied*, I am thinking especially of the children who appear in the above list of family members; of Derek Elliott and those with whom I meditate; of the Cultivate co-operative and Trevor at the Organic Deli who sustain me food-wise; the nearby River Thames alongside which I cycle or walk; and the Punter pub which is mentioned in the book but not named hitherto. All these I appreciate as essential supports for maintaining my fitness to write, think, and relax.

Self-recognising has been an intrinsic part of the journey – without the inner work I had to do, in dealing with the early trauma, progress would have been snail-like. I wish to express enormous gratitude to James Low, Caroline Ward, and James

Kepner, for their skill and understanding; and to the closest witness of my journey – my former partner and continuing friend for life, Sally Croft, to whom a huge thank you for your extended generosity, acuity, and care.

In terms of *experimenting*, I am thinking of those who have encouraged me the most to go to 'the edge' – and I am thinking of the opportunities I have had to do that in the last year. My thanks to Bob and Rita Resnick; to Daniel Donohue and Andrew Price; to Carmen Vazquez; and to Neil Harris, Christine Stevens, and Adam Kincel for arranging occasions when I could speak out the ideas of *Future Sense* to receptive audiences they had assembled.

With regard to experimenting I am also thinking of the many clients, trainees, group members, and supervisees, who – along with colleagues and conference attendees – have peopled my professional world for years, and whose explorations, struggles, and courageous meetings of 'what was next for them' have seeded and enriched the ground from which this book has grown. I have been privileged to know them. I particularly want to thank members of the Poulstone, Hawkwood, Manchester/Sheffield, and Holycombe long-term groups who have a permanent place in my appreciation.

Reading through the above, I am struck by the huge community of good people to whom I am indebted and with whom I feel connected. I am also aware that this is by no means a complete listing, and that others are constantly coming to mind. In fact, remembering and not forgetting are apt themes on which to end – not merely the *Postscript and Appreciations*, but the book as a whole.

Malcolm Parlett,
Oxford, August 2015

INDEX